# THE DOOR
# IN THE DREAM

conversations
with
eminent women
in science

elga wasserman

Joseph Henry Press
Washington, D.C.

**Joseph Henry Press • 2101 Constitution Avenue, N.W. • Washington, D.C 20418**

The Joseph Henry Press, an imprint of the National Academy Press, was created with the goal of making books on science, technology, and health more widely available to professionals and the public. Joseph Henry was one of the founders of the National Academy of Sciences and a leader of early American science.

**Library of Congress Cataloging-in-Publication Data**

Wasserman, Elga R. (Elga Ruth)
    The door in the dream : conversations with eminent women in science / Elga R. Wasserman
        p.  cm.
    Includes index.
    ISBN 0-309-06568-2 (hardcover : alk. paper)
    1. Women biologists—United States Biography. 2. Women scientists—United States Biography. I. Title.
    QH26.W375   1999
    305.43'5'0973—dc21
                              99-6428
                              CIP

Printed in the United States of America.

To
Lisa, Aaron, Rebecca, Sophie, Anika, Noah, and Sam

# CONTENTS

# PREFACE
## by Rita Colwell

A poster-maker in the 1970s created a timeline of prominent people throughout history. It included many of the great men—Gandhi, Socrates, Confucius, Shakespeare—but only a few women, notably novelist Jane Austen and chemist Marie Curie.

The same poster-maker, perhaps chastened by changing times, later published a timeline of prominent women. It included only two scientists, the ever-present Marie Curie and anthropologist Margaret Mead. Today, two decades later, there are still but a few women among the leading figures in science. Why? Because there are still relatively few women scientists. It is an underrepresentation that we cannot afford to allow to continue into the new century.

Intelligence is not linked to the Y chromosome; to exclude half the population from scientific inquiry is to deny us, as a nation, an extraordinary amount of ability and intelligence. The need for scientific brainpower will only increase as we proceed into an information age in which science and engineering will touch our lives like never before. Add to that the demands of global competition and it's clear that to prosper in the 21st century will require the broadest scientific contribution possible. The cost of excluding any group has simply become too high.

Why are women underrepresented in science today? I wish there were a single reason because then the problem could be easily targeted and changed. But the answer is not simple. In part, it lies in what I call the "valley of death" in education, when girls grades 4 through 8 are, in subtle and not-so-subtle ways, discouraged from pursuing science and engineering. Not only is the invitation not extended, but even those with a natural bent toward science are too often directed elsewhere. Add to this a dearth of role models (at least ones they might have been told about) and a lack of mentors, and it's no surprise that these girls pass science by.

I certainly felt this as an aspiring young scientist. I was—perhaps naively—puzzled when my ideas were not taken as seriously as were the ideas of the aspiring young male scientists around me. I second-guessed myself; I wondered whether my ideas were simply too strange to be taken seriously. But with the encouragement of a good mentor—Purdue University's Dorothy Powelson, a bacteriologist in days when women rarely held such titles—I became entranced by the world I saw through the lens of a microscope. My excitement fueled me as I scrambled over the roadblocks then facing would-be women scientists. My willingness to work hard (I counted 186,000 fruit flies as part of my masters degree research) served me well.

Now, having achieved success, I look back and realize that I was indeed climbing a steep hill and that someone was constantly rolling boulders into my path. Our task today is to prevent someone from rolling those same boulders into the path of young women who seek to make their contribution to the world in science.

But, you may ask, can this still be happening? Haven't we progressed beyond such narrow thinking? The answer is mixed; yes, we have progressed—but not enough. No one says, as they did to me in the 1950s, that they don't want to "waste" a fellowship on a woman. That's progress. But when the scientific establishment hands out the annual awards, it gives the top prizes to just enough women to avoid being sued for bias—but no more. That is not progress enough.

Even today, those of us who have made it in science feel the sting of prejudice. In meetings with (mostly white male) counterparts in government, I still find that all too often my statements are met with silence. But a few minutes later, when the same thought is expressed by a man in the group, the response is: "Oh, what a remarkable suggestion!"

This is both amusing and frustrating. Instead of letting it anger me, I redouble my efforts to make sure that my ideas, even if they are hijacked along the way, produce the outcomes I wanted. Such are the adaptations that we, as women in science, must make. The stories of many of the women profiled in "The Door in the Dream" parallel my personal trek. All have the mental toughness to passionately pursue interests they love, and to persevere in the face of obstacles. Eventually, like myself, they have reaped the rewards of being undeterred and true to themselves.

Enthusiasm is evident in the words of Mildred Cohn (pp. 43-46), who notes, "the most important aspect of my career is that it has been fun—the joy of predictive results materializing, the even more rewarding experience of serendipitously discovering an entirely unexpected phenomenon, and the special gratification of having the results applied to medical problems."

Or consider the story of hematologist and oncologist Janet Rowley (pp. 76-79), who initially completed only the minimal requirements to license as an M.D. Several years later, seeking a greater challenge, she broadened her work and ultimately discovered the abnormal rearrangements in cells of leukemia patients — a discovery that has greatly advanced diagnosis and treatment of the disease.

These women succeed by doing excellent work. When Gertrude Elion was thwarted in her efforts to earn a doctoral degree, she kept going. Eventually, the importance of her scientific contribution resulted in the bestowal of the Nobel Prize and more than twenty-five honorary doctorates.

These women are creative. After the birth of twins, Marian Koshland (pp. 53-62) was unsure how to handle five children and a career. Her husband suggested that if she were to work half-time—but spend all of that time on research—she could, as she put it, "do all the crazy things that nobody else can do." Which is what she did, trying experiments that others on a more solid career-track might not have dared to try. It paid off.

Like most women, these women were skilled in doing two things (or more) at once. Each raised a family with one hand while pursuing their science with the other. It's a balancing act that many women to-day, no matter what their profession, know well. *The Door in the Dream* provides readers, whether scientists or not, with a glimpse of the ex-citement and rewards to be found in scientific research as we confront a vast range of unsolved problems waiting to be tackled.

The tough challenges facing women in treks through science and education are still far from over. But, as scientists, we know the value of both reason and imagination and we know perseverance can carry us on great journeys.

# ACKNOWLEDGMENTS

I want to express my profound thanks to the women members of the National Academy of Sciences who, by graciously sharing their thoughts and experiences with me, helped me gain a fresh perspective on the complex issues confronting contemporary women scientists and other women professionals. Without their unstinting cooperation this book could not have been written.

This book was also shaped by many stimulating discussions with friends and colleagues. I am particularly grateful to Christine Chinlund, Dorrit Cohn, Faye Crosby, Patricia Graham, Dudley Hershbach, Lilli Hornig, Malkah Notman, Etta Onat, Edith Ruina, Carol Schreiber, Ellen Switzer, Sheila Tobias, and Susan Wolfson, for their insights and thoughtful comments about women professionals and for encouraging me to pursue this project. I thank Bob Lichter for keeping me current about the latest projects regarding the status of women scientists. I also learned much from observing my own children and their growing families as they try to find the time and energy to balance their personal and professional lives in such disparate disciplines as journalism, medicine, and science. I thank my husband, Harry Wasserman, for forcing me to clarify my thinking in response to his perceptive critiques and for enabling me to complete this project as a result of his volunteering to preside in our kitchen as a devoted, creative chef while I completed this book.

I am indebted to Stephen Mautner, executive editor of the Joseph Henry Press, for sharing my vision for this book and for guiding it to completion with unfailing encouragement and patience and to my editor, Gretchen Bratvold, for helping me create a coherent whole out of many disparate parts. I was especially fortunate to have had the able assistance of Mary Lou Oates and Sheila Klein, who proved indispensable in transcribing the interviews for this book.

I thank the Spencer Foundation for providing funding for this project and the Schlesinger Library on the History of Women in America, Radcliffe Institute, Harvard University, for agreeing to accept the original letters and interview transcripts on which this book is based as part of its archives.

# THE DOOR
# IN THE DREAM

# INTRODUCTION

In 1968 the president of Yale, Kingman Brewster, Jr., asked me to oversee the transformation of Yale College, then all-male, into a co-educational institution and to take whatever steps were needed to make Yale "a good place for women." For the next four years I urged Yale to add women to its faculty. I was promised that an effort would be made to hire female faculty but was told that in the sciences "qualified women" could not be found. I myself had earned a Ph.D. degree in chemistry 20 years earlier but had slowly drifted out of science into university administration. I knew that women could become highly productive scientists and began to wonder why women scientists could "not be found." What did it take for women to succeed in science, and why were there still so few? Why did women "drift" out of science as I had? I was determined to find out, and this book is the result of that quest. To find answers to my questions, I decided to contact women who had established successful careers as research scientists. I found such women at the National Academy of Sciences, an organization whose members are elected based on outstanding scientific achievement. I hoped to find answers in the stories of these women who forged their lives as successful women scientists.

## Personal Reflections

I myself am a "science dropout." As I look back on my career, numerous moments stand out at which my career could easily have taken a different course. When I started graduate study in chemistry in 1945, I never imagined that I would some day fill numerous disparate roles in addition to becoming a chemist, a wife, and a mother, all of which I had vaguely planned. I did not reflect on how and why I had slowly moved out of science into other challenging roles until many years later. Then I began to wonder what, if anything, would have persuaded me to remain a research scientist.

I arrived in the United States at the age of 12 with my parents and younger brother, having left Germany to escape Hitler. My parents settled in Great Neck, Long Island. Four years later, in 1941, I graduated from Great Neck High School near the top of my class. Except for the fact that I loved mathematics and French and disliked history, I recall relatively little of my high school studies. I worked on the school newspaper, played field hockey, and had numerous friends but was never invited to join the sorority crowd to which many of my classmates belonged. In my senior year, to my great surprise, I was named "Future Leader of Nassau County" based on a countywide test for high school seniors.

In high school I perceived being bright as a handicap. It was therefore a great relief to arrive in 1941 as a freshman at Smith College, where intellectual achievement was fostered and respected. I was lucky to have been awarded a scholarship by Smith, which I supplemented with a small local grant in aid and on-campus jobs. My parents were overjoyed at this opportunity for me since both placed a premium on education. In December of my freshman year the United States entered World War II, but this had little direct effect on campus life. There were officer training programs at neighboring colleges, women recruits were housed on the Smith campus, and younger male faculty entered military service, but for most Smith students education proceeded as usual.

Betty Friedan, who was a senior when I was a freshman, was the editor of our college newspaper. I had not yet given any thought to women's rights. I did, however, help organize a campuswide forum on race relations at which civil rights activist Roy Wilkins was the featured speaker. Several of us were troubled by a campus rule that required roommates to be of the same color, a rule that persisted even after a black student had been elected to head the student government. This mix of traditional and enlightened attitudes was typical of the Smith College I remember. I was by nature skeptical of authority and ready to question the status quo, perhaps in part as a result of my refugee status. I was and have remained somewhat of a rebel at heart.

None of my close friends in college were science majors, and I shared many late-night discussions with my nonscience friends. I took a wide range of nonscience courses and especially enjoyed art history, French, and symbolic logic, courses with outstanding teachers. I disliked physics and took very little math, probably because these courses were badly taught by faculty filling in for others who had entered military service. On the other hand, I thoroughly enjoyed biology and chemistry. I received particular encouragement from a young male professor of organic chemistry, although I suspected that the interest he took in me was not free of ulterior motives. In any case, I declined his suggestion that I stay on at Smith after graduation to earn a master's degree under his tutelage.

I had come to college with a long-standing interest in medicine, stimulated by extensive reading in the medical library of a physician uncle of mine for whom I frequently house sat. During my senior year I toyed with going into medicine but decided on graduate study in chemistry instead. I am often asked why. My reasons were twofold. First, I did not have the money to pay for medical school and the idea of borrowing money never occurred to me. Graduate study in science, on the other hand, was relatively easy to finance with teaching assistantships and fellowship help. The second reason was that I was passionately interested in medicine. I wanted equally passionately to marry and have children. Medicine, I feared, would confront me with the dilemma of choosing between raising a family or pursuing my career. I assumed that I could not do both. Since I was less intensely committed to chemistry than medicine, I could imagine forsaking chemistry but not medicine. I do not recall ever discussing this decision with anybody at the time, although I suspect that I might have changed my plans if I had received better counseling.

When I accepted an offer to enroll as a graduate student in the Harvard chemistry department, I was quite unaware that I was doing anything out of the ordinary. Even though I was technically a Radcliffe student, the only time I set foot at Radcliffe was to teach a section of chemistry to undergraduate women who at that time had separate laboratory sections from male Harvard undergraduates. I was one of only two women chemistry graduate students among a large group of post-war students on the GI Bill. I took it for granted that virtually all of my fellow students, my research supervisor, and all my teachers were male, yet I never wondered why my degree would be awarded by Radcliffe rather than Harvard. I welcomed the coeducational atmosphere after four years at a women's college, although in retrospect I realized that I had benefited enormously from my Smith years. Women at Smith were taken seriously, and I learned to be comfortable as a bright woman, something I had not achieved in high school.

On the advice of my Smith mentor, I decided to work for a young brilliant Harvard organic chemist who subsequently won a Nobel Prize—Robert Burns Woodward. He agreed to supervise my dissertation research on the condition that I not cry. A woman student of his had dropped out in tears the previous year, and he evidently wanted no repeat. I accepted these terms and kept my promise. At the time I never felt that my gender mattered to Professor Woodward, nor did I think that he treated me in any way differently from his male students. Not until the late 1960s, while an assistant dean in the Yale Graduate School, did I realize that he had lost all interest in my career in 1947, when I married a fellow Woodward student, Harry Wasserman. It took me 20 years to realize this fact, probably because even I did not take my future career very seriously while a student. Nobody advised or encouraged my husband and me to embark on a joint job hunt, although it probably would have been futile anyhow. Being a married female chemist did not help one's employment prospects in 1947.

I was recently invited to participate in a television program dedicated to Woodward as part of the *Nobel Legacy Series* on PBS. Since I had left chemistry more than 30 years before, I asked the producers

"Why me?" They confided that I had been the only woman they found who had completed doctoral work with Woodward. By the early 1990s, political correctness had evidently made a token female presence desirable.

In 1948, the year my husband and I both earned our doctorates, my husband joined the Yale faculty as an instructor. I found a position as a research assistant working for Professor David Bonner, a microbiologist, a position I thoroughly enjoyed. I shared a lab bench with Charlie Yanofsky, the geneticist, and now a member of the National Academy of Sciences. Mary Bunting, who later became president of Radcliffe, was working in the same laboratory. I saw her rarely because she had four young children at home and did not start her "day" at the lab until 6 or 7 p.m., when her physician husband took over the care of their children. When she heard I was expecting, she outfitted me royally with her old maternity clothes. She was helpful and kind to me in many other little ways. Despite the fact that I was excited by the research I was doing—using isotopic tracers to study metabolic pathways —I never thought of continuing once our first child was born. I could not see myself working double shifts, one as mother and the second as research scientist, as Mary Bunting was doing, and I do not recall anyone urging me to stay. I resigned from the assistantship voluntarily shortly before our first child was born.

For the next 12 years I kept my hand in chemistry by accepting part-time positions in industry and by teaching in community colleges at which there was no opportunity to do research. I was lured by the flexibility of part-time work and by the relatively high hourly wages I was able to earn freelancing for local industrial firms. I focused on the present rather than on long-term career goals. In the early 1950s, opportunities for women in science were virtually nonexistent, and my prospects of continuing a career as a female research scientist were dismal. Given these circumstances I was thrilled to have an opportunity to keep my hand in science and to earn extra money, especially since at that time the income of instructors, such as my husband, was barely enough to support a young family. The pressures to be a full-time mother were so strong at the time that I felt I was straying from the norm by working at all. Today it is difficult to appreciate how truly exceptional the women in my generation had to be in order to pursue scientific careers.

By the time our third child was in school, in the early 1960s, I could see no way to return to science while at the same time doing justice to raising our family. I could have looked for a position as a research assistant in someone else's laboratory but chose not to. I enjoyed the intellectual challenge of science, the excitement of posing and solving problems, but I did not want to be a helpmate working on someone else's problem. I was therefore thrilled when I was offered a position as assistant dean of the Yale Graduate School overseeing Yale's graduate science programs, a position that enabled me to work part time, to be home by the time our children came home from school, and to work independently. The position seemed tailor-made for my circumstances.

In the fall of 1968, when Yale decided to admit women to its undergraduate college, President Brewster wanted a woman administrator. I was on the scene and was invited to oversee the advent of coeducation at Yale. This was an opportunity to remake the image of old Yale, a challenge for which I felt ready and accepted gladly. I naively expected, however, that I would transfer my status as assistant dean from the graduate school to the undergraduate college. I was promptly informed that the assistant deans at Yale College—all of whom were male—would be too threatened if a woman were to join their ranks as a fellow dean and thus as a quasi equal. Brewster, trying to keep all parties happy, proposed that I serve as Yale's "Special Assistant to the President on the Education of Women and Chairman of the Committee on Coeducation." This was 1968, and I reluctantly agreed to this less than elegant title. I still had much to learn.

When I told my boss, the dean of the graduate school, that I would be leaving, he treated my departure as a personal slight. It took many years before he forgave me. Once a woman is given a position, he believed, she should remain loyal and grateful forever, even though this same dean had always encouraged male assistant deans to move on and upward at Yale or elsewhere. His expectations for me, a faculty wife, were clearly different than those for my male colleagues.

The next four years were the most exciting of my career. I had left science, but I had become an agent for change and a very visible one at that. Henry Chauncey, Jr., the secretary of the university, Brewster's right-hand man, and an old Blue who knew how Yale functioned, proved to be an enthusiastic mentor and adviser to me. I doubt whether I would have been able to find my way through the maze of such an established institution without his guidance and encouragement.

My mandate was to make Yale "okay" for women. I think that okay was supposed to mean full-length mirrors, bathtubs, separate lockers in the gym, and little else. I immediately realized, however, that in order to transform Yale into "a good place for women" we would have to enroll more than a mere 500 women among 4,000 male undergraduates and would have to recruit women to the faculty. At the time, there were 12 women among 672 tenure-track faculty members, including only two full professors, one in English and one in history.

Through regular networking with women in similar roles at other institutions—Sheila Tobias (Wesleyan), Adele Simmons (Hampshire College), Patricia Graham (Princeton), Jacqueline Mattfeld (Barnard) and others—I received much support and formed many new friendships. Unlike my Harvard years, I was now all too aware of the unique problems women face and was determined to set them right. That I would perceive "okay" to mean a more gender-balanced student body and the presence of women at all ranks of the faculty had not been anticipated. The response to my vision was the appointment of many committees to study such radical suggestions, rather than any visible progress. I grew increasingly impatient.

By 1973 Yale's initial transition to coeducation had been accomplished. I could not persuade Yale to hire the women it claimed could not be found and were not needed. It was time for me to move on. My growing interest in equal-access issues led me to enter Yale Law School, from which I graduated in 1976. After clerking for a federal appellate judge on the Second Circuit for one year, I spent the next 20 years away from science practicing law. I began my legal career as a tax lawyer. Tax law is intellectually rigorous, and I had always been attracted to concrete rather than more philosophical problems. The firm I joined, however, was hierarchical and male dominated. I was discouraged from having client contact but was expected to encourage the wives of the firm's male clientele to blindly sign wills and trusts, the terms of which often provided that, upon a husband's death, the wife's assets would be managed by a trustee her husband had named and that should she remarry she would be automatically disinherited under the terms of the trust. This was not why I had gone to law school. I left after one year and embarked on a very successful career as a family lawyer, doing divorces, real estate closings, and wills and trusts for clients who understood the documents they were signing.

I enjoyed the challenge of practicing law in which I used many of the skills I had learned as a graduate student, an administrator, and a wife and mother. Nevertheless the question I had begun to address earlier continued to haunt me: Why are there not more women in science? My own experience led me to reject the explanation that women either cannot or will not do "hard science." I suspected that many women drift out of science for reasons that have nothing to do with their innate ability or their interest in science.

At critical junctures in my life, my parents' support, financial help, and some wise mentoring from a college chemistry professor had encouraged me to move ahead. I am certain, however, that better guidance in college might have persuaded me to follow my first love and study medicine. I am equally certain that, if postdoctoral fellowships targeted to women trying to pursue science careers while raising children had been offered in the 1950s, I would not have left scientific research. The slightest encouragement from my thesis adviser, Bob Woodward, or from my research director, David Bonner, also might have changed the course of my career. During those years, my husband was struggling to survive professionally as one of eight young instructors in the Yale chemistry department, burdened with a heavy teaching load and a minimal salary. We were both trying to survive and take care of our growing family. Neither of us was looking far into the future, and, even though I had enjoyed science and had excelled at it, I, like many of my contemporaries, became a science dropout. The course of my career illustrates how promising women scientists can easily become invisible, part of the pool of women scientists who "cannot be found."

# The National Academy of Sciences

My personal experience, combined with an increased awareness of women's roles and men's reluctance to share power, led me to explore how some women have nevertheless managed to achieve outstanding careers as scientists. Few living women scientists are visible enough to serve as role models for young women. Unless women scientists have attained unusual success, their stories are frequently discounted as "merely anecdotal" or as "sour grapes." On the other hand, when hard statistical data about the status of women scientists is published, it fails to portray the reality of the lives of individual women scientists. For these reasons I decided to collect and disseminate the views of some outstanding women scientists. I made no attempt to obtain statistical data about gender differences among scientists, or to address the philosophy of science, the feminist critique of science, the history of science, and the careers of ordinary groups of women scientists. These are subjects for other books.

I found such a group of distinguished scientists among women who had been elected to the prestigious National Academy of Sciences. Each year 60 new members are admitted to the Academy based on nomination and subsequent election by Academy members. Election thus requires both outstanding achievement in science and the recognition of such achievement by one's peers in the scientific establishment. Since more than 25,000 science doctorates are awarded in the United States annually, only a tiny fraction of scientists can ever attain Academy membership. Academy members represent an elite minority among scientists, and their experiences are obviously not typical. Yet because of their elite status, they are highly visible, take active roles in shaping science policy, and indirectly affect the lives of research scientists, in and out of academia, at every level. The careers and views of women elected to the Academy therefore inevitably have an impact on all American women scientists.

I was eager to talk with the women who had been elected to the Academy in order to gain some insight into what had led to their success. How, if at all, do these women differ from women scientists who are less visible? What had attracted them to science? Where do they work? Are they married? Do they have children? If so, how did they find time to combine family and career? What concerns, if any, did they have as women scientists? Do they have any advice that could help younger women aspiring to careers in science?

The women members of the National Academy of Sciences whose stories form the basis for this book were born between 1898 and 1956, obtained their doctorates between 1930 and 1983, and were elected to the Academy between 1957 and 1996. Their lives and careers span the twentieth century. In 1973 there were only 10 women members in the Academy among 900 men. By 1996, when I had completed gathering information for this book, there were 86 women among the 1,600 natural scientists in the Academy, 5 percent of the total membership.[1] The biological sciences have the highest proportion of women members, while chemistry, engineering, and physics have the lowest. Except for two women of Asian descent, the group includes no minority women, reflecting the scarcity of minority women among U.S. scientists in this age group.

The women who were born in the early part of the twentieth century faced enormous difficulties and frustrations. They were told at every turn that they did not belong in science. Most felt lucky if they found positions working as research assistants to established male scientists that provided them with a modest income and an opportunity to work in a laboratory. Some worked as unpaid volunteers or as assistants to their husbands. Conditions for women scientists improved temporarily during World Wars I and II, but they did not improve significantly until the advent of the women's movement and affirmative action in the early 1970s. When the achievements of Academy members who had worked successfully behind the scenes became visible, these women were recruited to positions from which they had previously been barred.

The career patterns of the youngest Academy members, those who earned their doctorates after the mid-1960s, stand in stark contrast to those of their older colleagues. Overt barriers to women's entry into the mainstream of science crumbled as a result of civil rights legislation and the women's movement, and today women scientists hold positions at all levels of universities, government laboratories, and industry. Responsibilities for chairing departments and scientific societies and for serving on peer review committees are shared by women, an unthinkable situation only 25 years ago. The proportion of women among doctorate recipients in the sciences has grown fourfold since 1975. In the biological sciences, the area of science with the highest proportion of women, women now earn close to half of all doctorates. Although the number of women in the physical, mathematical, and engineering sciences and at the upper echelons of all fields remains low, this fact should not blind us to the progress that has been achieved.

I contacted all 86 living women members of the National Academy of Sciences in the biological, physical, mathematical, and engineering sciences who had been elected to the Academy between 1957 and 1996.[2] They include three Nobel laureates, eight MacArthur "genius" award winners, and 18 recipients of the National Medal of Science. I posed the following three questions to each member of this small but distinguished group of women: To what factors do you attribute your success in science? In your opinion, was your career affected by the fact that you are a woman and, if so, how? If you had money and power, what policies would you implement to facilitate science careers for women? I was overwhelmed by the warm responses I received from almost all of the women I contacted. They were welcoming, helpful, and eager to cooperate despite busy lives juggling teaching, research, travel, speaking engagements, committee work, personal responsibilities, grant application deadlines, and myriad other responsibilities. They gave of their time generously and talked candidly about their careers. Most of the women had spent their entire careers in predominantly male environments and seemed genuinely pleased that their voices as women would finally be heard.

Sixty-six of the 86 members (77 percent) answered my request for information. I interviewed 37 members, either in person or by phone, and received letter replies from 24 others.[3] Eighty-six outstanding women are not representative of the larger universe of women scientists, and the stories these women shared with me are obviously subjective and subject to self-censorship. Their optimistic outlook is one of the keys to their success. Since they are at the top of their professions, it is natural for them to minimize negative experiences rather than dwell on them.  Almost all of them, including the older genera-tion of women, remain active in research and have firsthand contact with students, postdoctoral fellows, and young faculty members.  They are therefore aware of the issues confronting today's young women scientists.

To capture the richness, variety, and poignancy of the experiences of these women, I have included 26 narrative profiles in the chapters that follow and shorter excerpts from interviews and letters through-out the text.  Each of these talented and creative women is unique, but each is also a product of her time.  The profiles of these scientists re-flect both their unique individuality and the culture of the era in which they lived and worked.  I would have liked to include the comments of every one of the women who wrote to me or whom I interviewed, but limitations of space and time made that impossible.  The profiles I se-lected for inclusion illustrate the variety of lifestyles and experiences of women in different age groups and different scientific disciplines.  An understanding of the obstacles encountered by all women scientists, even those as talented and outstanding as the members of the National Academy of Sciences, is critical in order to develop effective strategies to facilitate science careers for women in the future.

The profiles in Chapters 4 through 7 of women Academy mem-bers are arranged in chronological order to reflect the close links be-tween the careers of these scientists and the times in which they forged their careers.[4]  Chapters 2 and 3, preceding the profiles, describe the culture in which contemporary women scientists work and live.  Chap-ters 8 and 9 focus on common threads that emerged from the profiles of Academy members.  Chapter 10 contains suggestions made by mem-bers to attract more women to science careers.

I learned a great deal from my conversations with this group of outstanding individuals and hope that you too will enjoy listening to their voices.  I also hope that the stories of women who pursued their passion for science with such courage, zest, and enthusiasm will in-spire more young women and men to dare to follow in their footsteps, so that the community of scientists will become more diverse as we embark on a new millennium.

# A FIRMAMENT OF STARS

Our society puts an enormous premium on stardom, money, and success. Achievements such as those of Jackie Robinson, Michael Jordan, Arthur Ashe, and Tiger Woods encourage young African Americans to become athletes. Even though few will ever reach the pinnacles achieved by these stars, their examples inspire many to pursue careers that, in the absence of such examples, they might never have dared to enter. So, too, Sandra Day O'Connor's appointment to the U.S. Supreme Court, the election of Shirley Chisholm and Dianne Feinstein to the House and Senate, respectively, and Madeleine Albright's role as Secretary of State help young women envisage a future in law or public service, even though only a tiny fraction of women lawyers will ever serve as justices on the Supreme Court or as members of Congress.

Lawyers and physicians do not have to be giants in their fields to become visible to the average citizen. They are portrayed on *L.A. Law* and *ER*. We encounter women in doctors' offices, hospital emergency rooms, law offices, and courts. Close to half of all medical and law students are now female, not because women have suddenly acquired new aptitudes needed in these professions but because these professions have opened their doors to women and because women's roles in these professions are easily visible to the public. Women who achieve success in fields that have little visibility have far less impact on the dreams and plans of younger women. The visibility of successful role models seems to make a critical difference.

Science, like sports, Hollywood, and business, has its stars, but they are far less visible than athletes, movie actors, or business tycoons. Even the names of Nobel Prize winners in science are quickly forgotten once the initial excitement of an award subsides. Few scientists, no matter how distinguished, ever become household names. Whether male or female, they usually work behind the scenes, and the media tend to portray them as "nerds." Until very recently, distinguished women scientists were even less visible than their male colleagues. Since people assess a profession by its public image, by what they see and hear, it is not surprising that few women were brave enough to aspire to become scientists, a relatively invisible profession and one that, as women, they were discouraged from entering. It is unlikely that many women will choose science as a career in the future unless we enable them to see and understand how women live, work, and cope as scientists.

When we read about scientific achievements such as the cloning of a sheep called Dolly, the discovery of a new elementary particle of matter, or a promising approach toward the curing of cancer, we rarely understand how the individuals responsible for these developments became star scientists. We know even less about the careers of the many scientists who work behind the scenes making important contributions but who rarely achieve stardom. In fact, unless we happen to be scientists or have friends who are, few of us understand how a man or a woman becomes a research scientist in the first place. We assume that scientists must be bright and well educated and that they must work hard to achieve success. Most of us are also aware that without research scientists we would not have antibiotics, Prozac, Viagra, cell phones, computers, or jet planes. We vaguely remember the basic principles of science we learned in school, but few of us have more than a superficial understanding of modern physics, chemistry, or biology. To understand how one becomes a successful scientist, we must first understand how scientists are trained and how they work.

Scientists work in different capacities and in a wide range of settings, including government laboratories, industry, and educational institutions. A scientist may earn a living as a patent attorney, science writer, educator, researcher, marketing analyst, or any one of numerous other roles. A scientist may teach in primary or secondary school or at a college or university. She or he may head a large division of researchers at a pharmaceuticals firm, work as a technician in a chemical plant, or serve as a meteorologist in a government agency such as NASA (National Aeronautics and Space Administration). Scientists can become entrepreneurs and start their own biotech or software companies. The opportunities are boundless and constantly changing, each requiring different levels of training, skill, and commitment and each in turn offering different rewards and opportunities.

The "inner circle" of science consists of a subgroup of the larger universe of scientists, namely those men and women who work as independent researchers at the frontiers of science hoping to break new ground, often at elite institutions. The members of this inner circle, although numerically a small fraction of all science doctorates, influence the profession to a much larger degree than one would expect from their numbers. Because until very recently women were virtually excluded from this inner circle and because that is where scientists are most likely to gain visibility and influence, that inner circle is the focus of this book. I therefore deliberately highlight the careers of the few exceptional women who have joined this inner circle to demonstrate that women and men can be equally committed and successful as scientists and that stereotypical expectations regarding career paths based on gender are not appropriate for scientists at any level.

## Becoming a Scientist

A doctoral degree from a research university is the usual prerequisite for a career as an independent research scientist in government, industry, or academia. It normally takes four to six years to earn a doctorate. During this period, students take advanced courses in their chosen field and must demonstrate their mastery of the subject by a series of examinations. They must also carry out an independent research project under the supervision of a faculty member who acts as dissertation supervisor. They are expected to solve a problem that will break new ground, write a doctoral dissertation, and, if possible, publish a paper in a scientific journal based on their work. The outcome of a particular research project depends not only on the skill of a particular student but also on the complexity of the chosen problem and to a considerable extent on luck. If a problem appears insoluble, a student may be advised to embark on a new project rather than continue to struggle in vain.

Fortunately, financial support in one form or another is available to most science graduate students during the period in which they work toward a doctoral degree. The ablest students are awarded competitive national fellowships, which they may use at any university to which they gain admission. Fellowships may also be awarded to students directly by the institution to which they are admitted. Some students support themselves as teaching assistants; others receive stipends as research assistants from grants received by the professors under whose supervision they work.

The number of students working for a single professor varies enormously from discipline to discipline, professor to professor, and institution to institution, from a mere two or three to groups as large as 30 or more. Today, most professors also supervise one or more postdoctoral fellows, students who have already earned a Ph.D. but who want to add to their experience and publications. Most scientists complete one or more years of such postdoctoral study before seeking a permanent position. In some laboratories, especially in the life sciences, individuals who may have completed work for a master's or Ph.D. degree hold paid staff positions as laboratory technicians or research assistants. They carry out certain aspects of the research for others in the group, often the preliminary or somewhat repetitive steps required before new ground can be broken, although they may have an opportunity to do independent work as well. One or more advanced undergraduate students may also be permitted to do a limited amount of research under the supervision of a faculty member in the summer or during their senior year.

A faculty member and his or her postdoctoral fellows, predoctoral students, and technicians, if any, constitute a research group. Group members normally participate in regular group seminars, share laboratory space and facilities, and interact on a daily basis. The more experienced members of a group are expected to help the newer members, and much informal learning takes place this way. Unlike doctoral students in the humanities who often work in relative isolation, science students interact closely with their peers and are influenced strongly by the particular group with which they become affiliated. The specific nature of how a research group functions varies enormously by discipline and institution and from faculty member to faculty member. Some groups are very informal; others are very structured. Some give great latitude to students; others are very hierarchical. Some are relaxed, others extremely competitive.

## Competition

The pressure and competitiveness among scientists vary among different institutions, fields, departments, and professors. It is greatest for individuals who work on the "hottest" topics—areas that are expected to break significant new ground rather than refining current knowledge. When a topic is hot, several groups of scientists often compete to solve it. Since there is enormous prestige attached to getting there first, competition can be severe. Scientists whose work culminates in such "breakthroughs" become stars in their discipline and enjoy the benefits of stardom. They receive rapid promotions and lucrative job offers from rival institutions. They are invited as speakers to international symposia, receive prestigious prizes, are sought out as consultants by industrial firms, attract the brightest students, and, perhaps most importantly, are able to attract increased financial support for their research.

Research programs are enormously expensive. They require personnel, space, equipment, supplies, and support services. The days when a chemist needed little beyond a laboratory bench, some glassware, and a heating mantle are long past. The tools used in research today, such as nuclear magnetic resonance spectrometers, particle accelerators, computing facilities, and high-resolution telescopes, to name just a few, are enormously expensive. The three physicists who shared the 1990 Nobel Prize in Physics for conducting experiments that confirmed that protons and neutrons, once thought to be the fundamental particles of all matter, were actually made up of infinitesimally small bundles of energy, or quarks, used a 2-mile-long particle accelerator at Stanford University to conduct their research. They could not have made their discovery without this piece of equipment, nor could they have paid for such equipment without financial help from the federal government. The decision of Congress not to fund a planned new accelerator in Texas several years ago was a severe blow to particle physicists and their research, and it immediately affected the employment prospects of particle physicists. While this is perhaps an extreme example, scientists today cannot work effectively without grant support. Universities depend on outside agency funding to underwrite the expense of the research carried out by scientists on their faculty. We should therefore not be surprised that the ability of a scientist to attract outside funding has become a major criterion for deciding who is appointed to the faculty and who is promoted to tenure. Since money available from federal agencies and private sources is limited, the competition for such funds among researchers is fierce.

Only a tiny fraction of scientists ever become superstars, but, since research requires funding and stars attract money, a climate in which researchers dream of achieving stardom has a significant impact on all research scientists. The number of tenured faculty positions at leading universities is limited, and the competition for these positions is intense. Once a scientist achieves tenure, she or he has great freedom to pursue individual research interests, limited only by teaching responsibilities and by the ability to obtain sufficient funds to support students, postdoctoral fellows, and the costs of equipment and research. Nevertheless, at many institutions the pressures to achieve star status, to obtain funding, to win prizes, and to gain the perks that such status brings continue even after a faculty member is awarded tenure. These pressures can lead to long hours, six- and seven-day work weeks, and extensive travel, leaving little free time.

## Why Academia Matters

Roughly half of all science doctorate recipients enter academic life.

Although fundamental research in science is by no means restricted to universities, in most fields much of it is carried out there. Faculty members at research universities train the next generation of research scientists. Through their Ph.D. students and postdoctoral fellows, research professors exert enormous influence on the future course of scientific research beyond academia, in government and industry. The science faculties of our major research universities and scientists at leading research institutes tend to dominate the visible, influential scientific establishment. Granting agencies, editorial boards, and many professional societies also draw many of their members from academia. The majority of the members of the National Academy of Sciences are thus, not surprisingly, drawn from academic faculties and a few select research institutes.

Despite the influence of academia, many young scientists today, both male and female, seek positions in government laboratories or in industry—settings in which they are usually not directly responsible for obtaining funding, in which they avoid the struggle for promotion to tenure, and in which they have more regular hours—in order to have more time available for family and outside interests. Although most scientists are not employed at elite institutions, those who move away from the scientific center of gravity remain less visible and less influential.

## Women in Academia

The year 1968 marked the beginning of a period of enormous change in women's education and employment. The women's movement, sparked by the publication of Betty Friedan's *The Feminine Mystique*[1] was in full swing. President Johnson had just signed an executive order requiring that affirmative action be taken to bring the hiring of women into line with their availability in the relevant labor pool. Princeton University had announced that it would admit women as undergraduates, the first of the Ivy League colleges to take that step. Yale and other Ivy League colleges quickly followed suit. Before the late 1960s, only a handful of women a year had been admitted to professional programs such as medicine and law, and many graduate science departments admitted virtually no women. The few women who were admitted often found it difficult to find a willing dissertation supervisor, and those who earned Ph.D. degrees rarely obtained employment commensurate with their ability and training.

When the barriers to women's higher education and employment tumbled in the 1970s, almost no women scientists held positions at universities or in industry. The students who entered formerly all-male colleges or undertook graduate study at universities in the 1970s and 1980s were thus taught almost exclusively by male faculty. Minority women were doubly disadvantaged, since there were neither women nor minorities on the faculties of major universities. It is difficult for professors who have spent a lifetime working in an exclusively white all-male environment to envisage women or minority students as future colleagues or successors, and it is difficult for women who study in such male-dominated institutions to aspire to academic careers. It is unlikely that larger numbers of women will choose science as a career until more women are appointed to senior positions on university faculties.

Pressured by women's groups and federal legislation in the early 1970s, universities, for the first time, began to address the virtual absence of women from the ranks of academia. Leading institutions, including Berkeley, Harvard, Yale, and others, issued reports on the status of women on their faculties. Harvard had no women full professors and almost no women associate professors on its faculty. Fewer than 6 percent of its assistant professors were women. In the early 1970s, according to a graduate student survey at the time, the majority of Harvard professors still believed that women had to make a choice between an academic career and marriage and/or a family. The Harvard report concluded that "as long as such a choice is required, academic women will be, and will be regarded as 'exceptional'—a tag that few of us, male or female, can carry for long, and that inevitably means discouragement and frustration for married women, and even for single women, attempting to pursue careers."[2] The situation was similar at all other major universities. Given these employment prospects, it is not surprising that women were not rushing to earn science doctorates.

Although the total number of doctorates in all disciplines awarded to women annually in the United States has increased steadily each year since 1920, the percent of doctorates awarded to women has fluctuated widely. In 1945 women earned 20 percent of all doctorates, but this was only slightly higher than the proportion they had earned in 1920. After World War II the proportion of women earning doctorates plummeted and it took until 1975 before it again reached 20 percent. By 1995, however, women were earning 39 percent of all doctorates. A similar increase in the proportion of women earning doctorates has taken place in every branch of science.[3] (Figure 1)

Today, women scientists are represented on the non-tenured ranks of university faculties in almost the same proportion as they are among science doctorates, but the proportion of women on tenured science faculties at American colleges and universities remains far below the numbers that one would expect based on the proportion of women in the pool from which tenured faculty are recruited. It takes on average ten years after receipt of the Ph.D. for a scientist to attain tenure. It is evident from Figure 2 that the proportion of tenured women in 1995 was far lower than the proportion of women in the pool of doctorates ten years earlier.[4] It is obvious that factors other than the proportion

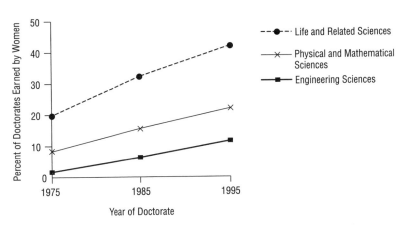

FIGURE 1    Proportion of doctorates earned by women in the United States in selected scientific fields.

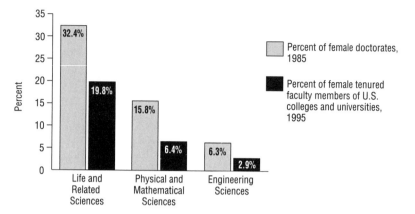

FIGURE 2    The percent of doctorates awarded to females in the U.S. in 1985 compared to the percent of female tenured faculty members at U.S. colleges and universities in 1995 in selected scientific fields.

of women earning science doctorates account for the dearth of women at the top.

The widely held belief that the scarcity of senior women scientists is caused by the failure of women to remain employed once they earn doctorates is unsupported by facts.  According to a recent study that examined the employment status of students who had received their doctoral degrees in the natural sciences at Harvard from 1988 through 1993, 90 percent of female and 89 percent of male doctorate recipients were employed three to five years after earning their degrees.[5]   Most women scientists remain continuously employed after they complete their training.  Even as early as the mid-1960s, when far fewer women were employed than today, more than 90 percent of all women who earned doctorates in the United States remained employed, most of them full time and without interruption.[6]

Today, the overt barriers formerly encountered by women who wanted to pursue scientific careers have almost disappeared, and the proportion of women science doctorates who seek academic positions is slightly higher than it is among men.  Since there continue to be relatively few tenured women even in humanistic disciplines in which women have been earning a high proportion of doctorates for many decades, it is apparent that the persistent scarcity of women scientists at the top must be the result of factors beyond the number of doctorates earned by women. The number of available tenure slots, institutional willingness to recruit and appoint women, the number of women seeking academic positions, and the retention rate among women faculty obviously all play a role.

The causes for the existing skewed gender distribution at the upper echelons of science are complex and not yet completely understood. It is, however, undisputed that today women as well as men can and do succeed at the highest level of science. The profiles of women members of the National Academy of Sciences that follow illuminate those factors that helped these women to excel as well as those factors that can deter women from pursuing demanding scientific careers. They contain valuable proposals for further leveling the playing field for male and female scientists in the future.

# NEW
# OPPORTUNITIES,
# TRADITIONAL
# EXPECTATIONS

Today, in the wake of civil rights legislation, affirmative action, and the women's movement, an ever-increasing number of women science doctorate recipients are being actively recruited by government, industry, and academia. Yet despite this obvious progress, the playing field for women research scientists is not yet level. Women's progression through the ranks remains slower than men's, the glass ceiling is intact, and in most fields the number of women in the sciences remains low in comparison with that of men.

Universities, research institutes, and industrial enterprises were established in an environment in which there were few if any women scientists. When these institutions opened their doors to women, women moved into a work environment that made no allowances for the fact that most women want children and that the period for childbearing, limited by the biological clock, coincides with the period for attaining tenure status or promotion.

Today, young women are entering formerly all-male occupations in ever-increasing numbers, and most working-age women fill dual roles as breadwinners and homemakers. The terms scientist, lawyer, surgeon, construction worker, police officer, and business executive no longer apply exclusively to males. Notwithstanding these changes, institutions have been slow to adapt to the needs of families with two employed parents, and women live and work in a culture that straddles the old and the new and clings to traditional attitudes concerning women's proper roles.

Many of the obstacles that contemporary women scientists encounter are rooted in this disconnect between the realities of women's lives and assumptions about their lives based on traditional stereotypes that remain entrenched in our society. I once asked an Israeli professor what he would do if he had two equally well-qualified applicants for a faculty position, one male and the other female. Without hesitation he replied that he would hire the male because, he said, "a woman would have to stay at home whenever a child or another family member became ill and that would be disruptive." When I reminded him that every Israeli male under 50 at that time was subject to six weeks a year of military duty he shrugged and added, "Oh, I never thought of that!" I am sure that this professor sincerely believed that his views were based on rational grounds. He was, however, so profoundly influenced by gender stereotypes that he could not perceive the irrational basis underlying his decision. The assumption persists that moms, rather than dads, remain the primary caretakers of the young.

Because old attitudes persist, the femininity of women embarking on scientific or other traditionally male careers remains suspect. We are still more comfortable with female flight attendants than female pilots, with female pediatricians than female surgeons, and with women artists than female scientists. The less a woman's chosen career is consonant with a "feminine" role the more directly her career may be viewed as in conflict with her role as wife and mother. The notion that women's primary role should be that of mother and nurturer persists even among those men and women who concede that women can become successful professionals.

It has been well documented that, as long as such attitudes remain ingrained in our culture, most working mothers or potential mothers cope not only with the dual demands of work and home but also with feelings of guilt and worry about their children's well-being.[1] Men have traditionally been expected to pursue careers without regard to family responsibilities. They tend to view every career advancement as an enhancement of their family's welfare and financial security because they are under societal pressure to be the primary breadwinners for their families. For women, on the other hand, a professional promotion can heighten the conflict between career and family. As a result, success has a different impact on the career decisions of men and women.

Studies have repeatedly shown that children are not adversely affected by working mothers provided the children are adequately cared for and the mothers are happy in their work environments.[2] The vast majority of women work because they need the income. Women who are assumed to work for personal rather than economic reasons are often criticized and described as selfish. On the other hand, our society expects or even forces poor women and welfare mothers to work. There is no rational basis for viewing women's roles so differently based on their socioeconomic class or for assuming that the children of middle-class women are harmed when their mothers work but that the children of poor women are not, especially since women scientists and other women pursuing freely chosen careers are far more likely to be content and to be able to afford adequate child care than mothers who must work in less skilled and lower-paying jobs.

Parents, teachers, friends, and even families often assume that to succeed as scientists women must sacrifice their relationships with friends, family, husbands, and children for the sake of their careers. Such assumptions are unfounded, but they continue to affect potential women scientists in profound ways at all stages of their lives and can dampen the aspirations of young women. In light of these attitudes it is not surprising that many people find it difficult to reconcile the image of a good wife and mother with that of a competent scientist and still regard women scientists with a mixture of awe and admiration, aggressive, masculine, and selfish on the one hand and intelligent, brave, and daring on the other. Women themselves often view such stereotypical portrayals as accurate and become reluctant to pursue their interests in science.

Such problems are not unique to science. A recent headline in the *New York Times* read "Missing: Great Women Chefs of New York." The article that followed quoted Pat Bartholomew, chairwoman of the Department of Hospitality Management at New York City Technical College, as saying:

> Through school and up to five years later, women have the
> same opportunities as men. . . . While they are students,
> women have the best grades, the best hands and are the most
> focused. When they leave school there is no problem getting
> the grunt jobs. But after about five years, lots of these really
> top young women have disappeared. They are out of fine res-
> taurants into all kinds of other jobs—catering, journalism,
> cookbook writing, restaurant consulting, . . . or they are pastry
> chefs.[3]

The reasons advanced for the "disappearance" of women chefs included long hours, brutal competition, and conflicts with family responsibilities. Many moved to places they viewed as more relaxed, less
competitive, and more tolerant of women.

Legislation outlawing discrimination does not automatically trans-
late into a change of entrenched attitudes and practices. Women now
account for close to half of all medical students in the United States.
Once they graduate they are in great demand. Nevertheless, as reported in a recent *New York Times* article headlined "For Women in
Medicine, a Road to Compromise, Not Perks," the top tiers of medicine have remained inaccessible to many women, and women hold few
positions as deans or tenured faculty. According to Wendy Chakin,
editor of the *Journal of the American Medical Women's Association*, the
main reason for the dearth of women at the top is that issues about
career pathways that are the least bit off track, like taking time off for
childrearing, persist.[4]

Health experts, both male and female, report that while sexism in
medicine still exists, particularly in the top echelons of academia, they
view the difficulty in combining a demanding profession with family
life as the single biggest hindrance to the advancement of female doctors. As one female physician and mother of four children commented:
"A lot of male doctors still have housewives at home. They can stay at
work until 10, and when they get home, their kids are bathed and there
is food in the house." Although in many respects culinary arts, medicine, and science are worlds apart, the issues for women in these fields
and in many other professions are strikingly similar.

Whenever I discussed the idea for this book with women friends and scientists, they responded with enthusiasm and encouragement. Men, on the other hand, wanted to know why I was writing a book on women in science, since, in their view, there are no longer any problems for women who want to have science careers, and there are already "several books on the subject." Inevitably they cited a token woman here or there to prove their point. Several implied that as the result of affirmative action women scientists now have an advantage over men.

Many men feel threatened by the ongoing change in women's roles, even though women's entry into the work force should lessen the financial burden our society places on them. Deviations from traditional norms easily spark conflict. The reaction to the 1997 Boston nanny murder case typifies the hostility toward professional working women still found among a large segment of the population. In that case the young child of two physician parents was fatally injured while in the care of a nanny. The father worked full time while the mother worked three days a week and often returned home for lunch. Nevertheless, the mother, not the father, was widely blamed for the tragedy that befell the child.

Harassment of women is one way some men attempt to maintain positions of authority. At the professional level and in academia, hostility toward women and attempts to undermine their ability to do their work often take subtler forms than the overt sexual harassment found among blue-collar workers.[5] My own experience of being stripped of the dean's title when my responsibilities shifted from Yale's graduate school to its undergraduate college arose out of the fear that I would have threatened the entrenched males had I been offered a title that until then had been reserved exclusively for men. It was a typical manifestation of subconscious efforts to keep women in their place. In many respects such relatively subtle forms of discrimination are more difficult to combat than the former outright exclusion.

In March 1999 the Massachusetts Institute of Technology, one of the most prestigious science and engineering universities in this country, issued a report, based on factual data, acknowledging that its female professors suffer from pervasive if unintentional discrimination.

The report documents discrimination in hiring, awards, promotions, in the allocation of laboratory space and research funds, and in women's underrepresentation on important committees.[6] The study and report were initiated after women scientists on MIT's faculty learned that a male faculty member had written a textbook based on a curriculum a female colleague had developed, without her knowledge or consent. MIT took a commendable and courageous step in issuing the report.

Similar problems exist elsewhere. One of the younger members of the National Academy of Sciences at another large university who asked to remain anonymous, and whom I shall arbitrarily refer to as J.S., related the following story: A prominent male scientist expressed a romantic interest in her, which she rebuffed. He then asked her to collaborate with him on a research project, but she declined to do so. After she refused to collaborate, he decided to compete with her by working on the same problem she and her research group were working on, a competition that he lost. When her results were published in a scientific journal but his work was not, he told colleagues that his work had not been published yet because J.S. had reviewed and rejected his paper, a story that was patently untrue. He then continued to circulate this story for months even after J.S. had confronted him and urged him to contact the journal editor so that he could assure himself that she had never even received his paper for review. After she had experienced a number of similar incidents, she concluded that:

> While one cannot unequivocally state that any of these events related to the fact that I was female, they left me convinced that if I did not speak up for myself and if I was not tough and aggressive in return, I would not survive in a scientific/academic world dominated by aggressive males.

Although each such event can be overcome, the profiles that follow make it evident that the cumulative effect of such incidents continues to handicap many women.

# FINDING A NICHE
## Women Born Before 1920

Women who were born early in the twentieth century forged their careers in the face of overwhelming obstacles. They were told at every turn that they did not belong in science. Most of those who dared to ignore this message remained essentially invisible and unrecognized. A tiny minority, however, found a niche here or there to carry on their work, and with persistence and luck they eventually entered mainstream science. The members of the National Academy of Sciences profiled in this chapter belong to this minority.

Academy members born before 1920 obtained their doctorates in the 1930s and 1940s, a time when discrimination against women was rampant. Women scientists were hired briefly during World Wars I and II to replace men who had gone to war, but in each case the doors that had been opened were slammed shut as soon as the wars ended. Employment prospects for women scientists, already severely limited in the 1920s, became dismal during the Great Depression of the 1930s. The women in this generation began their scientific careers unobtrusively, often hiding their gender to others, even to themselves, to the extent this was possible, in order to blend into a male-dominated profession. They walked a tightrope and could not afford to look around for fear they might lose their balance. It took unusual passion, luck, and stubborn persistence for these women to survive as scientists.

Fifteen of the 86 women members of the National Academy of Sciences were born before 1920. Ten of these 15 responded to my request for information, either by letter or in interviews. Over half of this group of women had been born abroad and had left their native countries for political reasons.[1] They came to the United States early in their careers, some even before they had completed their education. I suspect that their immigrant status helped them to persevere in a profession viewed as "inappropriate" for women, because as immigrants they were already outsiders, and it was therefore easier for them to defy cultural norms than for women who were firmly rooted in the prevailing American culture. The independence and self-assurance required of these women to pull up stakes in the face of political upheaval may also have contributed to their later success.

The group includes 11 women who earned Ph.D. degrees, three who earned M.D. degrees, and one who stopped her formal education after earning a master's degree. Each of these women scientists ultimately obtained permanent positions, but nine of them first spent many years working as research assistants or associates for established male scientists. Four of the 15 eventually obtained tenured positions on the arts and science faculty of a university. Seven others obtained faculty appointments at medical schools. Of the remaining four, three joined the staffs of government or private research institutes and one spent her entire career at a pharmaceuticals firm. That two of these women scientists were awarded the Nobel Prize and nine the National Medal of Science is a testament to the success they attained despite many obstacles.

The widely held belief that, in order to pursue careers in science, women in this generation had to remain single, or at least childless, appears to be without foundation. Two-thirds of these 15 scientists married, and almost half of them had children. Although neither of the Nobel Prize recipients ever married, five of the nine recipients of the National Medal of Science raised a family. For those who married, the choice of a supportive husband was often a key factor in their success. Husbands were instrumental in helping them find a place to work and frequently provided the sole source of family income in the early stages of the women's careers. On the other hand, one woman became a single mother of four children after her scientist husband left her to marry a graduate student, but she nevertheless continued a distinguished and uninterrupted career as a scientist. Eight of the women married men who also were later elected to the Academy. Most of the women who had children held off-ladder research positions during the early phases of their careers, before they entered mainstream science. Single women were hardly better off than married women. They did not confront nepotism rules, but neither could they depend on a husband for help or financial support.

The profiles that follow convey the obstacles that these pioneering women overcame in order to pursue their passion for science. I continue to be amazed that they succeeded.

## KATHERINE ESAU

Katherine Esau, a plant pathologist, came to the United States in 1923 with her family, which had fled from the Bolsheviks. She had studied agriculture in Russia and Germany and promptly found a position working for the Spreckels Sugar Company in California. She was hired to develop a sugar beet resistant to curly top—an economically ruinous viral disease spread by an insect called a leaf hopper. No one else at Spreckels was working on the project and Esau instituted a successful hybridization program.

When W. W. Robbins, then chair of the botany division of the University of California at Davis, paid a serendipitous visit to Spreckels, Esau asked him about graduate studies at UC Davis. He responded by offering her a graduate assistantship. Esau hoped to continue her research on developing the curly top-resistant sugar beet at UC Davis, but after her initial year of graduate studies she arrived at an impasse. Other UC Davis researchers had sugar beet fields they did not want infected with the curly top virus, which meant Esau could not release virus-laden leaf hoppers in the open. Undaunted, she decided to focus her research on the effect of the curly top virus on sugar beets instead, a decision that led to a lifelong career in pathological plant anatomy.[2]

Esau completed her doctorate in botany at UC Davis in 1931, joined its faculty the same year, and remained at Davis until her retirement. In 1954 she published a textbook on plant anatomy that became a classic in its field. She was elected to the National Academy of Sciences in 1957 but was not promoted to full professor at Davis until 1963, 32 years after she had joined the faculty and two years before she retired at the age of 67. Following her retirement in 1965, Esau continued her research at the University of California at Santa Barbara until three years before her death at the age of 99. Her work set the stage for modern advances in plant physiology and molecular biology. In 1989 President Bush awarded her the National Medal of Science for her work on the relationship between viruses and plant hosts.

Looking back on her education and career, she wrote to me in 1973 to tell me that scientific activities had dominated her life and that she had performed other aspects of academic life only out of a sense of duty. She added, "I found ways of maintaining spiritual independence while adjusting myself externally to established policies. . . . I have never felt that my career was being affected by the fact that I am a woman." Her terse comments throw light on how she and other women scientists in her generation coped.

## BERTA V. SCHARRER

Neuroanatomist Berta Scharrer was born in Germany in 1906. She came to this country in 1937, together with her husband, Ernst Scharrer. Although they were not Jewish, the Scharrers left Germany as a matter of conscience after Hitler came to power. Berta had earned a Ph.D. in 1930 from the university in Munich, where her husband was also a student, and they were married in 1934. The Scharrers, who had no children, worked in the same field and collaborated in their research. They decided early on that Berta would work as an unpaid assistant to her husband in order to avoid running afoul of nepotism rules. She would follow him wherever his career took him and pursue research in his laboratory. They began this arrangement in Germany and continued it in this country for almost 20 years. The Scharrers jointly made neuroendocrinology—a science that explores the relationship between an organism's central nervous system and its internal secretions—into an experimental and clinical science.

Between 1937, when they came to the United States, and 1946, when they went to the University of Colorado, the Scharrers were affiliated with three different universities in three different cities. Berta Scharrer was still unsalaried when her husband was asked to become chairman of the anatomy department at the newly established Albert Einstein College of Medicine in the Bronx in 1955. There she was finally appointed full professor. Although she now held a full-time position, she still received only a half-time salary.

When the Scharrers were attending a professional meeting in Florida in 1965, Ernst Scharrer drowned while swimming in the Atlantic Ocean. Berta Scharrer narrowly escaped the same fate. Now totally on her own, she was appointed acting chair of the department at Albert Einstein and, for the first time in her life, received a full salary. She took on administrative duties in addition to the research and teaching responsibilities she already had. In 1967, two years after her husband's death, Berta Scharrer was elected to the National Academy of Sciences. In a letter she wrote to me in 1973, Scharrer noted:

> My own activities have not been "typical" in that I was able to work with my husband providing the "milieu" until his death in 1965. It is only since then that I had to look after my professional career on my own. I do feel that in the U.S.A. women are not treated equally in academic circles, but this is hardly news.

In 1978, at the age of 72, Scharrer was appointed a distinguished university professor emerita at Einstein. She continued her research career for 17 more years, until her death in 1995. At the age of 76 she began new research and, in collaboration with two Danish scientists, worked on the identification and function of neuropeptides in invertebrates. She found that the same neuropeptides were present in invertebrates as in vertebrates, a discovery that provided evidence of a long evolutionary history of the neurosecretory system. At age 84 she moved into yet another emerging field—neuroimmunology. During the last six years of her life, she published 11 papers and three review articles and served as associate editor of the journal *Advances in Immunobiology.*

Scharrer received many honorary degrees and prizes. In 1983 President Reagan awarded her the National Medal of Science for demonstrating the central role of neurosecretion and neuropeptides in the integration of animal function and development. In a memoriam for Berta Scharrer, a fellow anatomist Steven Wissig, described her as a person of great humility and enormous concern for others. He remarked that Scharrer's lack of status prior to 1955 "reflected the strong prejudice against women as serious scientists."[3]

## RUTH PATRICK

Ruth Patrick is a distinguished limnologist, a scientist who studies rivers, lakes, and other freshwater bodies. She received a B.S. degree from Coker College in 1929 and completed her graduate study in botany at the University of Virginia, where she earned a Ph.D. in 1934. She then

held an unpaid position as curator of microscopy at the Academy of Natural Sciences for 11 years. In 1945 she was put on the payroll, and two years later she established the academy's Department of Limnology, which she has chaired from its inception. She has held a simultaneous position as adjunct professor in the Department of Botany at the University of Pennsylvania since 1948.

While still in graduate school, Ruth Patrick married Charles Hodge IV, also a scientist, but she decided to retain her maiden name in honor of her father. Widowed in 1985, Ruth Patrick married Lewis H. Van Dusen, Jr., in 1995. She has one son, Charles Hodge V, from her first marriage.

Patrick led an expedition to the headwaters of the Amazon River in 1955. She has been active in national societies concerned with ecology throughout her life and has served on many scientific advisory boards, among them President Reagan's Peer Review Committee on Acid Rain. Patrick has received numerous honorary degrees and other awards in the United States and abroad. In 1993 she received the Benjamin Franklin Award for Outstanding Scientific Achievement from the American Philosophical Society. In 1996 President Clinton awarded her the National Medal of Science for her research on rivers of the United States, for elucidating the importance of biodiversity, and for being the first person to use the ecosystem approach in studying the condition of rivers and the effects of pollution on them.

When I interviewed her in May 1995, Patrick was working on a multivolume treatise on the rivers of the United States. After trying in vain to mesh my schedule with her busy life so that we could meet in person, I accepted her suggestion to interview her via telephone. When I asked her when would be a convenient time, she immediately replied, "Two weeks from today at 8:30 a.m." She was 88 years old at the time and still worked a 10-hour day. In the course of our interview she talked about her childhood, her studies, and her career. Her recollections poignantly convey the atmosphere in which she and her female contemporaries pursued their passion for science. She noted several factors that contributed to her success as a distinguished scientist:

> One was my father, who, from the time that I was about six years old, encouraged me in the study of the natural sciences. Every Sunday afternoon he would take my sister and me with our little baskets and bottles out for an expedition. An expedition was going to the woods, where we would collect the flowers and the ferns and the mushrooms and the worms and the snails and all living things that little girls would be interested in or should be interested in. And then at the end he had a bamboo pole to which he would attach a can and he would reach down and scrape the rocks in the stream. He would bring the water up and put it in a bottle. We would then go home, and we would have our milk and crackers and he would have a cup of tea, and during that period of time we would pull the plants and animals from our baskets and he

would tell us what they were. Then, when this was finished, we would go into the library where he had a great rolltop desk. He would roll it back and I would climb up on his knees. He had four microscopes, and he would put out the appropriate one for what we were going to examine. He would make the slides and put them under the microscope and tell us what the things were: the protozoa, the nematodes, and the different kinds of algae.

Patrick's mother was a homemaker and a typical social lady of her time. She couldn't understand how her daughters could be interested in crawly bugs. But Patrick's father, though a lawyer by profession, loved science and encouraged his daughters' interest in it. By the time she was in high school, Patrick knew she wanted to study science in a serious way. She had a botany teacher who taught her how to identify trees by their buds and their bark and that intrigued her. Her father continued to foster her interest in microscopic things.

Patrick started college at the coeducational University of Kansas, but her mother would not let her go back there because she did not know the parents of the young men her daughter was dating. While at Kansas, however, Patrick had a botany professor who outlined the courses she should take if she wanted to be a scientist. When she ended up at Coker College, an all-girls school, for the rest of her undergraduate studies, her father noted that it was not big enough for someone who wanted to be a scientist, so every summer he sent her to research laboratories like Woods Hole and Cold Spring Harbor. For graduate school, Patrick went to the University of Virginia to study with Ivy Lewis, the foremost man in the country working on algae at that time.

Patrick married while she was a graduate student. Her husband, an entomologist, joined the faculty at Temple University in Philadelphia. She recalled:

Temple was then known as a poor boys' school. He had many offers from other places, but he believed firmly that, if he was a good teacher, and he was, that poor boys deserved a good education as much as wealthy ones. So he turned down opportunities at Penn and Princeton and so forth.

Patrick did her thesis research on the subject of diatoms, a class of unicellular microscopic algae. While in graduate school she started volunteer work at the Academy of Natural Sciences, which had the finest collection of diatoms in the United States. Upon completing her Ph.D. in 1934, she became a full-time volunteer at the Academy of Natural Sciences. She remained there as an unpaid volunteer until 1945, when she was finally put on a salary of $1,000 a year. She made a little money during the Depression by taking any work she could get, first at Temple University, then at the School of Horticulture. Later, in addition to her work at the Academy of Natural Sciences, she was named an adjunct professor at the University of Pennsylvania.

Patrick remembers how hard a time she had as a woman when she first entered her career. "Men at the time didn't really think women were as bright as men, and therefore women were never given the better positions." In a letter to me in 1973 she wrote:

> Most professors do not want to take on a woman as a Ph.D. candidate because they feel she will get married and they will have wasted their time, for such a person will not contribute to the professor's reputation. I also feel that when I was young employers discriminated against women, probably because they did not think a woman would stay on the job. Women have always had to work for less salary than men.
>
> The thing that is most essential is that we establish an environment whereby women when they are young are accepted with equal credentials as men, are paid the same salary, and given the same chance.
>
> Once you have established a reputation, it may help to be a woman. I have been most courteously treated by my colleagues and have felt that they have always respected my opinions, provided they were well founded.

Patrick believes that women are just as perceptive and work just as hard as men. She firmly believes in equal opportunity but feels affirmative action has "gone a bit overboard." She equates affirmative action with a lowering of standards. At the same time she concedes that, in her experience, when women who are not qualified are hired, they eventually "fade out."

Patrick tells her women students that if they decide to get married they should not use their income to have a better car, to join more clubs, or to have better clothing. She advises them to use it to provide good child care for their children and to hire somebody who will provide a steady home atmosphere for the husband. She added:

> I don't think a woman has the right to take on the vows of marriage and then go away so that when her husband comes home tired he has to scramble for his dinner. . . . You have to provide just like you do when you don't work. You delegate authority. . . . I do think so often women get inspired or stimulated by their careers and put their home and their children in the background.

Patrick herself deliberately delayed having a child until she and her husband could afford to hire help to take over her domestic responsibilities. They eventually had one son, born in 1951.

When Ruth Patrick was elected to the National Academy of Sciences in 1970 she was one of only 10 women out of about 900 members. I asked her whether there had been a sense of community among the small number of women in the Academy at that time. She responded with a quick categorical "no." When pressed, she conceded that they were "friends" but added that "of course each had separate research interests." Her ambivalence is revealing. To her, as to most women in her generation, the mere hint that women might act in concert presents a threat. Patrick's observations are typical for women in her age group.

Determined to pursue her love of science, Patrick ferreted out ways to do so. She was obviously keenly aware that women were not treated equally with men and that this had seriously circumscribed her own professional opportunities, but she never questioned the underlying assumption that she alone must assume the responsibility for seeing that her husband and child were adequately taken care of. She simply tacked her professional role onto her role as wife and mother.

# RITA LEVI-MONTALCINI

Neurophysiologist Rita Levi-Montalcini is another eminent scientist with foreign roots. She was born and educated in Italy, where she  graduated from medical school in 1936 with a summa cum laude degree in medicine and surgery. In 1947 a faculty member in the zoology department of Washington University in St. Louis invited her to come to the United States. She accepted the invitation and held a position as research assistant at Washington University for four years. In 1951 she was appointed assistant professor. By 1959 she had been promoted to full professor, a position she held until her retirement in 1977. Following her retirement, Levi-Montalcini returned to her native Italy and became director of the Institute of Cell Biology of the Italian National Council of Research in Rome. She retired from that position in 1979 but continued a position there as guest professor. When Levi-Montalcini was elected to the National Academy of Sciences in 1968, she became the tenth woman ever to be elected to the Academy.

Levi-Montalcini had shown early in her career that two tumors from mice transplanted into chick embryos induced potent growth in the chick embryo nervous system. She had discovered the nerve growth factor. She and her co-workers made fundamental and important contributions to understanding the mechanisms that regulate nerve cells belonging to the sensory and sympathetic ganglia (components of the peripheral nervous system). In 1986 Levi-Montalcini shared the Nobel Prize in Physiology or Medicine for this work with the American biochemist Stanley Cohen.

Levi-Montalcini wrote a moving autobiography in which she describes her early struggle with her father, to whom she was close but who believed a professional career would interfere with family obligations for his daughters.[4]  She prevailed and was eventually permitted to be tutored privately to prepare for university entrance.  In 1939, soon after she had earned her M.D., she was banned from the university as a Jew under Mussolini. Undaunted, she secretly pursued her research in her home.[5] She wrote to me from St. Louis in 1973:

> First of all, I must say that I do not believe my career has been affected by being a woman. A woman's career may be hampered in two ways: by her feeling of responsibility to her family and also by professional discrimination. In my case, I had no family obligations because I am single and therefore did not have that problem to face. As for the second difficulty, I have never felt, either in Italy or in the United States, any professional hostility because of being a woman.
>
> I do believe that educational and professional opportunities for women are somewhat improved today, and it is high time. There is no doubt that more women are now welcome in academic careers and they are entering in greater numbers. In the past, many fields were not open to women and in addition they were discouraged from preparing for a career that would interfere with home and family duties. Certainly I would like to see more women admitted to professional careers such as, for example, medicine, which is still in this country largely in the hands of men. I believe there should be more opportunity for advancement to top academic and administrative posts. . . .
>
> Furthermore, I would like to see many more women enter political life and take a very active part in government at all levels, which I strongly believe would have a salutary effect on society as a whole. Discrimination in this area is particularly evident and I believe that only through much greater participation by women will our country play a more constructive role both at home and abroad.

Levi-Montalcini chose not to mention, or simply blocked out, the fact that as a woman she was for years prevented from obtaining the education required for university entrance. Nevertheless, she is obviously sensitive to women's issues, although she denies, like so many of her contemporaries, that she ever experienced discrimination herself.

Whenever I meet someone who has met Rita Levi-Montalcini in person they immediately tell me what a strikingly beautiful and elegant woman she is, even at close to 90. Today she has a chauffeur for her Alfa Romeo Lotus and uses a car phone to keep in touch with the institute. She remains a vocal advocate for Italian science and for women scientists.[6] It is evident from her autobiography that Levi-Montalcini made a deliberate decision to remain single in order to devote herself to her work, and her 1973 letter intimates that she still believes that having a family inevitably detracts from a woman's career.

## MILDRED COHN

Biochemist Mildred Cohn grew up in New York City, the daughter of Russian immigrants. Her father was a man with inordinate respect for learning and scholarship who indoctrinated his daughter with the be-

lief that she could achieve anything she chose to, though not without some difficulty since she was both female and Jewish. She recalls that her mother had more conventional attitudes and more modest goals for her future.

Mildred Cohn graduated from public high school and attended Hunter College, an all-girls school, where she majored in chemistry and minored in physics. At the time, no physics major was offered. Writing about her career she remarked that her fascination with science was "sufficiently strong to withstand erosion by inferior education."[7] She describes Hunter's attitude toward science education as epitomized by the chairman of the chemistry department, who declared that it was not ladylike for women to be chemists and that his sole purpose was to prepare his students to become chemistry teachers. One can only wonder how many of her classmates were driven out of science altogether by these attitudes.

By the time Cohn graduated from Hunter in 1931 her father's business had failed as a result of the Depression and her family could not finance her graduate studies. Despite an outstanding academic record, her applications for scholarships or other financial aid to 20 or more graduate schools were unsuccessful. She managed to pay for one year of study at Columbia University by living at home, using meager savings, and earning money by babysitting. She could not hold a teaching assistantship because in 1931 Columbia offered assistantships only to its male students. As a result, she was forced to leave Columbia after the first year for lack of money, but she obtained a position at a government aeronautics laboratory in Virginia. There she was the only woman among 70 men. She found a supportive supervisor and was able to publish two papers, on one of which she was the senior author. Nevertheless, after two years she was informed that she would never be promoted.

Cohn decided to return to graduate school, where she again encountered discouragement. She persisted and, using her own money, earned her Ph.D. in physical chemistry under Harold Urey in 1938. Jobs were scarce. Industrial recruiters regularly posted notices on the bulletin board announcing that, "Mr. X of Y Company will interview prospective doctorate recipients—Male, Christian." She felt fortunate when, with Urey's help, she obtained a postdoctoral position in Vincent du Vigneaud's laboratory at Washington University in St. Louis. This marked the beginning of a period of 21 years during which Cohn worked as a research associate.

Soon after she had begun her new position, du Vigneaud moved his laboratory from St. Louis to Cornell Medical School in New York. Mildred Cohn had just married Henry Primakoff, a physicist who, luckily, also found a position in New York, and so the family moved. In 1946 Cohn's husband was offered a position in the physics department at Washington University in St. Louis, and she urged him to accept it. With du Vigneaud's help she obtained a position in Carl Cori's laboratory in the biochemistry department at Washington University Medical School, which at the time was the center of enzymology—the study of biological catalysts. During her years in Cori's department Cohn did independent research, and for the last six of those years she was an established investigator of the American Heart Association. In 1958 Cohn was promoted from research associate to associate professor at Washington University.

Cohn left St. Louis in 1960, this time to follow her husband to the University of Pennsylvania, where he had been appointed a professor of physics. She joined the biophysics department at the University of Pennsylvania Medical School and was promoted to full professor the next year. In 1982 she retired and became professor emerita.

Mildred Cohn was elected to the National Academy of Sciences in 1971. In addition to her many other honors, she received the National Medal of Science in 1982 for her pioneering use of stable isotopic tracers in metabolic studies and for the application of nuclear magnetic resonance techniques to the study of the function of enzymes. Today, Mildred Cohn continues her research, lectures on women in science, and serves on many professional committees.

Cohn's husband, the late Henry Primakoff, a theoretical physicist, also was a member of the Academy. They have three children, all of whom also earned doctorates, two in psychology and one in biochemistry, and each of whom has a spouse who also has a doctorate. All three have children, and Cohn recently became a proud great-grandmother. Looking back in 1992, Cohn commented on her career and on her status as a research assistant for so many years:

> In spite of the obvious disadvantages of my status, it held a number of positive features. I had no teaching or administrative duty; I was able to stay home if a child were seriously ill and could spend two months vacationing with my family every summer. Furthermore, I was not competing on the academic ladder, so I could choose technically difficult, long-range problems because there was no pressure to publish quickly. . . .
>
> In retrospect, the most important aspect of my career is that it has been fun—the joy of predictive results materializ-

ing, the even more rewarding experience of serendipitously discovering an entirely unexpected phenomenon, and the special gratification of having the results applied to medical problems. And I have been so lucky, always finding myself in a stimulating milieu, interacting with first-class minds, first my mentors, then my colleagues, and finally my postdoctoral fellows and students. My greatest piece of luck was marrying Henry Primakoff, an excellent scientist who treated me as an intellectual equal and always assumed that I should pursue a scientific career and behaved accordingly.[8]

In answer to my 1995 letter Cohn wrote, "The factors to which I attribute my success as a scientist: without undue modesty, native ability, self-confidence, a supportive husband, and great scientists as mentors." She then added:

> My career has been affected at every stage by the fact that I am a woman, beginning with my undergraduate education, which was very inferior in chemistry, and physics was not even offered [as a major] at Hunter College, unlike the excellent science education that my male counterparts received at City College. In my day, I experienced discrimination in academia, government, and industry.

Several Academy members recalled Mildred Cohn fondly as an early role model who had shown them how to juggle their careers and family responsibilities. Mildred Cohn pursued work she loved and put the best possible light on all of her experiences, however discouraging they were. She refused to get sidetracked by the numerous injustices that she had to overcome along the way to ultimate success. From early on she seems to have had the inner resources to overcome adversity. These traits undoubtedly contributed to her success.

## GERTRUDE B. ELION

Biochemist Gertrude Elion and her co-worker, George Hitchings, shared the 1990 Nobel Prize in Physiology or Medicine for their discoveries of "important new principles of drug treatment." Elion and

Hitchings were able to demonstrate the differences in nucleic acid metabolism between normal human cells, cancer cells, protozoa, bacteria, and viruses. Based on these differences they developed drugs that can kill cancer cells, viruses, and other organisms because they block nucleic acid synthesis in cancer cells and in noxious organisms without damaging normal human cells. Their research marked the be-

ginning of "rational drug design," that is, drugs designed based on an understanding of basic biochemical and physiological processes, rather than through tedious trial-and-error methods. The new drugs they developed include those used for the treatment of leukemia and malaria; azathioprine, a drug that prevents the rejection of transplanted organs; and acyclovir, the first selective and effective drug for the treatment of herpes infections.

Gertrude Elion was born in New York, the daughter of educated immigrant parents from Eastern Europe. By the time she had graduated from high school, the 1929 stock market crash had forced her father, a dentist, into bankruptcy. Fortunately, her grades were good, so she was able to attend Hunter College, which charged no tuition. In an autobiography she wrote for the Nobel Foundation in 1988, Elion recalled her days at Hunter:

> When I entered Hunter College in 1933, I decided to major in science, and, in particular, chemistry. . . . I remember my school days as being very challenging and full of good camaraderie among the students. It was an all-girls school and I think many of our teachers were uncertain whether most of us would really go on with our careers. As a matter of fact, many of the girls went on to become teachers and some went into scien-

tific research. Because of the Depression, it was not possible for me to go on to graduate school, although I did apply to a number of universities with the hope of getting an assistantship or fellowship.[9]

Instead, Elion looked for a job, but she recalled that the few positions that existed in laboratories were not available to women. After holding a number of low-paid and volunteer temporary positions she had saved enough money to enter graduate school at New York University in the fall of 1939. She remembers that she was the only female in her graduate class, but no one seemed to mind and she did not consider it at all strange. While doing research for her master's degree, Elion also worked as a substitute teacher in the New York City secondary schools, teaching chemistry, physics, and general science for two years. By the time she finished her master's degree in 1941, World War II had begun. Although there was a shortage of chemists in industry, Elion was still unable to get a research job and instead accepted a position doing analytical control work. The work was repetitive, and she left after a year and a half because she had learned all she could on the job.

In 1944, seven years after she had graduated from Hunter College, Elion was hired as an assistant to George Hitchings at Burroughs Wellcome Laboratories, a position in which she finally had an opportunity to do research. She had an insatiable thirst for knowledge and was fortunate that Hitchings permitted her to learn as rapidly as she could and to take on added responsibility whenever she was ready for it. Still eager to earn her doctorate, Elion took night courses at Brooklyn Polytechnic Institute. After several years of commuting, she was told that she would no longer be permitted to study part time and that in order to continue she would have to leave her job and study full time. Afraid of not being able to return to her position at Burroughs Wellcome, she decided not to resume graduate study. Elion never earned a doctorate, but she later received honorary degrees from more than 25 universities. Early in her career, her fiancé, whom she adored, died tragically of bacterial endocarditis and she never married.[10] She remained at Burroughs Wellcome throughout her life, becoming a scientist emeritus in 1983.

Elion received innumerable honors. In 1990, two years after she had received the Nobel Prize, she became a member of the National Academy of Sciences. President Clinton awarded her the National Medal of Science the same year. She was elected to the Engineering and Science Hall of Fame in 1992 and in 1995 was made a foreign member of the Royal Society, the British counterpart of the National Academy of Sciences. Until her death in early 1999, Elion continued an active schedule, teaching at Duke University Medical School, writing, and traveling. She served on many boards of cancer and health-related organizations and frequently lectured to high school, college, and medical school students. When she was given $250,000 by Burroughs Wellcome Laboratories to donate to a charity of her choice, she gave the funds to Hunter College to assist women graduate students in chemistry and biochemistry. In 1995 she wrote to me as follows:

> My success as a scientist probably stems from hard work, devotion and persistence. It also helped to discover some extremely useful drugs for the treatment of leukemia, gout, and herpes virus infections as well as a drug which makes kidney transplantation possible by preventing rejection.
>
> My career was affected in its early days by not being able to find a job as a chemist. This changed when World War II came and there was a shortage of chemists in the workplace. After I came to Burroughs Wellcome in 1944, being a woman no longer hindered me in any way.
>
> The opportunities for women in science have increased tremendously in the past two decades. This is perhaps more so in industry than in academia. We employ a larger number of women scientists at all levels, including some vice-presidents. I think women must have the confidence to pursue their goals without the fear that they cannot succeed.

When Gertrude Elion began her career she, as a woman, was literally denied access to a career as a scientist. Yet during the course of her life, she fulfilled her personal dream of making a useful contribution to humankind through science. Her achievements received the recognition they deserved, and she became one of the few women ever to receive the Nobel Prize. Based on conversations I had with Elion a few weeks before her sudden death, I believe that few things pleased her as much as the letters of thanks she received from individuals whose suffering had been relieved as a result of her discoveries and the dramatic progress for women scientists that she witnessed during her lifetime. She was a truly modest and caring human being.

⟫◆⟪

Each of the women profiled in this chapter found a niche in which she could pursue her scientific interests and make significant contributions. All ultimately achieved recognition. They had extraordinary talent, but this alone was not enough. They also had unusual determination, grit, flexibility, and luck. Some survived, as Katherine Esau did, by finding "ways of maintaining spiritual independence while adjusting . . . externally to established policies" and rarely if ever addressing the issues they faced as women. They focused on their work to the exclusion of all else. Others, including Rita Levi-Montalcini, Mildred Cohn, and Gertrude Elion were acutely aware of the obstacles facing women who wanted to pursue their love of science. They struggled quietly and in isolation while they were young in order to forge careers, but once established and more secure, they reached out to other women. Rita Levi-Montalcini became an advocate for women and wrote candidly about her experiences and struggles in her autobiography. Mildred Cohn lent a hand and offered advice to younger women scientists throughout her career. She spoke and wrote about her life, revealing negative as well as positive aspects of her life as a scientist, wife, and mother. Gertrude Elion took an active role in reaching out to high school, college, and graduate students by lecturing widely and setting up a fund for women students at her alma mater, Hunter College. Each of these courageous women maintained optimism in the face of the hardships they encountered, an optimism that enabled them to prevail.

# FIERCELY INDEPENDENT
## Women Born in the 1920s

Women born in the 1920s lived through several major dislocations during their formative years—the stock market crash of 1929, the Great Depression of the 1930s, and World War II in the 1940s. Financial fortunes were made and lost, unemployment was rampant, and young men went off to war. In this climate, many parents, especially immigrant parents who had been unable to obtain a college education themselves, urged their daughters to acquire marketable skills, "just in case." The availability of scholarship aid and tuition-free colleges made college an option even for women who otherwise could not have afforded a college education.

When the United States entered the war in 1941, women were recruited to help the war effort, and employers who had previously slammed the door in women's faces now eagerly hired them. Yet four years later when the war was over, the women who had been recruited were no longer in demand and instead were encouraged to return to their rightful place, to bear and raise children and to provide homes for their husbands. Colleges and graduate schools were filled with veterans on the GI Bill. When Adlai Stevenson spoke at a Smith alumnae reunion I attended in the late 1950s, he reminded us that women should be educated so that they could become society's "culture bearers." The feminine mystique was in full swing and almost a decade

would pass before Betty Friedan attacked it for what it was—a rever-
sion to the mores of the Victorian era and a retreat from the progress
of the 1920s that had been sparked by the individualism and activism
of the flapper years.

Twenty-four of the 86 Academy members in this age group were
born between 1920 and 1929. These women earned doctorates in the
1940s and early 1950s. Most did so before they turned 30, several
when they were still in their early twenties. Nineteen are biological
scientists, four are physical scientists, and one is a mathematician.

Two-thirds of these women married, either in graduate school or
shortly after they had earned their doctorates, all before they had begun their careers. The group includes five couples in which both
spouses are Academy members. All but two of the married women
had children. The number of children ranged from one to five and
averaged just under three. Their families are larger than those of members born before 1920, who averaged two children each, and reflects
the high birthrate among parents of the baby boomers in the general
population.

The women profiled in the previous chapter moved into science
unobtrusively and against enormous resistance. Like their predecessors, the women born in the 1920s often encountered discouragement
and discrimination, but an increasing number now succeeded in forg-
ing careers as successful, visible, paid scientists. Even though employment opportunities for these women remained limited, many managed
to have uninterrupted careers and to progress steadily to senior positions. Ultimately, 16 of the 24 women in this group obtained permanent faculty appointments, but only two, pediatrician Mary Ellen Avery
and mathematician Cathleen Morawetz, had professorships before the
enactment of affirmative action legislation in the early 1970s. Of the
remaining eight women, seven worked in government laboratories or
research institutes and one in industry. Nine women began their careers in various off-ladder research positions, but even they eventually
moved into the mainstream; they were more likely to be married and
to have large families than women whose careers were on track from
the start.

Two-thirds of the 24 Academy members who were born in the

1920s wrote to me or spoke with me about their careers, their research, their personal lives, and how they coped with their multiple responsibilities. All were elected to the National Academy of Sciences after 1973. I have tried to convey the richness and variety of their experiences in the profiles that follow.

## MARIAN E. KOSHLAND

Until her death in 1997, Marian Koshland was a professor of immunology at the University of California, Berkeley. The mother of five children, she was married to Daniel E. Koshland, Jr., a professor in the Department of Molecular and Cell Biology, also at Berkeley. She made major contributions to her field in the 1950s and 1960s, while she still worked part time and had five small children. By the late 1960s she had demonstrated that antigen receptors of certain cells are encoded by multiple rearranging gene segments, a finding that today is one of the cornerstones of immunology. She resumed a full-time academic career as full professor on the Berkeley faculty in 1970, when the youngest of her five children was 17 years old.

Koshland's first child was born while she was still a graduate student, her second just as she finished her doctorate at the University of Chicago in 1949. Two years later she became the mother of twins. Her fifth and youngest child was born in 1953. In addition to five children, the Koshlands have nine grandchildren.

"Bunny" Koshland, as she was known to her friends and colleagues, made major contributions as an immunologist and molecular biologist. As a graduate student at the University of Chicago, she worked on a vaccine for Asiatic cholera, work that led to her lifelong interest in the structure and origin of antibodies, proteins emitted by B cells to fight disease. In the early 1980s she discovered that different antibodies have different amino acid compositions, which makes them extremely efficient at fending off disease. She also discovered a molecular chain that allows antibodies to be exported from a cell and to circulate in the bloodstream. In 1991 she and her Berkeley colleagues described the characteristics of a pathway that apparently serves as an intracellular superhighway, bypassing normal intracellular communications channels, thereby making possible the proliferation of B cells essential in fighting off infection.

Koshland was elected to the National Academy of Sciences in 1981. She chaired the Department of Microbiology and Immunology at Berkeley from 1982 to 1989 and served as president of the American Association of Immunologists from 1982 to 1983. She received numerous honors and honorary degrees and served on many committees of the National Institutes of Health and the National Science Foundation. As a member of the National Science Board, she was involved in setting national science policy. At an annual meeting of the American Association of Immunologists, the Committee for the Status of Women in Science honored her for demonstrating that a woman could have a spectacular career while successfully raising a family. In a memoriam for Koshland, a friend and colleague wrote:

> If there is any single feature that marked Bunny's work, it was her ability to reduce complex phenomena to experimentally addressable components. She did this by putting a very high emphasis on experimental rigor and absolute scientific integrity. She was not affected by fads in science, but only by the bottom line—how well hypotheses hold up to hard experimental scrutiny. . . . Bunny was not at all shy in attacking and probing every assumption, every finding, every control. Merely surviving an encounter with Bunny always gave me the confidence that I could defend my ideas to anyone.[1]

I met Marian Koshland for the first time when I interviewed her in 1995. She impressed me as self-assured, forceful, stylish but at the same time self-effacing in light of her many accomplishments. We talked about her career and especially how she had managed to raise five children and to remain at the forefront of her field. Koshland belonged to the generation of women whose careers were launched before the 1950s and who seem to have been less conflicted about juggling career and family demands than women who began their careers later. It became obvious from her remarks that her husband was enormously supportive and from the outset encouraged her to remain active in her profession. As she noted:

> The arrival of the twins was a very important thing that happened to me. When I had the twins just before my thirtieth birthday, I remember that I cried, and I did not cry very often. I said to Dan, "You go out and get an academic job. I think I will quit." He said, "No way, because you will bore the bloody hell out of me if you stay home. I don't want you to stay home. How about working half time?" I said, "Everybody brighter than I, or as bright, is working full time, so how can I ever compete working half time?" Here was his reply: "You haven't thought it through. Most academicians love to do the teaching. They have committees and business and students and those students have to finish in a fixed amount of time and you have to give them problems that are realistic. If you would work half time but spend all of that time on research, and do all the crazy things that nobody else can do, I think you can make it." And that is what I did.
>
> My husband got a job at Brookhaven and, at that time, they had promised me a job. But when I arrived the head of the department said, "We are not going to have the wife of anybody." It was terrible. Dan was lucky to have the job at Brookhaven, so he said, "Let's stay here for a year or so, but if they don't give you something and you don't find something, we will move." You have to remember that Brookhaven was out in the country, and it was not easy to find an alternative place. I had four children under the age of 5, so I had plenty to do. I didn't mind hanging around the house for a year. I took a year off.
>
> My husband came home one day after we had been at

Brookhaven for about one year and said, "I heard that they put on symposia at Brookhaven and write up the proceedings and publish them in a nice little volume. They do them in physics, chemistry, and biology. The person who is running it is a physicist who does not know anything about biology and he needs somebody. So why don't you go out and say that you will take over and edit this thing, provided they give you a laboratory and a technician." So that's what I did. I told them, "I promise you I'll work half time and I don't want to be paid more than that, but I will probably work a lot more than that." I knew I could pay for half-time help. The first year it took me about a quarter of my time to get organized. After I was there for a while it became easier. So I keep telling people you have to take advantage of opportunities and you have to trust people.

I don't think it is as easy today because you no longer get grants as easily as in those days. Brookhaven was supporting me in those early years. I tried many crazy things and lots of the experiments did not work, but enough of them did so that nobody ever knew that I worked only part time.

When I asked Koshland how she managed with five children, she was very candid and said her husband's family was quite wealthy. He had additional income, which enabled her to secure adequate paid help when her children were young. She remembered:

The year that I had the twins, I had help but never live-in. I never had live-in help in my life. I was sometimes able to keep the same person for as long as 15 years. They would come in from 7:00 or 8:00 a.m. to 5:00 p.m., five days a week. I insisted that they be able to drive a car. They had to have a car and to drive the children, because in case of some emergency I had to trust them. But I always did the cooking since I love to cook. My children helped me. We always had show and tell at dinnertime because that was how we were raised. We did not go out for dinner, except rarely, on the weekends. Dinner was the only time we all saw each other. I had the two girls first, so of course they were very useful as helpful little mothers, particularly with the twins. When I look back, everybody says to me, "How did you manage?" I really don't know. I guess I had a lot of energy.

Koshland observed that people would laugh because her husband was not known as the "home type," and she was the one who always fixed broken bikes and other things. Her husband, however, helped out in other ways:

> We used to share things. For example, I don't particularly like to write, but he loves to write and he is good at it. So he always was the social secretary and did all the letters back and forth, all the bills, all the telephone calls. He has a big family and I had none, so that was appropriate. . . . He also used to read to the kids. That he was very good about. He would even sometimes bathe them. He was not much good about diaper changing, although with the twins he had to do some. But he did a lot of those things and they were very useful.

As her children reached adolescence, Koshland encouraged her husband to spend more time with the boys because they had reached an awkward age and didn't really talk to her anymore. None of the children had any serious problems, and she attributes this in part to the tightly knit group they were as both a nuclear and an extended family. The Koshland family is a very large and very well-established family, and the children had reinforcement from their many cousins who lived a very similar lifestyle.

> It is very important to have peers who do the things you like because that gives you the strength to say "no" when you should say "no." So none of the children ever had a drug or alcohol problem. When I came to Berkeley because my husband had been offered a full professorship here, they offered me tenure as well, right off the bat. That was in 1965. I said, "I'm very sorry. I still have four children at home in junior high and high school, and I just can't do it." I cannot move to a new community and do everything. I can do two things—

research and children, teaching and children, or teaching and research—but not all three and still make sure that these four children get proper attention.

When she went to Berkeley, Koshland gave a seminar about her work at the virus institute, which at the time was run by Nobel Prize winner Wendell Stanley. Stanley heard her give the seminar and as a result invited her to work on his grant half time. Because Koshland did not have an academic appointment, Stanley remained as principal investigator. She went on to describe their working arrangement:

> He permitted me to run the lab independently. I remember he came up after my seminar and he said "You are not what I expected. You are obviously an independent scientist. So I will offer you this, and this is how we will arrange it." He never asked me for an accounting, never asked me for anything. So you have to trust people a little bit that they are going to give you certain degrees of freedom. Everybody said, "You are absolutely crazy. Stanley will just use your money." In fact, he never touched it. They said, "Isn't it terrible that you had somebody else get your grant." But I did not care. I got the money and a chance to do research. Perhaps because he was named as principal investigator, I got much more money than I would have as a little person on my own. You have to think about that when you are a woman starting out. You have to be expedient. You have to find your niche.

Upon Stanley's death in 1970, Koshland called the Department of Microbiology and Immunology at Berkeley and said that her youngest son was now in high school and she was ready for the academic job they had offered her earlier. "Not much after that, I was a professor of microbiology, just like that," she recalled. She admits she was very lucky but attributes her luck in part to the messages she was given early in life:

> I went to Vassar College and got out in 1942. There is a big gap between our age group and the now 50 year olds, the newcomers. A lot of the [postwar] women settled down to be good mothers because that was what they were supposed to do or

told to do. I was from the prewar generation and we were not told that. We were told to get out there and have babies and fight the war. It was very different. There is a big hiatus in women in the sciences among those who finished college in the fifties.

I asked Koshland why there are still relatively few women in many of the sciences. She noted that since 1965 she had been involved with students, and women were represented about 50-50 through the postdoctoral level. After that:

> They just seem to disappear. I don't know where they disappear to, and I don't think anybody has the answer to that question. I do not know how many women do what I did for so many years, that is to work part time so that I could also be a good mother. You have to realize that when you do that you are then [in effect] not listened to on anything. You disappear. But these women may not have disappeared, in fact. Nobody has compiled that data. It would be great to know it. If you want to change policy then you have to find the answer to this question. We receive many applications for faculty openings, but there are not that many women among them. Microbiology always has a lot of women in it, and we traditionally count on a very high percentage. So there isn't any objection to women, but there are not that many applying.

Koshland noted that we need analysis to know why the number of women in the sciences seems to drop off. You cannot drop out, she says, because it is too hard to get back in. She attributes the low number of women in part to her observation that women from older generations are simply not that competitive.

> They did not have teams, and they did not play games. I would say that is true of me. I said to my husband once, "Supposing I had found something really fabulous before you did. How would you take it?" He said, "I do not know. I might have a very hard time of it." On the other hand, I do not know how to win very well.

Part of that competitive spirit, Koshland noted, includes the need for a killer instinct when a research topic is hot—the need to run experiments quickly and get published. She added:

> I am not talking about being aggressive in a nasty way. I am talking about pure instinct. Maybe part of that means that you cannot have children and a career, in a sense.

When I asked how women could follow their killer instinct and have children, she responded:

> Maybe they can't. Or maybe the husband is going to take care of the children. My niece probably has a pretty good killer instinct and she's pretty invested. Her husband did a lot of the child raising.

As a child Koshland found school easy. But although she got positive reinforcement for being a quick learner, she did not consider herself that bright. Koshland remarked that she was not as bright as her husband and couldn't do quantum mechanics at all, when he had breezed through it. (Dan Koshland vehemently disagreed with her assessment of her intelligence when he later saw a transcript of my interview.) She acknowledged that she did some things better than her husband, and in some ways it all balanced out. Originality was a trait that had helped her a great deal. She lamented that, in her opinion, women are not pushed to think as creatively as men. In 30 years of teaching grant writing, Koshland says she never had what she considered to be the very best papers come from women.

Koshland then reflected on a year she spent at the Massachusetts Institute of Technology in 1980. The young women there who were running a course on women in science wanted to know how she had managed to pursue science and raise a family. They had been told at MIT that they would have to work harder, longer, and not get married if they wanted to make it, that if they were expedient in what they did, they would be giving in. Koshland was perplexed by the messages these women were getting. She felt she did not talk their language and didn't want to have to argue with them. Again and again, in the course of my interviews with Academy members, striking a balance between career and family was an unresolved and highly charged issue. I was surprised that it remained so even for Koshland, who seemed to have navigated the problem so successfully.

I asked Koshland if it was easier for women in her children's generation to become scientists than it had been for her. She said, "Definitely yes." She pointed out that the availability of car phones is an enormous boon to professional women and cited her own family as an example. "If my daughter-in-law gets stuck in traffic, she can call home and say to her babysitter, 'I'm sorry, I'm late and I would like you to stay a half hour later. Please put the casserole in the oven.' How much difference that would have made to me!" While the example may seem trivial, it rings true for any professional woman with young children who has experienced the havoc even a slight disruption can wreak on her household.

We talked about other women scientists, and the name of Mildred Cohn, the biochemist, came up. Mildred Cohn was about 10 years older than Marian Koshland, who recalled Cohn fondly as a helpful role model. When Koshland was on a postdoctoral fellowship in Boston, her husband did some work with Cohn. They became friends, so Koshland knew that Cohn had three children. At the time, Koshland says:

> My children were in first, third, and fifth grades. I met Mildred and I said, "Mildred, what do you do? My children are after me because I don't go to the PTA meetings and I don't do all the things that mothers are supposed to do. What did you do about that?" She burst out laughing and said, "My kids, of course, are in high school and in college. I thought to myself, they won't be around long, I think I will take some summers off and we will spend them together, and it will be really nice. When I told my children this, they said 'Oh, mother, you are not going to be like all the other mothers, are you?!'" You can't win. I thought if you want a great story, that is a great story. It made a great difference to me and I decided to hell with the critics. I was going to live through these various periods.

Bunny Koshland, like Mildred Cohn before her, is an outstanding example of a woman who was not only a formidable scientist but also a devoted wife and mother. She found ways to open doors that appeared to be firmly shut and created an environment for herself in which she could pursue her scientific interests and still devote time to her family. What a loss to science and for herself it would have been if she had given up science, as she was tempted to do, after her twins were born.

Throughout her career Koshland was supportive of other women. She clearly believed, as she had told the women at MIT in the 1980s, that one could have a family and do good science. At the same time she realized, speaking as a woman, that she could only handle two responsibilities at a time, research and children, teaching and children, or teaching and research. In her role as department chair, however, her views of what she would accept from her staff were more conflicted. She spoke of needing a "killer instinct" to get hot research out fast and remarked that "some of the professors don't like it" if men take off time to help their wives with a new baby because "after all we pay our students." When I suggested that stipends could be prorated, she responded by saying that the students would then have insufficient funds. Her comments highlight the problems that need to be solved in order to make institutions responsive to the needs of young families.

Koshland was obviously a unique and highly talented woman, but that alone is not enough to explain her success. She was also energetic, well organized, and willing to take chances, to trust, and she was lucky. Her husband supported her career and encouraged her from the outset. This was of critical importance. In addition, as she herself remarked, the Koshlands were financially well off, and she could hire all the help she felt she needed and was secure enough to delegate some aspects of child care to others. There is simply no way Koshland could have achieved what she did had she tried to "do it all" without help.

## ISABELLA L. KARLE

Isabella Karle is a crystallographer and a senior scientist at the U.S. Naval Research Laboratory. She once described a crystallographer as someone who studies the interior of materials with crystal structure analyses, determining which atoms are connected to which, and how they are arranged with respect to each other in the crystal lattice. Her early research analyzed the structure of molecules in the vapor state by

measuring the degree of diffraction, or bend, in a stream of electrons passing through a molecule. She was instrumental in the development of a quantitative procedure by which vibrational motion as well as bond lengths and bond angles in molecules can be determined accurately.

Later her research was directed toward crystal structure analysis. Based on her husband's theoretical work, Karle developed practical procedures for determining the phase associated with each scattered reflection from a beam of x-rays directed at a single crystal, information that is required to determine the exact position of each atom in a crystal. These practical procedures have been adopted worldwide and have enabled scientists to perform structural analyses using x-rays on crystals containing only light atoms such as carbon, oxygen, and nitrogen. Karle has applied the techniques she developed to a wide variety of problems. Her techniques enable researchers to determine the geometrical arrangement of atoms in complex molecules such as steroids, frog toxins, alkaloids, and peptides. This work has led to determination of the structure of more than 250 frog toxins and has enabled researchers to identify frogs more accurately by their toxins rather than by their appearance.

Karle has received numerous honors, including the National Medal of Science and the U.S. Department of Defense Distinguished Civilian Service Award, both in 1995; the Bower Award and Prize for Achievement in Science from the Franklin Institute in 1993; and the Gregori Aminoff Prize of the Royal Swedish Academy of Science in

1988. She holds several honorary degrees and lectures widely through-out the world. She has served as president of the American Crystallo-graphic Association, on the editorial boards of scientific journals, and on national committees concerned with various aspects of chemistry and crystallography. She has been a member of the National Academy of Sciences since 1978.

Isabella Karle was born in Detroit, Michigan, to Polish immigrant parents. Her father was a house painter and her mother a seamstress. Her parents encouraged her and her younger brother to pursue aca-demic studies, even during the Depression. She recalled, however, that one of her high school teachers told her that chemistry was not a "proper field for girls."

After attending public schools in Detroit, Karle was awarded a scholarship to the University of Michigan at Ann Arbor, where she completed her undergraduate studies in chemistry in 1941. Although Ann Arbor did not offer graduate teaching assistantships to women at the time, Karle was able to attend graduate school with the help of fellowships based on her outstanding record. She completed her Ph.D. in physical chemistry in 1944 at the age of 22. While a graduate stu-dent, she married fellow chemistry student Jerome Karle. After work-ing briefly on the wartime Manhattan Project in Chicago and after a short stint teaching at Ann Arbor, she and her husband accepted posi-tions at the Naval Research Laboratory in Washington, D.C., where they have remained to the present time. They often collaborate and have published many joint papers. Jerome Karle was awarded the Nobel Prize in Chemistry in 1985. The Karles have three daughters, born in 1946, 1950, and 1955.

When I interviewed Isabella Karle in April 1995 I asked what fac-tors had led to her extraordinary success in science. She reflected on her childhood:

> I was never much interested, I don't know why, in dolls and
> girls' toys. I was off playing with the boys, shooting marbles or
> whatever they were doing. . . . It isn't that I wasn't interested
> in babies and children because . . . I was looking forward to
> having my own when the right time came. These were the De-

pression days and so my family was very much a do-it-your-self-type family. Those kinds of families survived better. I did an awful lot of home canning when my mother was working as well as a lot of sewing. She was a seamstress, and I learned how to sew and made all my own clothes from a very early age. These homemaking activities, in which I was well versed, were very useful. In creating a dress or a suit or a coat, much thought goes into how to lay out the pattern properly, how to put the seams together properly, and I think all of that was useful even though sewing may seem like girls' activity.

Karle recalled her first years out of graduate school. Because World War II had not yet ended and faculties had been depleted due to wartime assignments, she was able to get a short-term job teaching chemistry to engineers at Ann Arbor. The students were all 16 and 17 years old because the 18 year olds were being drafted. She noted why she and her husband left Ann Arbor in 1946:

> One of the reasons was that there were, of course, policies against both a husband and a wife being hired in the same university, let alone the same department. The institutions that had offered my husband a position often were in small university towns that had no facilities for my expertise or vice versa. We were quite fortunate that the Naval Research Laboratory (NRL) was most happy to hire both of us and eventually we worked together. NRL worried about this because there were also regulations in the Civil Service about a husband and wife working in the same area. The rules covered people without Ph.D.s, but the regulations did not say anything about people with a doctorate. So, at that time, the laboratory used that excuse to make it quite legitimate to hire both of us.

The Karles had many opportunities to go elsewhere, and in some places they had offers to come together. But they were both satisfied with their arrangement in Washington, D.C. Jerome had an adjunct professorship at the University of Maryland for 20 years, which satisfied his teaching desire. Isabella was too busy with family to have other extracurricular activities. I asked Karle how she had coped with children and two unusually high-powered careers. She noted:

> My parents helped in the summer, but they lived far away. . . . For 13 years we had a succession of mature women who lived with us during the week, and on the weekends they would go to visit their own families. We did not have any babysitters on weekends. The other source of help was that my children are spaced five years apart. The eldest one was always very reliable with the little ones when I needed extra help. The middle one was a nuisance until the eldest one left home to go to college, and then she took over. Fortunately, they were entirely reliable. We spent much time with the children on weekends and also in the summers when we often went to Europe and took the children along with us once they were old enough, old enough being about six or seven.
>
> Fortunately, my parents were quite willing to look after the little ones for several weeks in the summertime. They lived in Detroit, which always meant that our trips, no matter whether they were in the United States or in Europe, went from Washington to Detroit and then from there on. Although all our daughters are grown now, each remembers these very special trips.

All three of Karle's daughters studied science in college. The youngest has a bachelor's degree in geology, went to graduate school for museum studies, and is now at the Natural History Museum of the Smithsonian. The middle daughter received a Ph.D. in chemistry from Duke University. She works at the Walter Reed Institute in the Washington area. The oldest also has a Ph.D. in chemistry and is a professor at Stony Brook.

Karle feels that being female has had both positive and negative effects on her career, but all in all she thinks it balanced out. She added:

> I know that other women have run into all sorts of situations in which they were badly discriminated against. . . . I do not think I was promoted quite as fast as I would have been if I were a male, but the promotions came along two or three years

later. . . . I have known very capable young women who eventually gave up their science because it was just too difficult to continue. Some were expected to be assistants forevermore in their positions. . . . Most of them that I knew about from my era followed their husbands to where the husbands had positions. Some of them spent their entire lives very productively, but they . . . were supported on their husbands' grants. They never had the opportunity to be independent. On the other hand, they did continue with their research and there was no particular financial burden.

A number of them who were not that closely related to their husband's field did not get a position immediately. They decided to have a family. After [that], they thought either that they couldn't compete in the sciences or their interest changed or they remained as homemakers. Their lives might have been different had they been able to immediately step into a postdoctoral program.

Karle believes that with the advent of affirmative action some women have been chosen for faculty or committee positions not for their abilities but because they are female and would satisfy an affirmative action quota. She believes this has bred a certain amount of resentment. Whenever she was asked to serve on a committee, she did not accept the invitation if she felt she "was being used because of affirmative action." She is concerned about the sometimes unfair implementation of affirmative action:

The university is told that it needs a certain number of women on the faculty. Women who had been recruited for a position thought that they had the position, and that all that was required was the final approval of the highest authority at the university. But after all this, they were told that they were not suitable. This was really heartbreaking. If they had been told in the first place, "No, we don't have a position" or "You do not meet our expectations," that would have been easier.

Karle does not believe that the number of women will ever equal the number of men in the sciences. She notes:

Women are at a definite disadvantage at many universities because they have to compete with men . . . and having children just interferes tremendously with the kinds of demands that are put on young faculty people, such as getting grants, doing your research, doing something brilliant. How much the ratio will increase depends upon economic times. When the economy is not very good, the thinking often goes, "A man has a family that he has to support, so if a woman is already married, her husband should support her."

Karle spent the first half of her career in the days before affirmative action and like many others in her generation, remains skeptical of its benefits to women.

## ESTHER M. CONWELL

Except for a brief period after she had earned her doctorate in physics from the University of Chicago and taught at Brooklyn College, Esther Conwell spent her entire career in industry. A solid-state physicist, Conwell worked one year at Bell Laboratories, then 20 years at Sylvania (now GTE). From 1972 until 1998 she was a principal scientist and then a research fellow at the Xerox Webster Research Center. She has also been affiliated with the University of Rochester and was associate director of the National Science Foundation (NSF) Center for Photo-induced Charged Transfer, which is associated with the chemistry department at the University of Rochester. Upon her recent retirement from Xerox, she joined the chemistry faculty at the University of Rochester. She has continued her association with the NSF center, where she conducts research with the assistance of postdoctoral fellows.

Esther Conwell has made major contributions to semiconductor physics, a branch of physics dealing with the properties of solids such as germanium, silicon, and other materials of which transistors are made. Conwell's fundamental research has led to increased understanding of these materials, contributing to the better design of transistors and, based on that, computers. She has also made significant contributions to integrated optics. More recently she has focused on exploring the interaction between light and matter. Conwell is the author of a book on high-field effects on semiconductors that has become a basic text in the field.

Conwell was elected to the National Academy of Sciences in 1990. She is also a member of the National Academy of Engineering and a recipient of the Achievement Award of the Society of Women Engineers. She has been very active on numerous boards and committees of the American Physical Society and governmental agencies.

The experience of the Depression convinced Conwell's father that every woman must be able to support herself, and he encouraged her to have a profession. Her mother had more traditional views. She hoped that her daughter would get married and have a family. Conwell fulfilled the hopes of both her parents. She married in 1945, immediately after completing her master's degree, and three years later obtained her Ph.D. in physics at the University of Chicago. Her husband, Abraham Rothberg, taught briefly at Columbia but spent most of his career as a writer and journalist. This worked well because he was willing to move to Rochester when she received the offer from Xerox. He was always supportive of her career. Conwell and her husband have one son, also a physicist, who is a professor at the University of Rochester. Mother and son have collaborated in some of their work on conducting polymers and have published several joint papers.

When her son was little, Conwell had a full-time, live-in housekeeper. Before he was born, she had worried about the effect working full time might have on a child. She now feels that the children of working mothers can turn out well (as indeed her son did), often better than those of full-time mothers. When her son was six years old, Conwell spent one year in Paris teaching and doing research at the Ecole Normal Superieure. She found child care in France to be much better than in the United States. The children there received a hot lunch and were supervised in school until 5 or 6 p.m., if necessary, for six full days a week. I heard similar comparisons from several other women who had lived abroad when their children were young.

When I asked Conwell whether her career had been affected by being female, her reply was an unambiguous "yes." As a man, she would have gone into academia, but that opportunity was not available to her at the time. She quickly added, however, that "industry is not a bad place to be. I think there is more equal treatment of women, at least at good companies such as Xerox."

Conwell would like to see increased flexibility in the tenure track to avoid having the decision about tenure coincide with childbearing. She sees no reason why the nontenure years could not be extended. In her opinion, universities do not hire as many women as they should, and the allegation that good women cannot be found is simply not true. Affirmative action has indeed helped women she said. She also believes that girls often get turned off in junior high school because they are affected by the culture surrounding them. Her own career in engineering demonstrates that conventional assumptions about women's assumed talents and interests have no bearing on the talents and aspirations of individual women. When teachers or parents assume that they do, a great injustice results.

## CATHLEEN S. MORAWETZ

Cathleen Synge Morawetz is an applied mathematician whose research focuses on the scattering of waves and the mathematics of transonic flow. Mathematical analyses of high-frequency vibrational waves can be used by geologists to locate the presence of oil deposits. These analyses also form the basis of ultrasound techniques used in medicine to visualize internal organs and the fetus in utero.

"Transonic flow" is the movement of something at a speed near the speed of the local air (which at sea level is 742 miles per hour). Through Morawetz's work in the mathematics of transonic flow, engineers now better understand how airplanes generate drag from the shock waves they create as they move from subsonic to supersonic speeds. Engineers were struggling to come up with a design for wings with shockless airfoils so the surrounding air could continue to flow without shocks during this transition event. Morawetz, however, demonstrated mathematically that a shock wave must occur during the transition of an object from subsonic to supersonic speed. The resulting drag from shock waves therefore cannot be avoided. Instead, engi-

neers now settle for a "shockless" airfoil design that has greatly reduced the impact of transition to supersonic flow.

Cathleen Synge Morawetz was born in Toronto, Canada, and graduated from the University of Toronto in 1945. She earned a master's degree from MIT in 1946 and a Ph.D. in applied mathematics from New York University in 1951. The next year NYU hired her as a research associate. By 1965 she had been promoted to full professor. From 1984 to 1988, Morawetz served as director of NYU's Courant Institute. She has been a professor emerita at NYU since 1993.

Morawetz has been an editor of numerous mathematical journals and served as president of the American Mathematical Society from 1995 to 1997. She has also served on numerous boards, including those of Princeton University and the Sloan Foundation. She currently chairs the board of the School of Theoretical Physics of the Dublin Institute for Advanced Studies. She was elected to the National Academy of Sciences in 1990 and has received numerous other honors, including honorary degrees from universities in the United States, Canada, and Europe. In 1998 she was awarded the National Medal of Science by President Clinton. The National Organization for Women honored her for successfully combining career and family, and she was named Outstanding Woman Scientist for 1993 by the Association for Women in Science.

Morawetz is married to Herbert Morawetz, a professor of polymer chemistry at Brooklyn Polytechnic Institute. The Morawetzes have four children and six grandchildren. I interviewed Morawetz at her townhouse in Greenwich Village in June 1995. As I entered the living room and stepped around a child's stroller, she proudly announced that she had recently welcomed a new grandchild. She and I are virtual contemporaries and established an easy rapport.

I asked, as I often did at the beginning of my interviews, to what factors Morawetz attributed her success as a mathematician. How had it happened that she became one of only four women mathematicians in the National Academy of Sciences? She said that mathematics, like music, requires a special natural talent and that she was lucky to have inherited it. She was born in Toronto of Irish parents. There was a mathematics tradition in her father's family, and he himself was a distinguished mathematician who had been director of the Institute for Advanced Studies in Ireland before he moved to Canada. How had he influenced her career? She responded:

> He didn't particularly encourage me to make a career in mathematics. His attitude toward women was that if they would just give up all that nonsense about clothes and coquetry and that sort of thing they could be anything they wanted to be, but not both. So I was certainly encouraged to have a profession. Things might go wrong. You might be a widow or your marriage might not work out, so you trained for something.
>
> When I finished college, right after the war, in Toronto, I wasn't thinking of going on in mathematics. One day a woman on the faculty whom I had known for many years, a mathematician, bumped into me on the campus and said, "What are you going to do next year?" And I said, "Well, I'm thinking of going to teach school in India." She got very excited and upset, and she arranged for me to get a fellowship from the Canadian University Women's Association. So then I looked around and went to MIT because CalTech wouldn't have me.

At MIT, where she was one of very few women, Morawetz earned a master's degree in February 1946, less than a year after she had begun graduate study. While at MIT she married Herbert Morawetz, a Czech refugee who had fled from the Nazis and who was then working for the Bakelite Corporation. When he was transferred to New Jersey, she applied for a position at Bell Labs, where she was told she would have to work in a pool of women with B.S. degrees, an offer she turned down. Shortly thereafter, her father met a friend and colleague, the noted NYU mathematician Richard Courant, to whom he mentioned casually that his daughter was looking for a position. Courant interviewed Morawetz and promptly hired her at NYU, where someone was needed to solder contacts on an innovative new computer. When she reported for work, however, she discovered that her supervisor-to-be, on hearing that Courant had promised the job to a woman, had quickly hired a male in her place. The former supervisor admitted this fact to Morawetz many years later, but at the time Courant wondered what to do with his friend's daughter. He solved the dilemma by hiring her to edit his book on fluid dynamics, a book that is still the bible in its field.

Although Morawetz did not think she should get a Ph.D. because her husband did not have one, she caught the postwar excitement in the air about going to graduate school and decided to "take some courses." She soon found that she was enjoying the courses and, before long, was on her way to getting a Ph.D. At this point, in 1947, she discovered she was pregnant. Shortly before her first child was born, her husband had also decided to go to graduate school. They lived in New Jersey and were now both students commuting to New York. Before long she had three more children, a boy born in 1949, a daughter in 1952, and the youngest, another daughter, in 1954.

Morawetz's in-laws were not enthusiastic about her advanced studies, but they provided enough financial help to enable the young couple and their two children to live modestly in a one-bedroom apartment in Brooklyn during the year in which both Cathleen and her husband were graduate students. Her household help situation in this period was poor, and, as she recalls, "It nearly finished me. It was very hard . . . the hardest time in my life. I thought I'd have to give up." She worried that she might not be able to complete her degree. Despite all obstacles, though, she earned her doctorate in 1951.

Morawetz attributes her ability to establish a professional career while raising four children to luck and to her willingness to accept full-time household help, which she had for many years. Her husband had grown up in an affluent family in Europe in which household help was taken for granted. The notion of having household help was never an issue with her or her husband, so that she was able to raise her children with far less guilt than many working mothers. In her opinion, men in the United States are more helpful in the home but also more resistant than European men to having help in the house. This makes it difficult for American women to accept the help they really need to manage a demanding career.

After Morawetz and her husband had completed their doctoral degrees, they spent a year in Boston, she at MIT and he at Harvard Medical School. There they met Mildred Cohn, the biochemist, and her husband, Henry Primakoff. The families became friends, and she remembers Mildred Cohn as a wonderful role model who gave her lots of useful advice about coping with work and family.

She also recalls that Courant, in his own way, was very supportive. He had been very unhappy when she told him that she was pregnant with her first child, but then he gave her a small raise every time she had another child so that she could pay for extra help. When she left for MIT, he informed her that as soon as she completed her doctorate she would have to leave NYU. By the time they met at a conference several months later, however, he had changed his mind. He offered to find her a research position at NYU if she wanted to come back, which she wanted dreadfully. Her husband found a position at Brooklyn Polytech, and, when Courant came through with his promise, she accepted a research position at NYU. She voluntarily delayed accepting a faculty teaching position at NYU until 1957.

> I did not want to teach. I felt that family and research were sufficient, and that if I were to take a teaching job, I would have to give up the research. I had planned, when our youngest was full time in school, I would start to do something. In 1957 Courant was about a year from his retirement, and he came and asked me if I wanted to go on the faculty, and I decided "now's the time," and I went.

Morawetz was promoted to full professor eight years later in 1965. In her opinion her promotion was by then a little overdue:

> They had a funny setup at the Courant Institute. There was an undergraduate department and some people even told me, "You know, if you would go into that, then there would be no problem." But I was too proud, and I wouldn't do this. Any-

way, I was promoted eventually. I did have the embarrassing fact that two women—Russian mathematicians I know very well—both said to me when I visited Russia in '63, "How come you're not a full professor?" But, you know, looking back, there were some reasons for it.

What course might Morawetz's career have taken if she had not been virtually pushed into graduate study by a friendly faculty member who had spotted her talent? Would she have given up mathematics? She is one of the few women among the Academy members whose father was in the same field. At a crucial time he was able to put a good word in for her. Family financial help enabled her to survive the years when her children were small. As I spoke with her I wondered how many talented women had been derailed along the way because for them no door had opened. Perhaps they lacked a mentor, financial help, a lucky break, or just incredible grit.

I asked Morawetz whether she had any explanation for the relatively low number of women mathematicians. She pointed out that the number was increasing:

> The way mathematics is done has been changing. There is a lot more interaction and cooperation among mathematicians today, and women are no longer excluded from this interaction. Today, women are actively involved in the exchange and play of ideas and are quite relaxed about that.

When she was in Toronto, the male students never included her when they met to discuss mathematics. "Perhaps," she says, "I was too shy or too proud. . . . I really think it has changed, and there are some very good women coming up at this time."

I asked Morawetz how she felt about affirmative action. She said it had been useful but should come to an end, at least for women. The biggest obstacle she sees to the advancement of women in academia is the overlap of the tenure-promotion decision with the childbearing years. On the other hand, she believes that special dispensations aimed at women lead to resentment among men. She is unsure what the solution is but added that what bothers her the most is that she would like to see many of these able young women have children. Twenty years later, despite significant progress for women, it still is not easy.

Morawetz took real pleasure in telling me that all four of her children are now grown and launched on their own careers. The oldest, a daughter, is a retail executive; her second child, a son, has a degree in industrial hygiene and runs the education program for a major union; the third, a daughter, graduated from MIT, toyed with mathematics but went to medical school instead. She is now a psychoanalytic psychiatrist. Her youngest, a daughter, is a professor of law at NYU. Among them they now have six children of their own. I heard similar glowing accounts from many of the women I spoke with whose children are now grown.

## JANET D. ROWLEY

Janet Rowley is a hematologist and an oncologist. She completed her undergraduate degree at the University of Chicago in 1944 and obtained her M.D. from its medical school four years later. Rowley has spent her entire career working as a research physician at the University of Chicago School of Medicine. She was appointed associate pro-

fessor there in 1969, promoted to full professor in 1977, and is now the Blum-Riese Distinguished Service Professor of Medicine at Chicago. Rowley was elected to the National Academy of Sciences in 1984.

Rowley's research interests include chromosome abnormalities in human malignant hematologic (blood) diseases. She was the first person to discover abnormal rearrangements, called translocations, in cells from leukemia patients and demonstrated that such breaks and rearrangements in chromosomes can cause leukemia and lymphoma in humans. Her research has led to better ways to diagnose malignancies, to predict the course of a patient's disease, and to monitor treatment.

Rowley has published more than 380 papers in scientific journals, lectures widely throughout the world, and has been an active participant in many scientific organizations in genetics and cancer research. In 1996 she received the Gairdner Award for outstanding contributions to medical science. In 1998 she was the corecipient of the Lasker Award for Clinical Science and was awarded the National Medal of Science by President Clinton. In the past, many recipients of these highly prestigious awards subsequently won a Nobel Prize for their achievements.

When I asked Rowley, a married mother of four children, whether her career had been affected by the fact that she is a woman, this is what she wrote to me in 1995:

> It has had a major effect on my career. Growing up in the 1930s and early 1940s, I knew I was smart and I came from a professional family; my mother was a high school teacher. I wanted to be a wife and mother and when I went to medical school, I looked on being a physician as an interesting part-time job. As a consequence, I took the minimal post-M.D. training required to be a licensed physician. However, after about six or seven years of part-time clinical work (and two children) I realized I was very dissatisfied. I wanted to do something more challenging. I had that opportunity in 1960 and after a one-year fellowship I switched from clinical responsibilities to research, still working part time, now with four children. I intended to continue working part time, but I made some important discoveries that were so exciting that I changed to working full time (really more than full time) in 1975.
>
> I have spent virtually all of my educational life and my research career at the University of Chicago. This was probably my first stroke of luck (other than my family). The university had a tradition from its founding of accepting women and

expecting them to be successful. In 1944, they had a quota for women medical school students, namely three in a class of 65; so I had to wait nine months to start in the next class. That meant I was 20 when I started medical school in 1945, which was probably just as well. I had no sense of discrimination in college or medical school, but I was a relatively accepting person. I didn't expect trouble and I didn't encounter any.

Rowley's attitude toward her career was typical for the time and was common among women scientists throughout the 1950s and 1960s. When I asked her to what factors she attributes her success as a scientist she wrote:

> The first factor is incredible good luck, being at the right place at the right time as new technologies allowed analysis of material that was not possible earlier. Intelligence, determination, a supportive environment at home and at work were all important as well.

She then shared her views about changing opportunities for women since the 1970s:

> I think it is very much easier for women scientists in medicine and in the biological sciences from the standpoint of entry into training programs, finding good, supportive mentors both female and male, and obtaining postdoctoral fellowship positions. Unfortunately, a woman's biological functions have not changed. She is the one who has children, and who, in most situations, has the primary responsibilities for child care. This is not a trivial matter.
>
> To be successful today, an aggressive postdoc should work at least a 12-hour day and do this at least six days a week. In my experience, a wife will accept this for her husband's (and therefore her own) future success. Few husbands, especially someone not in science, will tolerate such a schedule for their wives. If one has children, it becomes even more difficult. My young female colleagues are painfully torn on the one hand by their desire to be with their children (and their guilt at not

being good mothers) and, on the other hand, their commitment to themselves to make the most of their ability and to succeed in science. The solution is to make the situation more humane for everyone, but as competition for fewer and fewer faculty positions becomes even more fierce, I think this sensible solution is very unrealistic.

Like many other Academy members, Rowley is aware of a disproportionate loss of women at every level after the postdoctoral stage and bemoans the absence of any good studies that have surveyed the "dropouts" to determine the multiple factors that cause women to disappear. She concludes:

> This is the most urgent piece of information required! If you don't know what is wrong, how can you possibly fix it? . . . Do women quit because a mentor discourages them? Maybe. Do they quit because they don't like the lifestyle they see as the accepted norm? Maybe. Are they repelled by the high level of aggressive behavior that is displayed by some colleagues for whom success is the only goal, no matter what the price? Maybe. We need solid information before we can move forward.

Janet Rowley speaks for many women members of the National Academy of Sciences, her contemporaries as well as younger members, when she raises these issues. Despite her own outstanding achievements, she is acutely aware of the serious problems women scientists continue to face.

## MARY ELLEN AVERY

Throughout her career Mary Ellen Avery has been active worldwide in neonatology, a field of medicine that concerns the care, development, and diseases of newborn infants. She was the first person to identify the deficiency of surface-active agents as the cause of acute respiratory distress in premature babies and subsequently developed treatments for this syndrome. Since 1974 she has been affiliated with the Harvard Medical School and Children's Hospital in Boston.

In 1991 Avery served as president of the American Pediatric Society. The same year she received the National Medal of Science for her discovery of the cause of respiratory distress syndrome in premature babies. Avery was elected to the National Academy of Sciences in 1994 and currently serves on its Executive Committee. She has also served on numerous international scientific bodies and is the recipient of many

professional honors. She has been a trustee of Wheaton College, Radcliffe College, and Johns Hopkins University, all three of which have awarded her honorary degrees.

When I talked with Avery in her office at Harvard Medical School in December 1994, I asked about her early interest in science. Neither of her parents was a college graduate, but both were very anxious that their daughters obtain a good education. She attended private school before entering Wheaton College. She had been raised to believe that she could do anything she set her mind to. Avery was introduced to medicine early when a neighbor, who was a professor of pediatrics at the Women's Medical College of Pennsylvania, took her along on rounds to visit sick children, and she decided to become a pediatrician early in her college career. This, Avery says, gave her the motivation to do well in college. She graduated summa cum laude from Wheaton College in 1948 and went on to the Johns Hopkins School of Medicine.

After attending a women's college, Johns Hopkins was a culture shock. Avery found herself one of only four women in her class, but she adjusted to the change and grew to love it. She remained at Hopkins after receiving her M.D. degree in 1952, first as an intern and resident, then as a fellow, and ultimately as a member of the faculty. The only gaps were a two-year fellowship at Harvard and a year during which she was recovering from a bout with tuberculosis. By the time she left Johns Hopkins in 1969 she had attained the rank of associate professor and had served for eight years as pediatrician in charge of the newborn nurseries. Her personal experience with tuberculosis led to her interest in pulmonary disease. In 1969 she moved to Montreal to accept a position as professor and chair of pediatrics at McGill University. There she also served as physician in chief of Montreal Children's Hospital.

While at Johns Hopkins, Avery was the first woman ever to be named a Markle fellow. This provided her with five years of research support during the critical postresidency years and gave her great freedom to pursue her own research. Avery regards the financial support that the Markle award gave her as critical to her career.

> To me, that sense of freedom was very influential. Nobody was telling me that I had to apply for a research grant or I wouldn't get my job next year. Nobody was pushing me to do more clinical things. I did all those things actually, but I did them because I wanted to do them. In retrospect, I always loved independence, as I think is true of many physicians. I always felt that I had lots of things that I wanted to do, and if I wanted to do them, I would work very hard and enjoy it, but if I were plugged in to somebody else's project, and felt obliged to do it because that's what I was paid to do, I would have been miserable.

> A lot of women are relegated to technician roles, regardless of their degrees, because often they do things very slowly, carefully, systematically. In the lab they're wonderful. I've seen over and over again the men striving to get ahead on the women's shoulders. . . . I was always striving to have greater independence and authority and, frankly, I kind of liked to be recognized. I have an insatiable appetite for praise, and that positive feedback did come.

Avery recalled that from early on she wanted to do "something important, something that mattered." She liked to do research and never considered going into practice. She also loved to teach. She attributes her success in part to Johns Hopkins Medical School, which she believes was a good place for women. It was founded in 1889 by two women, Elizabeth Garrett of B&O Railroad fame and money and Carrie Thomas, president of Bryn Mawr, on the condition that it would accept women on an equal basis with men. As a result it has always had women students. Although there were very few women full professors, there were women associate professors who were very highly regarded. These senior women went out of their way collectively to be nice to women students.

> We lived in a place called the "hen house," which was really subsidized by the senior women physicians. I remember Helen Taussig would always invite me out to her house for Thanksgiving or, if I were on duty at Christmas, she'd say "When can you get away?" because a lot of the time it was kind of lonesome and hard work, and I didn't have any family in Baltimore, so she just picked up the pieces.

In 1974 Avery moved to Boston, where she was appointed a professor of pediatrics at Harvard Medical School and physician in chief of Children's Hospital. Since 1985 she has held the position of physician in chief emeritus at Children's Hospital. She continues to be active at Harvard, where she was recently appointed Thomas Morgan Rotch Distinguished Professor of Pediatrics. More than many women of her generation, Mary Ellen Avery's career followed a straight line, similar to that of her male colleagues. I wondered whether she felt that her career had been affected by the fact that she is a woman.

> Initially, when people asked if I had faced discrimination I really felt I had to say, "not in any serious way," because clearly I had been promoted. When you are physician in chief of Children's Hospital and somebody says, "Have you been discriminated against?" and you say "yes," it doesn't fit. However, every woman who is rising to senior status and attains a leadership position, I think, encounters men who are envious or jealous . . . or who simply can't understand that a woman can do anything—the subtle put-down, not being heard in a

crowd, being the only woman in a room and never having your hand recognized. Or the opposite. If you are the only woman in a room, you are such an anomaly that everything you say is likely to be remembered, and some of the things I say shouldn't be remembered. . . . You realize that sometimes you are being heard too much and at other times too little.

I asked Avery whether she thought the atmosphere had changed in the past 40 years. She thinks that it may have changed in some dimensions but that old attitudes still persist.

If I walk into a room where nobody knows me . . . there are usually several other women, but even so the men almost always dominate the conversations. If you try to get a word in, the conversation doesn't pick up on what you said. It goes back to where it was before, as if they would politely listen to you but they didn't give a damn what you said. . . . The way it has improved for me lately—the last decade—is that most of the time I am identified and known, and it is so much easier. . . . I can't be totally discounted. They can argue with me, but they can't totally ignore me.

Avery then commented on women's tendency to be less competitive than men, a topic several other Academy members raised. Women need money as much as men, but, in her opinion, they do not use money in the same competitive way as men. They welcome a raise, but they rarely came to her as chairperson to say "I *need* a raise." Men, on the other hand, had all sorts of reasons why they *needed* a raise—a new baby, a divorce, etc. This made it difficult for her to achieve salary parity between men and women, especially since there was an enormous disparity between men and women when she arrived, first at McGill and then at Harvard. Even today men tend to have more perks than women. They are, she thinks, more likely to be invited to distinguished lectureships with substantial honoraria or to have their way paid to meetings. Research space and even grants tend to correlate with rank, and at the Harvard Medical School in 1994 there were only about 20 women among a total of 400 professors.

A major concern raised by Avery is the number of women who

leave faculty ranks after holding assistant professorships. She thinks that only a small number of women leave strictly for family reasons. The few who do are explicit that they want large families and eventually want to return to 9-to-5 jobs, such as at health maintenance organizations. She believes that the majority leave for other reasons.

They don't want to face the highly competitive kind of stress. They don't want to feel that they have to get grants and have to write papers. I think that many of them think in less competitive terms. Their egos don't require it. As long as they have some space and some money, they will generate some grants, but they don't want to build a big program with 20 people. They don't want a whole floor of a building. They simply opt for a less competitive lifestyle. If someone had encouraged them and said, "We'll allow you to work half time for the next three or four years," or "We'll promise you reentry," for example, I think they might reenter, but very few department chairmen—all of whom are men in the Harvard clinical departments—do that. The power structure at the medical school is entirely men. The boards of trustees at hospitals have a couple of women on a board of 10 or 12 men, so they are often just sitting there as decorations. The faculty women are so few at the senior level that they cannot influence the policies of the school. Even if we formed a union we would have no clout except in our individual capacity to relate to another individual. It has to all be done on that sort of underground basis, case by case. . . . It takes a lot more effort. There is an enormous old boys' network with respect to promotions.

There are plenty of candidates. The pool is increasing. There was a point when there were very few. Now the pool is there, but there is always a reason why "this department is too big to trust to a woman." A woman does not have a place at the table with the trustees. She can't do as much for the hospital. . . . Even though I was on the board of trustees, I knew that I was not part of the weekend phone call circuit, that I was not able to connect as well, so that many people dependent on me did not see me as as strong an advocate for them as the person who succeeded me. He was a very aggressive man.

Avery, like Koshland and Rowley, believes that the message such a competitive male-dominated atmosphere sends may lead younger women in science to decide that they do not want to put up with a similar struggle.

## ELIZABETH D. HAY

After graduating from Smith College summa cum laude in 1948, Elizabeth Hay became a classmate of Mary Ellen Avery at Johns Hopkins. Hay is a professor of embryology in the Department of Cell Biology at Harvard Medical School and a former chairman of its Department of Anatomy and Cell Biology. At the time she was appointed to this position in 1975 she was the first woman ever to chair a department at the Harvard Medical School. Hay was elected to the National Academy of Sciences in 1984. She holds several honorary degrees and has received numerous other honors, including the E. B. Wilson Medal of the American Society for Cell Biology and the E. G. Conklin Award of the Society for Developmental Biology. She has served on many editorial boards and has also been a member of numerous scientific boards and committees. From 1981 to 1982 she was president of the American Association of Anatomists.

Using the newly developed techniques of genetic labeling and video microscopy, Hay's lab studies the complex interactions between cells and their surroundings that allow cells to reach their ultimate homes. Elizabeth Hay has likened the developing embryo to Rome at rush hour, with cells of all types from Alfa Romeos to motor scooters zooming around in all directions. Each cell must carry inside it complex instructions that allow it to determine how to reach its appropriate destination. When the instructions are absent or are not carried out properly, accidents, such as cleft palates and cataracts, result.

When Hay was in her early thirties, she moved from Baltimore to Cornell Medical School in New York City in order to be at the cutting edge of electron microscopy, an exciting new field that matched her talents and interests to an unbelievable degree. She had to sacrifice friendships and comforts in Baltimore to make this move and soon had to relocate again when the Cornell department moved to Harvard. She has been on the Harvard Medical School faculty since 1960.

Hay attributes her success to a love and talent for science, a very strong ambition to achieve, and the luck to find and be able to join the right department. In 1995 I asked her whether her status as a woman had affected her career. She wrote to me:

> My status as a woman delayed the launch of a productive career in science. I was not in the "network" (no ads in *Science* then) and when I did hear about a job it was usually much worse than the one I had in my department at Johns Hopkins. I sought out a job in New York City very actively and the department chief who hired me appreciated my developing talents in electron microscopy and needed my teaching experience. . . . When he stepped down as chairman, he asked me to take the job. I never thought about discrimination against me as a woman during this period but, in retrospect, I see that I was not getting the outside offers that many of my colleagues were.

As physicians, Avery and Hay seem to have had a somewhat easier time finding positions commensurate with their training than women who earned Ph.D. degrees. Nevertheless, in contrast to most women in the previous generation, they are acutely aware that they were disadvantaged at certain stages of their careers by the fact that they are women.

## VERA C. RUBIN

Vera Rubin is an astronomer whose research has focused on the orbital velocities of stars as they orbit the centers of their galaxies. Her discovery that stars at the outside of galaxies travel as fast as those near the center has led to understanding that most of the matter of the universe is not radiating at any wavelength—that it is dark. She has also studied the large-scale systematic motions of galaxies, motions superimposed on those arising from the expansion of the universe.

Rubin graduated from Vassar College in 1948 at the age of 19. The same year she married biophysicist Robert J. Rubin. She earned a master's degree at Cornell in 1951 and a Ph.D. in astronomy from Georgetown University in 1954. The Rubins have three sons and one daughter. Two children were born before she received her doctorate, the third in 1956, and the youngest in 1960. Of the three sons, two are geologists and one is a mathematician. Their only daughter is a professor of astronomy at the University of Massachusetts.

Immediately after she earned her doctorate in 1954, Rubin taught mathematics and physics for a year at Montgomery County Junior College in Maryland. She spent the next 10 years at Georgetown University. She was a research associate in astronomy and from 1959 to 1962 also was a lecturer in astronomy. In 1962 she was promoted to assistant professor. Three years later she joined the Department of Terrestrial Magnetism of the Carnegie Institution of Washington as a staff member, a position she still holds.

For more than 25 years Rubin has been actively involved in professional activities on both the national and the international levels, lecturing widely in the United States and abroad. She was elected to the National Academy of Sciences in 1981 and has received numerous other honors, including the National Medal of Science from President Clinton in 1993. In 1966 she was awarded the Gold Medal of the Royal Astronomical Society (London), the first woman to have received the award since 1828, when it was awarded to the English astronomer Caroline Herschel. Rubin holds honorary degrees from many universities, including Harvard and Yale. In 1996 she received the Women and Science Award, a pandisciplinary prize established in 1994, sponsored by the Weizmann Institute in Israel. The latter is particularly appropriate for Rubin, who not only has achieved distinction in her field but also has been active in her support of women throughout her career.

When someone asked Rubin what had been the greatest help to her career, she said above all the continual encouragement she received from her husband. She also especially valued the support of fellow astronomers, Geoffrey and Margaret Burbidge, who gave her confidence early in her career by treating her as a real astronomer. When asked what had been the worst hurdle in her career, she answered:

Being a student and a mother at the same time and finding adequate care for the children. . . . It was a constant worry and I was paid and treated as a part timer for many, many years.[2]

Until her last child entered high school, Rubin held a two-third's-time appointment at the Carnegie Institution so that she could be home at three o'clock. She then often worked at home for hours after her children were in bed. She never had live-in help. Eventually, a new director at the department was shocked to learn that she often worked long hours plus weekends but received only a part-time salary. He promptly put her on a full-time salary.

Only two women astronomers have been elected to the National Academy of Sciences since Rubin was elected in 1981. One of the two, Sandra Faber, is a former summer student of Vera Rubin. Rubin thinks it is a tragedy that hundreds of women who could have become outstanding astronomers never made it because they were discouraged all along the way. She believes that too few astronomers are being trained by women. "We are kidding ourselves," she says, "if we don't realize that science is still a male-dominated profession and some of the males enjoy this dominance."[3] She wonders how many of the increasing number of women currently studying science will make it.

———◈———

Four of the women profiled in this chapter—Avery, Conwell, Hay, and Karle—followed straight-line career trajectories once they completed their training. Conwell married a man who was able and willing to relocate with her. Karle married a fellow scientist who agreed not to accept a position unless his wife also could be hired, a tough condition in the days of antinepotism rules. Both Avery and Hay were physicians and neither chose to marry.

Rowley, Koshland, Morawetz, and Rubin found ways to work part time while their children were small and waited to step into senior positions until they felt ready to do so. Eventually each of them moved into the mainstream of science. For them the switch from part-time position to senior appointment worked well—whether at a university, a medical school, or a research institute—because it permitted them to devote time to their children in the early years. It is, however, easy to overlook the many other talented women in the same generation who remained marginalized because they were never able to secure permanent positions.

It is apparent that each of these women is exceptional—talented, well trained, doggedly persistent, passionate about her work, and lucky. Absent a considerable amount of luck, however, it is doubtful that they would have succeeded as scientists. Many equally talented women in this generation remained in marginal, poorly paid, often dead-end positions or dropped out of science altogether because of the obstacles they encountered.

# CAUGHT IN A
# TIDAL WAVE OF CHANGE
Women Born in the 1930s

Women born in the 1930s experienced the Depression as children, World War II as adolescents, and the postwar period while in college. By the time they graduated, Dr. Spock's *Baby and Child Care*[1] had become the bible for the parents of the baby boomers, and a life of suburban domesticity had become the norm for women. The pressures to become full-time homemakers and to raise large families were immense, and women whose interests ranged beyond domesticity did not have an easy time.

The decrease in the overall percentage of doctorates earned by women in the United States from 20 percent in 1945 to 10 percent by 1950 reflects the postwar emphasis on domesticity. The percentage did not return to the 1945 level until the 1970s. That only 15 of the female members of the National Academy of Sciences were born in the 1930s compared to 24 in the 1920s and 26 among women born since 1940 is probably attributable to the low birthrate during the Depression and to the ethos of the 1950s rather than to a statistical fluke.

I interviewed eight women in this age cohort and received letter replies from five others. All but one of the 15 Academy members born in the 1930s married and 12 raised children. Most married before earning their doctorates. Most married fellow scientists, including three who married men who also became members of the Academy. These women had slightly fewer children on average than the Academy members born a decade earlier. They were swept up in the changes of the 1960s and 1970s that came about as a result of the women's movement and the extension of civil rights legislation to women, changes for which neither they nor their husbands were prepared. Given the turmoil of this period, it is not surprising that some of their marriages did not survive. In stark contrast to the older married women scientists, six of the women in this age group eventually divorced; several subsequently remarried.

Today, one of the 15 women in this age cohort is president of a major research institute, one has a position in industry, and 13 hold professorships at universities or medical schools. Most are in one of the biological sciences, but the group also includes an engineer, a geoscientist, and two physicists. Unlike the women in the older age groups, an increasing number moved directly up through the ranks without first spending time in peripheral positions. Two of the women who now have tenured appointments in academia earned their doctorates late, one at the age of 37 and the other at the age of 40, reflecting the influence of societal changes on their aspirations. Like the women of the previous generation, these women demonstrated that one can succeed as a scientist without following a traditional career path.

## MAXINE F. SINGER

Maxine Singer is an eminent biochemist whose wide-ranging research on RNA and DNA has advanced scientific understanding of the role that nucleic acids play in the genetic makeup of viruses and humans. After graduating from a large public high school in New York, Singer received her bachelor's degree from Swarthmore College in 1952 and her Ph.D. from Yale University in 1957. After completing a postdoctoral fellowship at the National Institutes of Health, she held a position at NIH as a research biochemist in the Institute of Arthritis and Metabolic Diseases until 1975, studying the synthesis and structure of RNA. From 1971 to 1972 she took a year's sabbatical to pursue a new interest in animal viruses at Israel's Weizmann Institute of Science. In 1975 Singer moved to the National Cancer Institute, where

she continued work she had begun in Israel. These investigations led to an interest in the genetic makeup of primates and ultimately to her discovery of a transposable element, or "jumping gene," in human DNA on which much of her research has focused in recent years. Currently, Singer is president of the Carnegie Institution of Washington, D.C., a research institute that she joined in 1988, and continues her status as a scientist emeritus at NIH. She is married to a lawyer and is the mother of four children.

Maxine Singer has been a member of the National Academy of Sciences since 1979. She has served on the editorial boards of several scientific journals and is a former chair of the editorial board of the Academy's journal, *Proceedings of the National Academy of Sciences.* Singer has also served on the governing boards of Yale University and the Weizmann Institute. In 1988 she received the Distinguished Presidential Rank Award, the highest honor given to a civil servant, and in 1992 she was awarded the National Medal of Science for her outstanding scientific accomplishments and deep concern for the societal responsibilities of scientists.

Singer has had a long-standing commitment to influencing public awareness of scientific issues. In 1975 she was one of the organizers of a conference that drew up the nation's first guidelines for recombinant DNA research, research that focuses on molecules formed by combining DNA from different sources. She has also developed training programs for teachers of elementary school science and started an imaginative Saturday science school for third- through sixth-grade students. When I talked with Singer in April 1995, I asked her what factors had contributed to her success.

There were two I think, three perhaps. I did have a terrific
high school chemistry teacher. She wasn't very friendly, but
she was a very good teacher. She made chemistry very interesting. . . . I had decided to be a chemistry major before I went to
college. . . . I also took physics and all the math that was offered, which wasn't a whole lot in those days. That was before
calculus was offered in high school.

Maxine Singer majored in chemistry at Swarthmore, but by the
time she graduated she had decided to switch to biology. She views her
years at Swarthmore as "probably the most important experience" contributing to her success.

In my class there were six women who were primarily interested in science in one way or another, and we were all good
friends. Six people in a Swarthmore class in those days was a
significant group, and I essentially learned science in that con-
text. It was in the background of a coeducational school with
men majoring in chemistry, biology, everything. None of them
were any better than these six women. They were also my best
friends.

In a very real way that was my life there, except for the fact
that I met my future husband, Dan, a political science major,
there. I started going out with him when I was a freshman. My
community was a scientific community and one in which
whether you were male or female just didn't figure. It was between 1948 and 1952, and we didn't spend any energy at all
thinking or worrying about the fact that we were women. . . .
We received a lot of encouragement because Swarthmore is a
very small place. . . . It was always assumed that we would all
go on. . . . That was, I think, an extremely important experience for me. By the time I left Swarthmore, I had a lot of self-
confidence about what I was doing. . . .

We graduated college in 1952. It was the first class that was
offered National Science Foundation predoctoral fellowships.
That year there were 600 NSF fellows. Thirty-two of them
were women. Five of them were these women in my class in

this tiny school. We weren't aware of all of that at the time. . . .
Of the six women in our group, one went to medical school
and five went to graduate school.

Singer noted that all of these women went on to have professional
careers, and several became professors. She married immediately after
graduating from Swarthmore and entered graduate school at Yale,
where her husband was attending law school. When he went into the
army for a couple of years, Singer stayed in New Haven as a student:

> I went to graduate school in biochemistry at Yale and worked
> with Professor Joseph Fruton. I didn't find the coursework
> part of graduate school difficult or demanding, and I think
> that is the experience of a lot of Swarthmorians. In the group
> that came to graduate school with me in the fall of '52, half of
> us were women. I didn't find that strange. I just did what I
> wanted to do. . . . I had all of these terrific experiences in my
> education, and nobody ever suggested to me that they were
> anything but normal.
>
> I then got a very fine postdoctoral position at the NIH.
> Dan had a clerkship in Washington. We had intended to stay
> here in D.C. a couple of years and then go somewhere else,
> but we really liked it. By the time it was time to move, I was
> already aware how hard it was for a woman to get an academic
> position. I was very well set up, because by that time I had a
> permanent job at the NIH and my own lab. NIH was in a
> period of enormous growth, and if you were decent they of-
> fered you a job. People now can't believe the way we got jobs
> then. Dan found a law firm he liked and so we stayed.

Between 1959 and 1964, the Singers had four children, three
daughters and one son, all of whom have now established their own
careers. Her son is an entrepreneur working with new biotechnology
companies on the West Coast. The oldest daughter is on the history
faculty of Tel Aviv University, the middle daughter does research and
teaches equine surgery and orthopedics at the University of Liverpool,
and the youngest daughter is a tenured member of the mathematics
faculty of Haverford College. She and her mother are the first mother-

daughter pair to be awarded National Science Foundation predoctoral fellowships and as such were honored in 1992, the fortieth anniversary of the fellowships.

I wanted to know how Maxine Singer had coped with a full-time career. She told me that she did absolutely nothing except for her research and the children. She also had lots of household help, which they managed to pay for out of their combined incomes by restricting all other discretionary expenses. They had no financial help from their families. She commented that young people today have much higher expectations with respect to their own standard of living than her generation had. Maxine Singer worked full time at the NIH. The fact that her husband was always very helpful at home, although he too had a busy schedule as a lawyer, made a big difference, she says. Good friends who were also juggling careers and family provided another source of support.

I asked Singer to comment on efforts to help women reenter after they had taken time out to have children. She did not see this approach as a good solution:

> I see a lot of problems. Dropping out is really difficult, and there is no way to keep a foot in. It is just not a plausible thing. As it is, even if you get a full-time job, it is very tough.

Maxine Singer was unusually lucky to have found such a supportive environment during her undergraduate years at Swarthmore, at a time when such support and encouragement for a woman in science were rare. As a result she embarked on her graduate study without having the internal conflicts about becoming a scientist that many other women had. By working at NIH, she was able to avoid the dual pressures of raising a family while struggling to achieve tenure that she would have faced in academia. As she reminded me, her and her husband's willingness to spend money in order to have adequate help at home while their children were small was key to enabling her to maintain a full-time career from the outset. She was fortunate to have a close circle of women friends who also were pursuing careers while raising children, thereby providing a valuable support network. Few women in her generation were that lucky.

## MARY-LOU PARDUE

Mary-Lou Pardue is a geneticist and cell biologist who studies how chromosomes affect the inheritance and expression of genes. She also investigates the molecular mechanisms by which cells respond to stress,

thereby enabling organisms to cope with varying environmental conditions. Pardue graduated from the College of William and Mary in 1955 with a bachelor's degree in biology. She earned a master's degree in radiation biology from the University of Tennessee in 1959. After working for several years she returned to graduate school and received her Ph.D. in biology from Yale in 1970. She then spent two years as a postdoctoral fellow at the Institute of Animal Genetics at the University of Edinburgh in Scotland.

Pardue joined the faculty of the Department of Biology at the Massachusetts Institute of Technology in 1972 and has been a full professor there since 1980. She has been a member of the National Academy of Sciences since 1983. Pardue is past president of the American Society for Cell Biology and the Genetics Society of America and has served on numerous editorial boards and been a member of many national scientific organizations. She holds an honorary degree from Bard College. In 1977 she received the Esther Langer Award for Cancer Research. I spoke with Pardue in December 1994 and asked her when she first became interested in science:

> I have always liked nature and the outdoors, and I liked building things. I debated between engineering, biology, English, and history. At William and Mary everyone urged me to go to graduate school, so I applied to a number of graduate schools. All of my applications were successful, but at that time I had no intention of going on for an advanced degree. . . . I wanted to get a job in research. Somebody had told me that Oak Ridge, Tennessee, had a good biology research program, so I applied for a job there as a technician. This was 1955.

I worked as a technician for a couple of years and then was again encouraged to go to graduate school. I applied to graduate school and was planning to go to Harvard. I was also awarded an NSF fellowship, which had a big effect on my career. But soon after making plans to leave Oak Ridge to go to Harvard, I decided to marry an engineer scientist who was working in Oak Ridge. I was just going to forget graduate school. Then I found out that the NSF fellowship could be moved to another institution, so I moved it from Harvard to Oak Ridge and studied at the University of Tennessee.

I had a wonderful time studying during the three years of the fellowship. At that point they wanted to give me a Ph.D., but I didn't want to take the Ph.D., so I talked them into giving me a master's. In the society I was in it was quite all right for a wife to be going to school, but getting a Ph.D. was a little too serious. . . . After enjoying graduate study for three years, I decided to take the master's degree and go back to work. My marriage broke up not long after that.

Pardue is uncertain whether her career was a factor in the breakup of her marriage. In any event, she kept working as a technician for a couple of years before returning to graduate school in 1965 for a Ph.D. By then she had been in the field long enough to know who was good to work for and who wasn't:

I decided right then and there that I was going to go get a degree at Yale with Joseph Gall, and that turned out to have been a marvelous decision. . . . Most of the women who came to Yale and worked with Joe Gall came because of the scientific work that he was doing. . . . One of the things that also attracted me to him was the way he presented seminars and the way he answered questions. . . . He had a very scholarly outlook, and he wasn't trying to put his questioners down. If someone asked him a dumb question, I saw him turn it into a good question. . . .

At William and Mary, where I went as an undergraduate, I saw a few, very few, women faculty members, but they were not in the same category as the men. The women faculty members were doing the heavy teaching. The male faculty members in those days tended to be young people who had just gotten their first jobs as Ph.D.s. They were doing research, and most of them went on to get faculty jobs at other places and did well in research. So I saw two streams of people.

In the late sixties, being a research associate looked like the most realistic goal for a woman. That is what I expected to be. I wanted to do science and to be where the action was, but first I wanted to go to Europe for a couple of years and then I planned to do postdoctoral work in the United States with a senior scientist. I knew it would be harder to look for a faculty job from Europe, but I didn't think a faculty job was likely anyway. The males in my class tended to stay in this country because it would make their later job hunts easier. . . . The four people in the world that I wanted to work with were all in Edinburgh. So I went to Edinburgh to Max Birnsteil's laboratory. I had a wonderful time there.

Pardue was eager to do science, but she saw no career ladder ahead of her. As a result she felt free to indulge her yen for a year abroad, something her male colleagues aiming for faculty appointments did not dare do. Pardue did not think it would be smart to do her postdoctoral work with the person who had supervised her doctoral dissertation. She also knew that when she returned from Europe she wanted to find a postdoctoral position with someone who would appreciate her for what she could do and someone who was outstanding enough that she would not be a threat to him. Before she left for Edinburgh, she found a senior scientist who met those criteria with whom she planned to work upon her return. When she wrote to this scientist after her first year in Edinburgh to ask if she could postpone her postdoctoral assignment another year, he told her that she really should apply for faculty positions. He suggested she send him her curriculum vitae so that he could forward it to people who asked him for names of potential job candidates. This suggestion set off a chain of events:

I sent him the c.v. At about the same time, an article appeared in *Science* about the handicaps women face in getting jobs in academia. Boris Magasanik at MIT wrote a letter to *Science* saying that the MIT faculty thought that part of the solution lay in hiring more women faculty and that MIT was looking for a developmental biologist. The person who had asked me to send him my c.v. clipped this letter out and sent it to me with instructions to send my c.v. to MIT, which I did . . . at the end of my first year at Edinburgh. That summer I was invited to go to Cold Spring Harbor to teach for a few weeks. So I arranged a trip back to the States, and then I started getting invitations from places all over the country to speak. This was really good. This was the summer of '71 when everybody was really being pushed to hire women, and so I went around the States and gave seminars in lots of places, and more and more places asked me.

At the end of the summer I stopped to visit Joe Gall, just before leaving to return to Edinburgh. When I arrived, there was a letter that had chased me around the country and had caught up with me. The letter was from MIT, responding to my application for a job. It was obviously a form letter. The first paragraph said that they had gotten my letter but that they had received lots of letters and wanted me to know that therefore they were definitely not interested in me. I showed the letter, which was very blunt, to Joe Gall, and he was also appalled. Then I left and went back to Edinburgh.

By this time I had lots of other places to be and I had a whole pocket full of job offers, so I was having a pretty good time when I got a phone call from a man at MIT. He wanted me to come and give a seminar and visit. I was going to interview at Harvard, so I said I'd be happy to stop by and see him at MIT. He then said, "I think there's a letter that we'd better explain to you." I learned later that MIT had called Joe Gall and had asked him how to get in touch with me, whereupon he told them that they'd better be careful because they had already been in touch with me (via the blunt rejection letter).

I don't know why the letter that I got was so poorly worded. I think if the letter had been written to a man, they would have worded it differently, but they saw all these women out there and didn't quite know how to say "No." Nevertheless, the story ends well. When MIT got in touch with me the second time, I enjoyed the visit and they offered me a position as an associate professor.

Pardue was in her late thirties when she received the MIT offer of an associate professorship. While she had a lot of experience, she was still an unknown quantity. All her other job offers were at the assistant professor level, so she accepted the MIT offer, but she notes that it was a calculated risk:

This department did not have people who were doing the sort of thing that I was doing. There was very little cell or developmental biology in the department then. I figured it was exciting to go someplace where I hadn't lived before and to work with people that I didn't communicate with otherwise. The other reason for coming was that several other women were already here—Lisa Steiner, an immunologist, and Annamaria Torriani-Gorini, who had been at MIT for some time as research associate and had recently been made a faculty member. . . . I liked two things about MIT. It was nice to have several women in the department, but the more important thing was I knew that MIT wasn't desperate to hire a woman because they had more women than any of the other departments that I was looking at, places where I would have been the first and the only woman.

While accepting the MIT offer initially felt risky for Pardue, she observed that as a woman she felt freer to take risks than her male colleagues.

One of the things that contributed to my success was that, as a woman, I never had any expectation that I was going to be on a faculty; therefore, I did what I wanted to do without worrying that it might affect my chances for the perfect job. I think I took more risks than I might have taken had I thought I was going to be a success. I did science that I thought was interesting because I didn't see myself as ever being a professor at a big university.

Mary-Lou Pardue's early career was typical for the period. Her expectations for the future were shaped by what she saw, not by what she was told. She watched male faculty move on from her college to do research elsewhere, while the few women on the science faculty at William and Mary stayed on and taught. When she came to Yale, she again saw men who were professors and women who were research associates. Despite the encouragement she received from various mentors along the way, she first refused to study for a doctorate and later turned down a doctorate she had earned. She had never set her sights on a faculty position until she was actively recruited.

Throughout her career, however, Pardue deliberately sought out congenial work settings. She was drawn to Professor Gall in part because he did not put students down, but rather used their questions constructively to foster understanding. She realized that bright women threaten frail male egos and considered this fact in her choice of a postdoctoral position. She deliberately chose to accept a position at an institution where she would not be the only woman in a department. She wanted to have female colleagues, but, more importantly, she did not want to feel that she had been hired primarily because she was female. She bore no grudges and forgave MIT's tactless response to her initial inquiry. Pardue was also willing to take risks along the way, in going abroad, in choosing the areas of her research, and in joining a department in which she would have few or no colleagues in her own field. Luck also played a role, when, just as she entered the job market, the barriers to the hiring of women in universities crumbled as a result of newly enacted affirmative action policies.

## MARGARET G. KIDWELL

Margaret Kidwell is a geneticist and a population and evolutionary biologist who was born in England in the 1930s. She came to the United States in 1960 on a Kellogg Foundation fellowship to earn a

master's degree in animal breeding at Iowa State University and planned to resume her British civil service position the following year. While at Iowa, however, she met her future husband and "got turned on to doing research," something she had not previously realized that she could or wanted to do. She earned her master's degree in 1961 and married the same year. Her two daughters were born in 1962 and 1964, respectively. After several years in Canada her husband accepted a faculty position at Brown University, where Kidwell began to work as a research associate in 1966.

In 1970, when her younger daughter entered grade school, Kidwell resumed graduate studies at Brown and obtained her Ph.D. three years later. In 1984 she became a tenured professor at Brown. She is currently a Regents' Professor in the Department of Ecology and Evolutionary Biology and Interdisciplinary Program in Genetics at the University of Arizona in Tucson, where she has been a professor since 1985.

In addition to her election to the National Academy of Sciences in 1996, Kidwell has received many other honors. In 1984 she served as vice-president of the American Society of Naturalists. She served as president of the American Genetics Association in 1992 and of the Society for Molecular Biology and Evolution in 1996. She is currently serving a three-year term on the Board of Directors of the Genetics Society of America.

Kidwell's research focuses on population and evolutionary biology and the evolution of transposable genetic elements—DNA sequences that can move from one site in a chromosome to another or between different chromosomes. They are similar to the "jumping genes" in corn made famous by Nobel laureate Barbara McClintock. Kidwell's work is the direct outcome of observations she made during her Ph.D. thesis research, when she discovered that a number of very peculiar genetic effects were produced when flies of different strains were crossed, or hybridized. Jumping genes in fruit flies have been used by others as molecular "vehicles" to move genes from one individual, or species, to another—a technique known as genetic transformation. This is a very powerful technique with multiple uses in basic and applied biological research. As Kidwell noted:

> Although in the short term the jumping of these elements from one location to another can have quite severe detrimental effects for the host, in the long term they can be important sources of new genetic variability, which may provide an organism, and perhaps a species, with a better opportunity to survive and prosper under new environmental conditions.

When I interviewed Kidwell in January 1997 she spoke about the early influences in her life that led to her career as a scientist:

> I think my family background had a big influence. I grew up on a farm in England and I was the eldest of two girls, and there weren't any boys. I just loved farming and helped my father a lot. I think had there been a boy in the family the situation would have been different. But I was given significant responsibility, which I loved. I developed a lot of independence and self-confidence and learned how to work in a whole range of activities, including driving a tractor by the time I was 10 years old.
>
> There was also the role model of my parents. There were few jobs that were viewed exclusively as women's work or men's work. My parents pretty well shuffled the chores and responsibilities. Each of them did what they did best. I remember my father's main job in the house was washing dishes, and he also did the shopping, and my mother helped with many tasks on the farm. It was a small farm specializing in poultry, pigs, vegetables, and fruit production. My father was a pedigree breeder of Rhode Island Red chickens, so I developed a very early interest in genetics from a practical point of view. I little thought that I'd eventually spend much of my life pursuing genetics as a science.

Kidwell had only eight years of formal schooling before she entered university at age 17. She completed her undergraduate degree in three years, her master's in a little over one year, and her Ph.D. in under three years. In retrospect she views growing up on a farm with limited formal education as an advantage:

> The formal education I did have was excellent in quality, but, most importantly, I learned how to teach myself a lot of things, which for continuing success in life is very important. I have this great love of research which I discovered late, not until I was almost 30. I love puzzles, I love challenges, and I think I'm fairly persistent. I think persistence is really important. I don't ever think of myself as a brilliant intellect or anything like that. . . . I think I do have a good left-brain/right-brain connection. I can think well at different levels, first at detailed levels, and then pull back and get the big picture.

Kidwell worked very closely with her husband on joint research projects in the 1960s. Much of the work was unpaid, but that didn't bother her because she was learning all the time. Her husband taught her the basics of the genetics of Drosophila. Later, as she developed her own particular interests, he gave her "full rein" to pursue those interests.

> There was a whole period there of nearly 10 years between my master's degree and starting my Ph.D training. During that time I was also raising the children and getting them into grade school. I worked mostly part time, but I was able to do a whole lot of interesting things. For example, I helped my husband arrange a summer institute for college teachers to which world experts were invited. All great experiences.

After Kidwell earned her Ph.D. in 1973, she spent the next 11 years doing research supported by grants. During that period her husband developed Parkinson's disease. He was able to continue to work until 1984, when he retired on a disability pension. In the same year Kidwell was appointed to a tenured position at Brown as professor of biology. One year later, in 1985, she was recruited by the University of

Arizona in Tucson, where she accepted a position as professor of ecology and evolutionary biology. By that time her daughters were grown and she was free to move. I asked her what it had been like at Arizona when she arrived and how the department reacted to having a woman on the faculty.

> When I first came here there was only one other woman in this department, an assistant professor who subsequently left. I was the only woman for a short time. Now we have six women in a department of 22. So there has been great improvement in biology, at least in this university, and I've seen it in others, but the physical sciences I'm not so sure about.

I asked why there is such an enormous difference between the physical and the biological sciences. She speculated that women seem more attracted to biology, where so-called math phobia is less relevant. She noted, however, that both she and her daughters had always done well in math and that women are capable of excelling in the physical sciences but that they seem to be more drawn to biology.

Both of her daughters pursued biological sciences. The older one has a master's degree and works for the U.S. Department of Agriculture. The younger daughter went to medical school and is a neurologist at UCLA. Kidwell commented that her younger daughter had felt that she was being forced to be much more aggressive than she would naturally be while she was in medical school, although she is now happy in her field and enjoying her work.

While Kidwell believes the difference in the numbers of women in the physical and the biological sciences has more to do with women's interests than with factors in the field, she observed that brilliant mathematicians often do their best work early in life, a time when women who have children are unable to concentrate fully on their work. In biology, on the other hand, she personally felt no disadvantage by waiting until later to engage in full-time research. She noted:

> In biology a certain maturity can be a great advantage. . . . I really felt I was hitting my prime around 40 when I got my degree. In a way I found it was an advantage to have the years when my children were young behind me before I went into

research in a very concentrated way. By then I was really raring to go and had a tremendous amount of pent-up energy and interest.

As a student in England, Kidwell had never felt in any way disadvantaged because she was a woman, even though women were in a minority in most of her classes. She thought that women might even have had a slight advantage. When she worked in the British Civil Service her male boss always pushed for opportunities for her. After she married, her experiences became more complex:

> After I was married, I certainly felt discrimination in hiring, but it gets complicated. I think I can say that I have not personally been subjected to anything that I could knowingly call discrimination on the basis of sex alone. As a graduate student I became aware of the difficulties faced by professional couples in finding positions together. I also became aware of the political complications that can arise when a couple works in the same administrative unit. When I came here, I did start to realize that many other women were having serious problems, particularly with respect to hiring.
>
> The biggest question in hiring is often the spouse situation. What do you do when a prospective hire has a spouse? It goes right across the spectrum of possibilities. The very best outcome is to hire both members of a couple if they are fully qualified. It often depends on the initial level of communication. It is important for both to communicate up front about their needs and expectations. Some find satisfactory employment in the community. Some do not come because the needs of the spouse seem unlikely to be met. So it's right across the spectrum.

When I spoke with Kidwell, she was finishing her seventh year as department chair and had just made a decision to give up the chairmanship and had resisted considerable pressure to continue. She had not been able to keep up her science at the level she wanted to while chairing the department and was eager to return to full-time research. I asked her what she would do to help women succeed as scientists if she could really dream. She noted the tremendous need for better child care on an institutional basis, as well as the time needed to fully realize the goals of affirmative action. She fears that the high dropout rate among women in science may get worse because there is a glut of postdoctorals trying to get jobs.

> I think flexibility—willingness to be flexible about what kind of opportunities to seek or willingness to change course in midstream—is important. I have found, as I've gone along, that it is important to be willing to shift direction if you see opportunities or you see your interests changing. To make up your mind early on and stick with that inflexibly can be a mistake. That's not the kind of persistence that pays. When I am talking to young women, they find it very interesting that one can start late . . . and even when you are recognized late, one can still really make it. I think that is very important for them to understand.

However, when I asked Kidwell whether she thought that somebody applying to the University of Arizona today who was five or 10 years older than the average applicant would get a fair shake, she was not sure:

> I was particularly fortunate in being available at just the right time, when they wanted to increase the number of women and were open to hiring a more senior one. Now, in general, the preference is to hire at the junior level. On the other hand, because of the dearth of leadership, if a woman could come along who really wanted to take a leadership role, an opportunity might be found. It's very hard to get people to take that kind of responsibility and to devote themselves to administration to the extent required.

When we discussed the need for maternity leave and child care, Kidwell cited the example of a tenured faculty member who had recently had a baby and had never even asked about a leave of absence. She was keen to get back to work after two or three weeks and apparently didn't want to take time out.

People have been very helpful. An informal atmosphere really makes a difference. She'll often come in and feed the baby while we're having a conference, and her husband, who is a graduate student, will frequently look after the baby. He's in the same building, so it's working out really well. . . . I think the biggest thing is a change in the attitudes of some men. That's what can help women the most. Some of the old school will never change; they will just die away.

I was curious whether Kidwell had found differences between the opportunities for women in the United States and in England. She responded:

I have felt very fortunate to be in this country. If I had stayed in England, I think I would never have had the opportunities that I've had here in this profession. Every time I go back, I feel that they're so behind the times in their attitudes. . . . As president of the Molecular Biology and Evolution Society, I made a tremendous effort here when we ran a meeting last year to include really good women. We had an excellent meeting, and everyone was very happy with it. Yet next year it is being arranged in Germany, and we find that there are very few women on the program. Somehow they just haven't moved very fast in this direction. There are obviously a lot of fairly broad-minded people, but there's still tremendous resistance. I see it there and I often feel quite uncomfortable. I get the feeling of not being treated quite equally, both on a professional and a social basis. There's a barrier. In this country, most of the time, I feel I am treated by male colleagues very much as an equal. In Europe there's the attitude, "You're a woman and I'm a man, so we can't meet at the same level, even professionally."

Margaret Kidwell did not get her career off the ground until she was over 40. Although she never abandoned research entirely, she remained on the periphery until her personal circumstances enabled her to devote full time to science. She would like to enable other women to follow her example, but she concedes that it would be difficult for anyone to do so in today's climate. Even though she was actively engaged in research after she earned her Ph.D., she was not offered a faculty position at Brown until 11 years later, when her husband was forced to retire for health reasons. I wonder whether Brown would have ever offered her a tenured position if her husband had not retired.

## MYRIAM P. SARACHIK

Myriam Sarachik, an experimental physicist, was born in Antwerp, Belgium. Her elementary school education was temporarily interrupted by the outbreak of World War II, when she and her family left Belgium to escape the Nazis. They arrived in Havana, Cuba, in November 1941 and immigrated to the United States in 1947. She became a naturalized

citizen in 1953. Sarachik attended the Bronx High School of Science in New York City and continued her education at Barnard College, where she earned a B.A. in physics in 1954. She earned a master's degree in 1957 and a Ph.D. from Columbia in 1960.

After a year in New York City teaching at City College while working as a postdoctoral research associate at the IBM Watson Laboratories at Columbia University, Sarachik joined the technical staff at Bell Telephone Laboratories in Murray Hill, New Jersey. In 1964 she was appointed assistant professor at City College of the City of New York. She was promoted to associate professor there in 1967 and to full professor in 1970. Sarachik has been a distinguished professor in the department of physics at City College since 1995.

Sarachik was elected to the National Academy of Sciences in 1994. She has been active on numerous national scientific bodies. Sarachik is on the board of directors of the Committee of Concerned Scientists and on the Council of the American Physical Society. She currently chairs the Solid State Sciences Committee of the National Research Council.

Sarachik is an experimental physicist working on solids and chooses experiments to test or challenge current theoretical advances. She has studied electrical transport and magnetic properties of a variety of materials, mostly at low temperatures. Some of these materials have potential applications for memory storage and quantum computation. Much of her research has centered around semiconductors, which are the basis of the solid-state optical and electronic devices that have revolutionized communications, computation, and information gathering during the twentieth century. In her own words: "The better we understand their fundamental properties, the better we can utilize them to full capacity."

Myriam Sarachik is married to Philip Sarachik, a professor of electrical engineering at Brooklyn Polytechnic Institute. The Sarachiks have one child. When I interviewed Myriam Sarachik in May 1995 I asked what factors had contributed to her success in physics. She responded:

> A love of science is absolutely indispensable, but in addition to that there absolutely has to be the drive to succeed, the will to move. . . . Tenacity, and the fact that I have finally learned how to do it well, really well. I guess I was always pretty good, but I didn't really put it all together very well, and there were a lot of things that I didn't know. There are still a lot of things that I don't know. It is inexcusable not to know, but I have learned not to be derailed by it. I think that tenacity is an enormous part of it.

When I questioned whether that drive might be greater for people who are immigrants than for people who are firmly established, she noted:

> I think there are other differences in people who have emigrated. It may depend on how old they are when they come. In my case, my travels when I was young sort of left me a misfit to begin with. . . . I think the struggle to accept not

fitting in is something that people who change cultures have to deal with earlier and with a great deal more attention. . . . I was eight years old when I left Belgium. I spent the next five and one-half years in Cuba, where I didn't fit in very well either. I then came to this country when I was almost 14. . . . In my middle teens, when it came time to make various choices, I had already come to terms with not quite fitting in. So going into science was just a small additional step. For many women it may actually represent a much larger transition.

As a child, Sarachik loved arithmetic and algebra. As she moved from one country to another, she kept finding that she was faster and better at math than anybody else in the class. That gave her a sense of worth and pleasure. But she had other interests, too, and when she went to college she was torn when it came time to select a major.

I was trying very hard to decide between romance languages, literature, music, math, and physics. I had a broad range of interests. I think one reason I chose physics was that it was by far the hardest of all the subjects. It was something that had really challenged me. I had almost failed. The other thing is that my father thought that physics was absolutely the discipline of all disciplines and that, had he been able to get an education, he would have become a physicist. Romance languages and literature were too easy for me, and I decided that if I really wanted to be a musician that I would want to be an outstanding musician, and the chances that I would make it to that level were really rather minimal. Being a reasonably good physicist was okay—somehow I was not aspiring to be the great physicist.

As an undergraduate at Barnard, Sarachik took the more advanced courses in math and science at Columbia, because as a women's college Barnard did not offer many courses in these areas. When she enrolled in the middle of Columbia's first-year physics course, somewhat of a repeat of a course she had already taken at Barnard, she was almost knocked out of the class because the Columbia standards were so much higher. She liked that because it showed her what she needed to do to compete with men. I asked her whether she thought, as some have suggested, that women do better in mathematics when there are no men in their classes. She said she didn't think so but then continued:

> I must tell you that it is a very personal sort of thing. I felt that being put in the larger pool and having had to compete from the beginning worked well for me, although it is true that I was never able to ask a question in class. It is not until recently that I am able to freely and comfortably ask questions at seminars with colleagues. It told me where the real world was and what I was going to have to measure up to. Since measuring up was the game for me, it worked well. But there are studies that indicate that some women are more comfortable, make better progress, and ask questions in class much more easily if they are in a class with all women.

While Sarachik enjoyed the coeducational peer group at Columbia, she found that the male faculty at Columbia were very much products of their time—fair minded but not very encouraging to women. She also felt the weight of her family's traditional influence.

> I came from an orthodox Jewish background, where women were not supposed to do anything at all. However, for the time being it was okay if I did something because I had not yet found my proper husband and all that. My father really wanted a son to do what he would have done, but his two sons were not interested. And they didn't particularly like physics. I am the middle child, but I am a girl. His only daughter seemed to have the aptitude and the motivation that he wanted. So I got very mixed messages. A very large part of that message was that even though I wasn't really supposed to be doing anything, what I was doing was very much worthwhile. I think that did play a very large role.

Directly after completing her bachelor's degree, Sarachik married an engineering student at Columbia. She went on for her master's degree and then quit. In her words:

The reason I quit was that it was not appropriate for a woman to go any further. I had already exceeded all proper bounds for a woman. I took one or two courses just because I loved it. My intention was not to go on. But, you know, why not take some courses? Then I looked at a good friend of mine, who was a year ahead of me, who was going straight on for her Ph.D. and it suddenly occurred to me one day, "If she can do it, why in heaven's name can't I?"

But everything changed just after Sarachik got her Ph.D. in 1960. She discovered she was pregnant. She met a fellow woman student at Columbia who had just had a baby who warned her, "Don't make any commitments. You don't know how you are going to feel after the baby is born." Sarachik remembers the impact of that encounter:

I really believed that some transformation was possible and that what I wanted to do with my life would really get totally altered, transformed into something else. I decided maybe I'd better do the wise thing and not line up a job, which I might not have been able to do anyway. But then the baby was born and I almost went out of my mind for awhile. Here again my husband comes into the picture. He was working and he would come home and look at my miserable face and he would become miserable. After about five to six months he said, "Myriam, you've got to go out and get a job." I said, "Look, Phil, how am I going to do that? In order to look for a job I have to have somebody to take care of Karen and we don't have the money." "Never mind," he said. "You go look for a job. We'll put the money into it. There is just no way that we can continue this way because we are just miserable together." So that is what I did.

It was at that point that I had a miserable time getting a job because nobody would touch a woman with a baby. My supervisor, my former thesis adviser, did not think I should work. I went to an American Physical Society meeting, and there I met a friend who had not succeeded in getting his degree at Columbia. He had worked for the same adviser I was working for, but couldn't get along with him, so he just moved to another graduate school. There he got his degree, and, believe me, he was certainly not better than I was. He was looking for a job at that point. He got 20 requests for interviews. I got zero. It was really rough.

A reporter for one of the TV stations came to talk to me about what it was like to be a woman in physics. I was so upset and I felt in such jeopardy of being squeezed out of the field. I tried to talk to him, but I told him so many things, which I asked him not to print because I was afraid it would shock people, that he never published the article. I could understand it very well. But I was afraid. Quite frankly, becoming a troublemaker would have been the kiss of death.

Finally, Sarachik persuaded Nobel Prize winner Polykarp Kusch at Columbia to help her find a job. He did not understand why she wanted to work when she had a baby, but he eventually relented: "We trained you and we gave you a degree, and if you want to do it you have a right." Soon thereafter Sarachik was hired as a postdoctoral fellow at Bell Labs. She would have loved to have stayed at Bell, but she was not offered a permanent position. I asked Sarachik if she thought she had not gotten an offer because they thought her personal life would prevent her from being serious about her work. She insisted that the decision had not been made on that basis, saying:

> The degree to which your being a woman colors their view of how good you are is intangible. . . . I was not regarded very highly, at least not compared to the real hotshots. They had some very sharp guys. . . . I really wasn't that good. . . . I was very bright. I was very sharp in many specific ways, but I hadn't quite put it together.

Sarachik noted that, after her two years at Bell, she and her husband "had the two-body problem":

> He was looking for a job at the same point that I was. In those days it was not only hard, it was unacceptable for the woman to really insist on having a job. So he got offers in places where I didn't have anything at all.

She felt guilty about denying her husband a good opportunity at the University of Maryland because they offered her only a postdoctoral position. "But," she said, "Phil was quite remarkable for his time. He just felt that we had to maximize our joint chances." Finally, they both found employment in New York City, he at NYU and she at City College. Sarachik recalls:

> The person who was largely instrumental in getting me that job and really pushing for it was the guy with whom I had collaborated on my thesis. He had done a postdoc at IBM and then he had moved to City College. He told everybody that I was just crackerjack. I didn't think I was. But he said, "Yes, she is crackerjack."

Sarachik has been at City College ever since. I remarked that she must have done really good work because it is not easy to get into the National Academy of Sciences. She was more modest:

> Well, I did good work in those days. It was not spectacular, but it was highly regarded in the field that I was in. I started winding down a little bit and then, because of a personal tragedy, I pulled out of research pretty much for about 10 years. During those 10 years, I chaired the Ph.D. program in physics at the City University, that means not just City College but also Brooklyn, Queens, and Hunter and so on. It was really a bad business because there is a lot of dissension in the program. The administrative structure was Byzantine and it still really is. There was a lot of enmity, and there were no real resources to work with. I hated it. I surmised that I hated administration, but it may actually not be true. It may just be that that job was undoable.
>
> At the end of that time, I decided that the one thing that I had always really loved the best was research, and I decided to get back into it. I found that on my second go-around I did it a lot better. I was at the time close to 50. It was hard. I really worked like a fiend for a while. Whatever got done in the lab was basically me getting it done, because I didn't have anybody else, no personnel, except an undergraduate who was

very keen on helping me. So I really had to get back in there and do it. . . . It was hard getting back in because I was not at the forefront anymore. I picked a new field, but it took me a good two or three years to really realize exactly where the forefront was. Then, when I submitted proposals, I had this gap in publications, like "What's she been doing?"—which doesn't help. But there was a fellow at the Department of Energy . . . who dispersed research funds. On my first go-around, he was doing work in the field where I had been doing work, and he was very impressed with me. He gave me my chance. He said, "I know her. She is going to do good things." He funded my research proposal.

Sarachik then explained to me why she had left research earlier:

I should tell you something else for completeness. I had another baby, and that child died tragically in an accident when he was little. I think things happen in a very strange way. One of the reasons that I am so good at what I do now is that the fear that I used to have is just not there anymore. The fear of making a fool out of myself, the fear of failing, which was never enough to stop me but which really got in my way very seriously. I had been through something that was so bad that nothing else compared to it. So I'll make a fool of myself. I survived that; I can survive this.

We then talked about how balancing family and career is a major problem for women. While in some exceptional cases men really do feel an equal responsibility at home, in most cases, she said, that is not so. Sarachik noted:

In our case it was not so for two reasons. One of them had to do with the fact that my husband was willing to let me do as much as I felt that I should do, and the other end of it was that, because of my background, I really felt that I should do everything, even though my head told me, "Oh why?" The problems are just so deeply internal. The battle was really not with him; it was in me. . . . I don't think we are going to change attitudes very soon. I think that women are as culpable in this as men are. Women contribute to the image of who women are as much as men do. To sit and say it's the lousy unfair men who are doing this to us is absolutely not true. I think that respecting the self is absolutely the very first step. Once you do that the rest is doable. If your sense of who you are is really 100 percent healthy, then when you encounter overt discrimination you can look this person in the face and say, "That's your problem."

I asked Sarachik if her career had been affected by the fact that she is a woman. She responded:

No question. No question at all. I had at various junctures to fight extremely hard to stay in the field. A man would never have had to do that. I was just simply unwilling to give up, and I was not going to take "no" for an answer.

Sarachik recalled how she had stood her ground as a postdoctoral fellow during a disagreement with a faculty member in her department, that she had been "gutsy." She continued:

When I was growing up I was extremely shy, and I thought of myself as the passive woman that I was supposed to be. But when I tell you about such incidents, I realize that my self-image was very far from reality. I simply was not going to be pushed out of the field.

Being a woman was different from being a man. It also had its advantages. When I went to a conference or when I gave a paper I was noted. I was noted for better or for worse. I was not likely to disappear into the crowd, particularly in those days when there were so few of us. I have often said that the men in the field at that time tended to fall into two groups. There were those who thought that, given the fact that I was a woman in physics, I clearly had to be better than most men. Then there was the other group that felt I was a woman and therefore, "How good could I be?" The truth of the matter was that I was no better and I was no worse. I was just very tenacious. I think that the women that survived in those days had tremendous tenacity.

There are striking parallels between the careers of Myriam Sarachik and Mary-Lou Pardue. Both overcame internal barriers. They were drawn to science but hesitated to make serious commitments because they saw a conflict between their roles as women and scientists. Mary-Lou Pardue completed her doctorate after she was divorced, when she realized that she wanted to become an independent researcher. Myriam Sarachik came from a family in which women were expected to assume the role of wife and mother, without more. She tried hard to conform and might even have abandoned science if her husband had not realized how unhappy she was as a homebound mother. He encouraged her to find a job, even though it was extremely difficult at the time for a married woman with a baby to find a position. She followed her husband's advice, just as Marian Koshland had done after the birth of her twins. Eventually, with much persistence and the help of a former colleague, she found a position commensurate with her training. She then described very movingly how, as a result of a devastating personal tragedy, she eventually lost the fear of failure that had haunted her until then and was finally able to delve back into research after a 10-year hiatus. She blames the values she had internalized, rather than the external barriers she encountered, for her struggles.

## P. S. GOLDMAN-RAKIC

Patricia Goldman-Rakic, a neuroscientist, received her undergraduate training in experimental psychology at Vassar College and a Ph.D. in psychology at UCLA (University of California at Los Angeles). She then spent one year as a postdoctoral fellow at the Brain Research Institute at UCLA and another year at New York University in the Department of Psychiatry before moving to the National Institute of Mental Health in 1965. She became chief of the NIMH Section of Developmental Neurobiology in 1978. One year later she moved to Yale University, where she currently holds joint appointments as professor in the departments of neurology, psychiatry, and psychology.

Goldman-Rakic serves on numerous advisory committees, including the National Advisory Council of the National Institute on Aging

and on the Scientific Academic Advisory Committee and the Board of Governors of the Weizmann Institute and has served on the editorial boards of major neuroscience journals. From 1989 to 1990 she served as president of the Society for Neuroscience. She lectures widely in this country and throughout the world. She was elected to the National Academy of Sciences in 1990 and has received many other honors, including the Karl Lashley Award of the American Philosophical Society, the Lieber Award of the National Alliance for Research in Schizophrenia and Depression, the Distinguished Scientific Contribution Award of the American Psychological Association, and the John McGovern Award of the American Association for the Advancement of Science.

Goldman-Rakic has made major contributions to our understanding of the cellular mechanisms of information processing in the cerebral cortex of the brain, especially the process of working memory upon which human language, reasoning, and cognition depend. The research in her laboratory has placed the study of the most complex area of the brain on a firm neurobiological foundation and has helped to elucidate the role of the neurotransmitter dopamine on processes relevant to Parkinson's disease and schizophrenia. Her work provides the neurobiological foundation for understanding cognitive processes in psychiatric and neurological disease. When I interviewed Goldman-Rakic in May 1995, she talked about her background and factors that contributed to her success as a scientist:

> I always tell my students that success takes three things in equal proportions: hard work, native ability, and good luck—being in the right place at the right time. I think that I have had some of all of these elements in my own career. However,

I am beginning to have second thoughts about this formula and giving more weight to the factor of ability and perseverance in the face of obstacles. I never dreamt of being a scientist when I was young. I had more artistic aspirations and fantasies. I studied piano and dance. It has been a curiosity that I have three sisters and all four of us obtained Ph.D.s in science.

After college Goldman-Rakic succumbed to the prevailing pressure to get married. She came from a large family and did not view childrearing as all that challenging. She continued:

I was just convinced very, very early that I wanted to do something else, that I wanted to do something important. I wasn't thinking in terms of a scientific career. I just had a feeling that there was broader scope to life than what I had been exposed to.

In retrospect, getting married immediately out of college was probably not a good idea. However, my first husband was a scientist and very supportive of my graduate education and, in fact, he was very interested in a career but not so much in having a family. I was already going to graduate school and thinking only about graduate school and not thinking about a family. Basically, during the early part of my career, I was very much oriented toward supporting my husband's career, which was not uncommon for the time. At that time I was still under the assumption that my career would be secondary to his, and I and he expected that. Rather gracious of me, perhaps too gracious. I can't believe that I accepted it, but I did. What happened was that I followed him to places where I had nothing to do. That was a really bad time for me. At that point any prediction that could have been made about my career would have been that it was finished, totally off, totally bad, going nowhere.

My husband, at the time, took a position in Maryland, and again it was up to me to find something. I had no mentorship whatsoever, and I felt that it was really my responsibility to find a position. . . . I was on my own, and I just had to scout for myself. I inquired around. I would look up places in a directory and just write blindly to people not knowing who they were, what they did, but just going on minimal cues.

Through this process I came into contact with Dr. Rosvold, who headed the Laboratory of Neuropsychology at the NIMH. He was looking for a postdoctoral fellow who was experienced in statistics. My experimental background gave me excellent training in statistics, so I thought I could definitely qualify. Apparently I did qualify, and I was given a staff fellow position in the intramural program at NIMH. We went to Maryland, and I showed up in Dr. Rosvold's laboratory, and he took me under his wing. Neither he nor I could have predicted that I would stay there for 14 years.

During that whole time, from entering the door, when I knew very little about the brain, particularly about the cerebral cortex and the importance of the frontal lobes, to when I left, when I knew quite a bit, I always considered this period as a great educational experience. Everything I did and learned was completely dictated by my own immediate interests and by what I myself zealously wanted to know. Dr. Rosvold was helpful and supportive and encouraged me to follow my interests in development, which had already been established during my graduate training. This was very generous as his laboratory was not working on developmental issues. I was following my own instincts, and I found that I was learning avidly in this new field. Looking back, I was reading the right things, but at the time I would not have known that they were the right things.

In the meanwhile, my marriage dissolved. As a result of this and other personal experiences, I more and more put myself into my work and more and more recognized that it was a central and sustaining part of my life. I accepted that I could be successful in this work on my own terms and not just as a helper. I felt natural leading the research, planning it and carrying it out, and I felt that my ideas were good. . . . They led somewhere, and they were validated by what I was doing.

Goldman-Rakic, who had started working at NIMH in 1965, was promoted to the tenure track in 1973. She was made a section chief in 1978, the year before she left NIMH. By that time she had been working as an independent investigator for about eight years, although her leadership had not been formally recognized. She recalled:

> That should have happened earlier. I had been de facto leading a large group of people for many years, but the administrative nature of this role was taken for granted rather than reflected in my title. I had several times asked the chief of the laboratory to put me forward for a promotion, and he said he would, but he never did. For a long while it wasn't so greatly important to me because I was able to do what I wanted to be doing. It became important as more conflicts developed in the laboratory between personnel. When the situation became politically charged within the laboratory, I started to push. I asked him to put me forward, and he said he would, but he did not act. I believe that saying you will attend to a problem and then doing nothing is commonly evidence of administrative frailty. In retrospect it probably did not ultimately affect my career. It might have helped me earlier on.

The people above Goldman-Rakic at NIMH were men. While she felt they had good intentions and supported and valued her work, they did not recognize their responsibilities to women. She added:

> I am giving you this background because I do remember going to the director of the intramural program and the deputy director, both very kind and gentle people, and saying, "I have done this and that. I have done some pioneering studies in developmental plasticity (now a very "in" domain of neuroscience). I have supervised a large number of people and assumed many administrative duties. Their promotions and the success of our laboratory are in large part a result of my activities. I did all the administrative work, and I am writing this many papers and I'm doing a terrific job."
>
> And they said, "Pat, stop. You do not have to convince us

that you deserve this." I said, "Well then, why not do it?" Finally, they did it. But it was hard for them because they saw it as maybe something of a threat to others. I was surprised to realize that they knew it was the thing to do but still did not act. This episode in my life revealed to me that silence and passivity are a powerful administrative mechanism for ignoring or postponing what is right and proper to do.

The long overdue title reflected the successful administrative and scientific contributions Goldman-Rakic had already been making for years. She does not even remember whether she received a substantial salary increase because that was never important to her. She noted that for many years she had already been at the highest salary level in the civil service, short of being a laboratory chief. "The nice thing about the government," she said, "is that salary increases are stepwise and very regular. It is almost an inevitable sort of thing." While money wasn't an issue for Goldman-Rakic at that point in her life, she valued the promotion to section chief because it reflected her administrative and scientific contributions to the laboratory where she worked.

A year later, in 1979, Goldman-Rakic moved to Yale. Her decision to move was very difficult. She was giving up her position at NIMH, friends, a large scientific and support staff, very substantial technical and financial support, and a good government retirement plan. She had literally built up all this from nothing over the course of 14 years. She recalled: "It was wonderful and I loved those people." At Yale she had to start all over again. She recounted:

> As I look back, it was tremendously difficult to pick up and start from scratch all over again. I received no seed money and inadequate space, even though I was recruited as a full professor and had an independent career.

Nevertheless, she was drawn to Yale for two reasons: personal and professional. Yale had a long and eminent tradition in primate research and a primate breeding colony. She and a developmental biologist at Harvard Medical School, Pasko Rakic, were the only two people in the country working on primate brain development. In her words: "That is how I met him. We could have been colleagues in another life if we had not married." They had been seeing each other for several years and had been traveling between Boston and Washington. She noted:

> It was inevitable that at some point there should be some ac-commodation on both of our parts. We were committed to each other. What could be more ideal than halfway between Boston and Washington, in New Haven? And I, having grown up in Massachusetts, felt there was a romantic quality to com-ing back to New England. So this was going to be a chance to develop neuroscience at Yale. I thought that I could be of help.
> . . . Pasko was extremely generous and easily shared his labo-ratory space and equipment with me. Without that it would have been impossible.

Pasco Rakic preceded his wife to Yale, where he founded the Sec-tion of Neurobiology. For her this was an opportunity to do something different professionally. Both the academic and the medical school en-vironments were new for her. It came down to:

> "Should I just do what I know how to do and keep doing this the rest of my life?" or "Should I take this challenge, should I opt for having a personal life, although I had already accepted that I might not have had a personal life?" or "Should I just stay in the comfort of what I have developed?" "Should I do it?" Well, it really wasn't a decision. The decision was made. It was just a question of how I could execute this because it was tough leaving everything I had built behind.
>
> Only one postdoctoral fellow came with me to Yale. I had to learn to write grants and teach medical students for the first time. I encountered a new and less inviting environment than I was accustomed to. It was psychologically harder than I ever thought it was going to be, but in spite of everything I think I can say that I have been successful. I was able to rebuild a well-funded laboratory with talented students and postdoctoral fellows and to enjoy the excitement and pleasure of tackling challenging scientific issues.

We discussed the impact of gender on career. Goldman-Rakic believes there is still considerable gender discrimination at work in academia. She noted:

> Virtually every chair and most important positions in this school are held by males. The preponderance of real power in this and other universities is in the hands of men. That has to have an isolating impact. I certainly felt the lack of women colleagues and women friends in the medical school.
>
> I don't think women as a class are yet fully treated without regard to gender, either good or bad, although there is a tendency to give preferential treatment to some women who become banner cases. I still feel that gender discrimination is possibly an issue, but I have to add that it has never been foremost in any of my interactions or activities. Sometimes it comes as an afterthought or sometimes it comes as a feeling: "Oh, I'm not feeling that comfortable. Why?" But it has never been in the forefront for me. I have always felt here I am doing what I want to do. I am interested in the intricacies of brain structure and function and in achieving new insights and taking on challenges with my students and colleagues. I have received many accolades and honors, and I am recognized in my field for my work.
>
> Maybe I don't recognize sex discrimination as much as I should. It does affect certain things. I see it in certain ways, those things that I have been deprived of because I am a successful woman. By and large, I am just saying that when I wake up in the morning and when I go to bed at night, I am not thinking about gender prejudice at all. I am not letting it interfere with my activities, and I think that achievement is the best antidote to gender discrimination.

Patricia Goldman-Rakic's reflections on her career show unusual insight into the issues women scientists confront in the course of their lives. She is acutely aware that the playing field for male and female scientists is not yet level, although she personally was able to rise to the top of her field. Even though she decided early on that she did not want a family, her career was influenced by the fact that she had internalized prevailing attitudes about a woman's role in relation to her spouse. She is also aware of the adverse effect that male-dominated institutions can have on women's status even in the absence of any intentional discrimination. Before moving to Yale from a position at NIMH in which she had achieved prominence and in which she was very happy, she struggled with the questions all dual-career couples face when an opportunity to relocate arises. For Goldman-Rakic, as for so many other women members of the Academy, achieving a harmonious balance between professional and personal lives was not always easy.

## MARY K. GAILLARD

Physicist Mary K. Gaillard was born in New Brunswick, New Jersey, in 1939. She received a bachelor's degree from Hollins College in Virginia in 1960 and did graduate work at Columbia University, where she earned a master's degree in physics in 1961. While at Columbia she married a postdoctoral fellow whom she then followed to France. She earned doctorates in physics from the University of Paris in 1964 and 1968.

From 1964 to 1981 Gaillard worked as a theoretical physicist in Geneva. Since 1981 she has been a professor of physics at the University of California at Berkeley. Her research involves the theory of elementary particles, a field of physics that seeks to identify the most elementary constituents of matter and the forces that govern their interactions. She has worked on the implications of theories of elementary particles for high-energy physics and cosmology. Her goal is to reconcile theories about the constituents of matter with experimental observations by linking particle theory to phenomena that may be detected in accelerator experiments and through cosmological observations.

In addition to receiving many honors in her field, Gaillard has served on national scientific committees since the early 1980s, among them the Fermi Laboratory Physics Advisory Committee from 1986 to 1990, the Executive Committee of the Division of Particles and Fields of the American Physical Society from 1990 to 1992, and the High Energy Physics Advisory Panel to the U.S. Department of Energy from 1991 to 1994. She is currently a member of the National Science Board. In 1985 she served as chair of the Status of Women in Physics Committee of the American Physical Society. She was elected to the National Academy of Sciences in 1991.

Gaillard is the mother of three children, all born while she lived in Europe. Her oldest child was born in 1962, the youngest in 1967, and there is one child in between. She divorced her first husband in 1981 and recently married Bruno Zumino, a theoretical physicist and a professor in the graduate school at Berkeley. When I interviewed Gaillard in March 1995, we talked about the early influences in her life. I asked her what factors had contributed to her success as a scientist. She responded:

> I think family is part of it. I grew up at a time when it was very rare and unusual to go into science. My family was an academic family. My mother had been a teacher and a girl's counselor. She did not have a real career, but she always worked, more or less. My father never treated boys differently from girls.

Gaillard's father was a historian. Only a cousin shared her interest in science. Although she did not get explicit encouragement to pursue science, she was not discouraged either.

> It was expected that you went to college and did something. Dorothy Montgomery, a teacher of mine at Hollins College, put me in the right places at the right times. When I came to Hollins, I vaguely knew that I wanted to major in physics, but I did not think beyond that. There was one physics major at Hollins every two years. When I went into the Hollins Junior Year Abroad Program, Dorothy Montgomery got me into a lab in Paris at the Ecole Polytechnique because she did not want me not to do physics. What was very important was that

she sent me to Brookhaven National Laboratory as a summer student. I worked in a high-energy physics group and that is what really got me into physics.

After finishing my undergraduate degree, I went right on to Columbia University. . . . I always had an inclination to do theoretical physics, but when I got to Columbia they gave you this lecture that very few people will be able to do theory. . . . Then I married a postdoctoral fellow at Columbia, a French-man. That is how I ended up in France. That was both good and bad. The good part was that it is easy to get child care in France. We lived in the countryside. I had a next-door neigh-bor who did housework everyday. She also took care of the children when they were very small. Then I started using au pair girls as well because we needed somebody when we went out in the evening.

The bad part was that I was basically told, "We only hire graduates of Ecole Polytechnique and Ecole Montmarte." . . . I simply couldn't get into an experimental group for one rea-son or another. . . . Finally, my husband decided to hire me because he thought what was going on was ridiculous. He had not wanted to hire me in the first place because he thought it would be better if I worked somewhere else. Any-way, I was taking courses and I did well and by default ended up in theory, which was actually what I always wanted to do. Somebody told me once that I have some kind of survival mechanism.

Gaillard then followed her husband to Geneva, where he had ac-cepted a position at the European Laboratory for Particle Physics (CERN). She ended up living in Geneva for nearly 20 years. During that time she worked for the French National Center for Scientific Research (CNRS) in Geneva, although she was never offered a posi-tion. She was paid by France and was going up the ladder of the French system. She summed up her frustration:

It was a patronage system. . . . I was getting increasingly un-happy with working in Geneva. There were a lot of things.

The salary I made was much lower because it was a French salary. I didn't have all the benefits of the CERN people, and yet I was one of the more prominent people there. . . . Eventually I just felt that I could not stay there anymore. It was really a question of deciding where to go. Eventually I got a job offer at the Fermi Laboratory in Chicago. That first offer came a year or two before the Berkeley offer. I had two solid offers, and I was getting hints when people heard that I was moveable. I started getting phone calls.

In 1981 Gaillard was offered an appointment as a full professor of physics at Berkeley. At the time, her oldest child was already at the University of Washington, and her daughter was about to start undergraduate studies at the University of California at Santa Cruz. Her youngest was still in high school and had a harder adjustment to make.

Gaillard was happy to be at Berkeley after the bitterness at CERN. She had been recruited and was wanted, even though some people on the Berkeley faculty still harbored old ideas. She was the first woman on the physics faculty, but several women joined the department later. She does not think that her gender has played a major role in her career at Berkeley, except for the fact that she is on too many committees.

Salary-wise I think I have been treated fairly. When I first came I was naive and I did not know the ropes. I was happy to leave CERN. . . . My salary was higher than my French salary, but the cost of living here turned out to be much higher than I had anticipated, and I was not convinced that I was being paid on a par with my colleagues with the same level of achievement. Then I got an offer from another university which I was first thinking of immediately turning down, but then I decided to use it, and I got a significant raise after that.

I asked her what she thought about allegations that men's and women's brains are different.

There are feminists who muddy the waters by arguing that there is no absolute scientific truth. Science is done by men and, therefore, it is masculine and is defined in masculine terms. This upsets me terribly. I think it does a terrible disservice to women and to science.

I asked Gaillard to speculate on why there are even fewer women in physics, particularly in theoretical physics, than in science as a whole. She observed:

> When I went to Columbia, you got the feeling that doing theory is really hard. At every level women tend to value themselves less than men do. I mean people with the same grades and the same experience. . . . If the goal is made to look further away and much harder to do, then a woman will more easily become discouraged.

Gaillard remarked that she can almost count the women theoretical physicists on her fingers but added, "There are a lot more young women in the field now. . . . Professor Howard Georgi at Harvard has had lots and lots of students who do very well, and he in particular has produced a number of women students." She thinks that because women are not encouraged to take the necessary math early on, they cannot handle physics, in particular theoretical physics, when they get to college. She noted that in Italy everyone is required to take the same courses and, as a result, more women go into the sciences. When asked what would help women to become scientists she said:

> Require more of everybody. Certainly improving the education everywhere and making it more rigorous is an important thing not only for women in science but for the country. . . . I am still puzzled why there are not more women in science because I think many of the barriers are gone. You will still meet some old fogie who says, "Women cannot do science," but by and large they are gone. . . . But you still don't see the women. They are not coming down the pipeline. Why?
>
> I am a little bit alarmed about the trends today about reversing affirmative action. I am absolutely in favor of taking the best candidate. I do not want to push people who aren't good enough, but affirmative action has done so much good

in just the way people talk. In Europe I would be on a jury committee or at a committee meeting and people would just sit there as though I weren't there and make these absolutely sexist remarks. . . . Here, men hardly ever do that. There has been a change in the way people talk.

Gaillard noted that no one has ever made her feel that she has gotten where she is because she is female. She does think, however, that some of the younger women graduate students worry about this. In general, though, she thinks women have made huge inroads into physics. When she started out in the field, she could count not only women theorists but every woman in the field on her fingers. She was amazed that 125 women physicists had recently signed a letter to the women in Congress to stop a funding cutoff in high-energy physics. Gaillard noted that the biggest difficulty in her field now is that "we are scrambling to get funding to support our students. We have trouble placing the students. The loss of the supercollider was a big blow to our field. A lot of positions all over the country dried up." I asked Gaillard where she sees the future going. She responded:

> I'm pessimistic. This goes way beyond feminism. I'm just pes-
> simistic about science, about scholarship. Maybe this is some-
> thing that will reverse itself, but there is such a trend against
> science. I cannot jump up and down and get enthused about
> encouraging women to be in a competitive marketplace. I
> mean it's just not my thing. The reason I got into these issues
> was because I believed that if a woman wants to do science
> she should be able to do so. If there is no science to do, then
> what?

The defeat of funding for the supercollider, a facility essential for carrying out research in Gaillard's field, may account in part for her pessimistic view of the future, but it also shows how closely the course of science is tied to the economic climate and to the public attitude toward science. Women are often the first to be hurt when there is economic retrenchment.

Each of the women profiled in this chapter followed a different career path. Maxine Singer and Myriam Sarachik earned their doctorates while they were still in their twenties, married, raised children, and had uninterrupted careers from the beginning. Mary-Lou Pardue and Margaret Kidwell did not decide to earn doctorates until they were in their thirties, and nevertheless eventually attained tenured faculty positions. Patricia Goldman-Rakic, Mary K. Gaillard, and Mary-Lou Pardue made decisions based on their husband's career plans at the early stages of their careers but shaped their own careers after they were divorced. To a greater or lesser degree, the lives of every one of these women and of others in their generation were affected both by the traditional culture in which they were raised and by the changing climate for women that came about beginning in the 1970s.

# THROUGH OPEN DOORS
## Women Born After 1940

The world encountered by women born after 1940 was vastly different from that inhabited by their mothers and grandmothers. Unlike their predecessors, they found newly opened opportunities as graduate students, as postdoctoral fellows, and as new recruits to industry and academia. For the first time their careers as scientists, launched after the advent of affirmative action in 1970, began to resemble those of their male contemporaries. For the first time ever the résumés of these women are virtually indistinguishable from those of their male colleagues.

Thirty-two of the 86 Academy members I contacted were born after 1940, 26 in the 1940s and six in the 1950s. One-third of this group are physical or mathematical scientists, and the rest are biological scientists. The group includes astronomers, geologists, mathematicians, a chemist, a geophysicist, geneticists, biochemists, and cellular and molecular biologists. Many of the biological scientists work in interdisciplinary areas bridging the physical and biological sciences. Two of the members hold positions at research institutes, two are at government laboratories, and 28 hold professorships at universities.

I interviewed half of the 32 women in this group either in person or by telephone and received written comments from six others. Three members responded to my inquiry but, as a matter of principle, chose not to participate in a study restricted to women. Twenty-eight of the 32 women in this age group married, and 20 have children. The women in this age cohort have smaller families than the women Academy members of previous generations; they range from one to three children and average two per family. Eight of the 32 women born in the 1940s had been divorced; three of them subsequently remarried. All six members born since 1950 had married, four of them have children, and none had been divorced.

The disappearance of overt barriers has altered the climate in which women scientists work, so for the first time women feel at home in many areas of science. Women's professional organizations have sprung up in many disciplines, enabling women to network and to share their experiences both as scientists and as women. The profiles that follow reflect the shift that has taken place since the early 1970s in the lives of the youngest women members of the Academy.

## JUDITH P. KLINMAN

Judith Klinman is a chemist and biochemist. She majored in chemistry at the University of Pennsylvania, from which she graduated in 1962. In 1966 she received her doctorate in organic chemistry, also from the University of Pennsylvania. She then spent four years as a postdoctoral fellow; one year at the Weizmann Institute in Israel; one year at the Department of Chemistry at University College, London; and two years at the Institute for Cancer Research in Philadelphia. In 1972 she joined the research staff of the Institute for Cancer Research in Philadelphia, where she was promoted to tenure in 1978. She was also a member of the faculty at the University of Pennsylvania. In 1978 Klinman moved to the University of California as a professor of chemistry. Since 1993 she has had a joint appointment there in the Department of Molecular and Cell Biology. She was elected to the National Academy of Sciences in 1994.

Klinman lectures widely in the United States and throughout the world and has a long list of publications. She currently serves on several editorial boards, including those of the *Annual Review of Biochemistry* and *Current Opinions in Chemical Biology*. She was president of the American Society of Biochemists and Molecular Biologists from 1998 to 1999.

Klinman has made major contributions to our understanding of the relationship between protein structure and function. She characterizes proteins that contain copper and iron and facilitate the production of hormones and neurotransmitters. Her work addresses fundamental questions such as how proteins can act on molecular oxygen without undergoing oxidative damage themselves and how proteins invoke quantum mechanics to catalyze hydrogen transfer. Klinman and co-workers have discovered a new class of cofactors (commonly known as vitamins) within proteins, designated quino-proteins, that have been found to be ubiquitously distributed in bacteria, plants, and mammals.

Klinman raised two sons as a single mother. Both her sons are now grown; one is a sociologist, and the other is in business. Her former husband, an immunologist, works at Scripps Institute in La Jolla. She wrote to me recently to tell me that she is in a new long-term relationship and has two stepchildren.

I interviewed Judith Klinman in March 1995. She is warm, pleasant, and most modest about her achievements. I asked her to what factors she attributes her success in science. She told me that she had known she wanted to be a scientist at a very early age and had always been ambitious. She loved school, which for her provided a refuge from her home and whatever "craziness" was going on there. She attended a large inner-city public high school with good teachers. When she took high school physics and chemistry she felt as if a light had come on. This is how she recalled her high school years:

> There were 25 of us who were kind of the "nerds." . . . It was extraordinary. We hung out together, and we were very competitive with each other. . . . We enjoyed the group and each other. We explored jazz. It was kind of a new generation, the fifties. . . . The group was about half male and half female. A lot of the women have gone on to have professional careers. My best friend at the time is now an obstetrician, and others became lawyers. They went out into the world. . . . We've kept track of each other.

Klinman knew that she wanted to go to the University of Pennsylvania. Her high school friends encouraged her, but her parents were not supportive. They urged her to get married, to become a medical technologist, and to forget science. Eventually her parents, who did not have a great deal of money, agreed that if she could get a scholarship she could attend Penn. To do this, Klinman figured she needed to be first in her class of 1,200 people. When she came in second, she remembers thinking "Oh, no!"

> I can look back on my career now and see that what I took to be normal was not what the average person was doing. . . . It turned out that I got a partial scholarship, and my parents said, "Okay, you can go." My mother went to work to provide additional income. When I think back to my drive to be first in this class of 1,200, it didn't come from my family at all. Quite the opposite. They were saying, "Oh, what are you working so hard for?"
>
> At that point, there was still a college for women at Penn, which was perfect because there was a group of people that you could retreat to. It was smaller than the rest of the campus. . . . I knew immediately that I was going to major in chemistry. I took an A.B.; I didn't take the B.S. I had lots of art and literature. Penn was a very good place for me. It wasn't so high powered. It was a bigger world but not so big that I felt that I was going to drown.
>
> When I was ready for graduate work, all my friends were getting married. I remember thinking of myself as an old maid. Imagine that. I was 21 or 22 and thinking of myself as an old maid. I look at the young women today, and I am so in awe of the changes that have taken place. Marvelous. In some ways it is much harder now, I think, because the expectations are much higher.
>
> I decided that I wanted to go to New York, which was not very far from home and yet I could be in a big city. So I wrote to Columbia and NYU. Columbia did not give me an assistantship and NYU did. I don't know how many women were

getting accepted into graduate school. It was 1962. There were practically no women. I remember going up to see a friend of mine who was going to Harvard, and he said, "Why don't you apply to Harvard?" I thought about it and I said, "No, I don't have the self-confidence to go to Harvard." I figured, okay, NYU you want me, I'll come. I moved to New York. It was fun, but I really had a lot of doubts whether I would ever make it. I met my future husband, and we decided to get married.

So here I was, 23, doing what all my friends were doing, getting married. My husband was in graduate school in Philadelphia so I moved back to Penn. I think it was lucky because it was the right place for me, the right level. It was not so high paced. I got my Ph.D. in chemistry at Penn in three years because I had already had one year at NYU. I worked with Ed Thornton (a physical organic chemist) who was a great choice for me. He has chosen a low-key career, but he is a real scholar and taught me how to think. It is interesting how I learned to think with Ed, critically, and then in my postdoctoral fellowship I learned how to be experimentally bold.

I had my first child while I was in graduate school, and I was under pressure to finish my Ph.D. so that my husband could go to the Weizmann Institute for postdoctoral studies. I ended up doing a lot of my experiments in the wee hours of the morning, but I would never recommend that route to anyone. I feel that I missed out. I didn't have the time and luxury with my son that I would have had, and should have had, if I'd had the intelligence.

In 1966 Judith Klinman, her husband, and their son went to Israel. Her second child was born there in 1967. Judith and her husband both worked at the Weizmann Institute in Rehovot. She recalled their life there:

There was a nursery school there. In Israel it was a Zionist goal to have everyone working. I remember Andrew, the older, used to go to school with this plastic bag around his neck with his clean diapers. He would come back in the afternoon and it would have the dirty diapers. All these little kids with plastic bags around their necks. He thrived in that period. All the women were working, so I fell into an environment that was very supportive. The Weizmann Institute was in its heyday at that point, a very exciting place to be. There were people from all over the world there.

The Klinmans spent a year and four months in Israel and then went to the MRC Laboratory in London for eight months. Klinman's husband had a position there, but she did not. When she showed up at University College she was able to get some space to do research but no stipend. She describes the scientists there as "quite hospitable." A physical organic chemist whose wife was also on the faculty was especially helpful to her. This was one of many coincidences that enabled Klinman to get some reinforcement. At the end of two years, she and her family returned to Philadelphia, where her husband had accepted a position at the University of Pennsylvania. Klinman took a postdoctoral fellowship at Fox Chase Cancer Research Center, which she once again found to be a very good choice for her.

> The wife of the man I chose to work for was also a Ph.D. biochemist. She was in the laboratory also. Then there was this whole history of women there. Beatrice Mintz who later got into the National Academy of Sciences, a cell biologist, is still at Fox Chase. It was a terrific choice for me. A small enough place with very smart people who loved science. I really caught fire there. I learned how to do experiments. I had always been trained in an intellectual physical organic tradition, but Irwin Rose, he is just an experimental genius! I have never seen anyone who could solve problems in as original and rigorous a way as he did. So another stroke of luck, he supported me in my own position. He let me be a research associate in his lab for two years, after a two-year postdoctoral. He permitted me to do my own research and let me publish without his name. So another stroke of luck, if you want to call it that.

At this point I interrupted Klinman and pointed out that she had selected this man as the person for whom she wanted to work and that she must have known what she was doing. She had not picked someone who would make her into a mere pair of hands. She conceded that he had been very highly recommended to her by a lot of people, and they all thought she was very lucky to get into his lab.

In 1978 Klinman was divorced and left Philadelphia with her two sons to accept a tenured faculty appointment at the University of California in Berkeley. I asked her whether she thought the fact that she was a scientist had anything to do with her divorce.

> Who knows? We were working so hard. We were raising children, and we were exposed to all the stresses that all young families feel now. That was fairly unusual in those days; it wasn't so common. We were really trying so hard to do everything. We never took the time to nurture the marriage, and we were also competitive with each other. The world changed midway through our marriage. I started out being a much more traditional wife, and then as I went along I got my own position and became more ambitious. It was a wild time; it was the 1970s. Everywhere we looked everyone was getting divorced. It was a time of tremendous upheaval, and we were not immune from that.
>
> At that point I decided, I'm out of here (the Institute for Cancer Research). I'm going to change my life. I've had 10 good years. There is something heartbreaking about divorce for everyone. In retrospect it was the best thing that could have happened for me. At the time it was just pain, for the children as well. So I decided, "Okay, I'm free. How far away can I get?" I wrote to two places at that point, to UCLA and Berkeley. I thought it would be wonderful to be at a university, to have graduate students, and to get as far away as I could. UCLA wrote back and said they weren't interested. Berkeley said "Come out for an interview."

When Klinman moved to Berkeley in 1978 she became the first female member of the chemistry department (and of the other physical science departments) at Berkeley. I asked her how she thought the fact that she is a woman had affected her career.

When I came here I was a great white hope in the West and I resented it. At that point I had two adolescent sons and not a great deal of money. I had no full-time help or anything like that, and I was teaching for the first time in my career and also putting together a lab. I made a lot of very clear choices at that point. I decided that there is a certain level of collegiality that is expected from people, and I really backed away from that. I decided I did not have the time. I felt uncomfortable, anyway, with a lot of my colleagues. I think that was a very smart decision. I have been called on that since then.

I have only recently found out that I was not promoted at the normal rate, and I am still considerably behind my male peers. The expectation was that I would be a good mother and a good teacher and not rock the boat too much. Instead, I decided to focus on my research and my family. Those were my decisions. That was all the energy I had. I was blamed for the fact that I did not interact sufficiently with the department and the fact that my teaching was not strong.

I did some committee work but not a huge amount. To look at research proposals on the weekends as a single parent with two children, that's crazy. So I backed off from that. I would run the seminar program connected with science, but I did keep a low profile. Also, I did not particularly like the committees I was being asked to join. I thought they were kind of twiddling your thumbs type of committees. I also felt my voice was not being listened to to a very large extent. So I thought, "Okay, fine. I have control over this area of my life, and this is where I'm going to focus my energy." The other thing is that I have never published at a fast rate. Only in recent years when things started to explode has my publication list grown at a fast rate. I usually published three or four long papers a year. Not little communications but full substantial papers. That was the way in which I worked for many, many years.

My younger son went to college in 1986, and at that point I really started to make a push for my science. It was a deliberate decision on my part. I had never before had the luxury of devoting myself completely to my science and at that point I decided to do that.

After Klinman was elected to the National Academy of Sciences in 1994 she found out that her salary was far below that of her male colleagues. She went to her chairman to discuss the matter, and he brought up the fact that students in the large organic chemistry course she was teaching thought her exams were too hard and had criticized her course. She found this was ridiculous and became annoyed, at which point the chairman asked her whether she had considered the possibility that she had too high an opinion of herself, a question she says he would never have asked a male faculty member. She then went to the dean and asked to see the record of age versus salary, a matter of public record at a state university. She never received the information she requested, but the dean admitted that she had been promoted at a slower rate than her colleagues.

Klinman reminded me how important it is for women to get together, to exchange information, and to be in positions of responsibility. When she first came to Berkeley she was invited to join a women's group made up largely of fellow scientists but declined because she was not interested. She eventually joined the group several years later at the suggestion of a friend and was still a member 13 years later. The group has become very meaningful to her.

Like the women born a decade earlier, Judith Klinman subordinated her career to that of her husband's at its early stages, but the world changed midway through her marriage. By the time she moved to Berkeley in the late 1970s, she was secure enough to set her own priorities so that she could manage both work and family, even though she was penalized for her choices. She had the courage to confront her department chair when she learned that she was paid less than her male peers—a sign that women were beginning to feel that they belonged rather than being interlopers who must not rock the boat. She eventually overcame her sense of isolation by joining a women's group.

# JOAN A. STEITZ

Joan Steitz was born in Minneapolis, Minnesota. She earned a B.S. degree in chemistry from Antioch College in 1963 and a doctorate in biochemistry and molecular biology from Harvard in 1967. After completing three years of postdoctoral work at the MRC Laboratory of Molecular Biology in Cambridge, England, she joined the Yale faculty in 1970, where she is a professor of molecular biophysics and biochemistry. She is married to Thomas Steitz, a structural biologist and professor of biophysics and biochemistry at Yale. Joan and Tom Steitz  have one son, currently a Yale undergraduate.

Steitz studies the organization, control, and expression of the mammalian genome (genetic makeup), with a particular emphasis on understanding the molecular aspects of differentiation and development. Her laboratory is investigating how a number of small RNA and protein-containing particles found in all cells contribute to basic life processes. Understanding the nature of these particles is important not only for basic molecular biology but also for improving the diagnosis and treatment of rheumatic disease.

Steitz has been a professor of molecular biophysics and biochemistry at Yale since 1978 and a Howard Hughes Medical Institute investigator since 1986. She currently serves as chair of her department. She was elected to the National Academy of Sciences in 1983 and has received numerous honors, awards, and honorary degrees. In 1986 she was awarded the National Medal of Science, and in 1994 she was the first woman to be awarded the Weizmann Women in Science Award. She currently serves as nonresident fellow of the Salk Institute, as scientific director of the Jane Coffin Childs Memorial Fund for Medical Research, as a member of the External Advisory Committee of the Dana-Farber Cancer Institute, and as a member of the Board of Scientific Advisors of the Whitehead Institute. Since 1994 she has served as associate editor of the journal *Genes and Development.* She was chairman of the President's Committee on the National Medal of Science in 1998.

Steitz attended Antioch College at a time when it had a strong science program and sent a lot of students to graduate science programs. Antioch has a work-study program in which students alternate three months of work with study, and Antioch students often rotate through the same job in succession. This is how Steitz managed to obtain a position in a laboratory at MIT doing research in molecular biology before this subject became part of the undergraduate curriculum. This experience is what first got her excited about molecular biology. When I interviewed Steitz in New Haven in December 1994, she described her experience as follows:

> I had seen that people who were molecular biologists worked awfully hard. They worked for nothing; they worked nights; they worked weekends. They were totally absorbed in their work. I thought to myself, "Gee, it doesn't sound like you can balance this and be a woman, and be a wife, and have a family. So I'd better go to medical school because it will be much easier to categorize my time."

Steitz had planned to go to medical school, but in the summer before she was to start she obtained a position working for an embryologist, Joseph Gall, who was then at the University of Minnesota. Gall gave Steitz her own project to work on, and she described him as "wonderful, an incredible supporter of women." She soon found herself working nights and weekends. By August she had switched her plans and decided to go to graduate school.

Steitz enrolled at Harvard and did her doctoral work under the supervision of biochemist James Watson, who, together with Francis Crick, had discovered the double helix and constructed the Watson-Crick model of DNA. She was the first woman graduate student to work with Watson and received the highest grade in his course during her first year of graduate study. She thinks Watson accepted her as a student because he was impressed with her academic ability. Steitz described Watson as the sort of person who is uncomfortable in relationships with almost all people, who hates some while others "are on his good list." She ended up on his good list and had a wonderful experience in his lab. He has always been very supportive of her, and he has subsequently had other women as graduate students and postdoctoral fellows.

Shortly before she earned her doctorate, Joan Steitz married. Her husband, Tom Steitz, who had already completed his degree, remained at Harvard an extra year to allow her to finish her dissertation. Steitz was surprised when I asked her whether being a woman had affected her career. She said "yes" and observed that in the many interviews she had given she had never been asked to comment on the effect of her gender on her career. She then elaborated:

> The beginning of my career was very much affected by my being a woman. I did my graduate training in the 1960s when there were no women on faculties of major universities. I had a completely different attitude about what my life, my career as a molecular biologist, would be like; therefore, I focused on different things and put out effort in different areas than my male colleagues, who were my peers. I did not expect that I would ever be a faculty member at a large university. I presumed that I would be a research associate in somebody's lab because that was what all women did and therefore what was very important was for me to learn how to do research very well. I had the idea that it was possible to be respected as a woman by doing very good research but that it wasn't so important to learn about political dealings, broadening my view of things, because I was never going to need those qualities or to be a professor teaching.
>
> I went off to the Cambridge MRC, where it was quite clear that I was accepted only because my husband had been given a postdoctoral position. When I got there, there wasn't any space for me and Francis Crick said, "Well, why don't you think about a literature project? You can do it in the library." I knew I wasn't going to be any good at thinking theoretical biology thoughts in the library. I wanted to do research. Luck-

ily a couple of the younger staff members took pity on me and came up with a little bench space.

The other thing that happened that I wouldn't have done if I weren't a woman was choosing a very risky research project. It was a project that a lot of people had discussed that somebody ought to do, but none of the men dared take it on because they knew that in one or two years they had to finish their postdoc and land a job. So I took this project on. After a year of being very depressed because it didn't seem to be working, I started to have success with it. In the meanwhile, Bella Abzug and Gloria Steinem had gotten the women's movement going in the United States and all of a sudden universities were saying, "Gee, we don't have any women on our faculty. We've got to have women." Tom had a position fixed up at Berkeley, and I had found a second postdoctoral position there and was assuming that I would go on being a research associate.

In the meantime we were traveling and both of us gave seminars and all of a sudden people started offering me jobs. I was flabbergasted. Even though I wasn't anticipating it and was very scared, I wanted to undertake the challenge. Berkeley didn't offer me a job, but several other places did, and that's why we came to Yale. So I was very lucky.

The second way that being a woman has affected my career was that the field of molecular biology was in its nascency at the time that I went into it. Departments in molecular biology were just starting to be formed about 1970, about the time that I started out in academia. As a new field it was started by people who came to it from other disciplines, and the people who were adventuresome enough and courageous enough to make this sort of switch were the type of people who are willing to evaluate things on their merit. They don't come in with a lot of hide-bound ideas about the way things should be. I think that this tradition continues even now, and that makes it a very good field for women. I think it has been even easier for women in molecular biology than in standard biology, certainly than in medicine or than in the more physical sciences. Most of the people in molecular biology evaluate things in an objective way based on one's scientific contributions. It is important that other people can reproduce your work and quote it. A woman gets as much credit as a man does, but that doesn't mean it's easier. That's my explanation for why women perform well in a particular area.

Also, because there weren't many women, if you were out there and did something really nice you didn't blend in with the crowd. You got noticed more because you were different, and therefore people were more likely to remember you, and that is an advantage. That is still the case. If we have two job applicants and we can't decide between them, and one is a woman and one is a man, the pressures are to offer the job to a woman. I still think it is very much an advantage to be a woman.

I asked Steitz whether being a woman has made any difference to her as a faculty member. These were her comments:

I have never felt any overt discrimination in my department. The only person that I ever felt that with was the former dean of the Yale Graduate School. At the time I had been a full professor for over 10 years. I was a member of the National Academy of Sciences and was serving as director of graduate studies for the Department of Molecular Biophysics and Biochemistry at Yale. There had been a divisive meeting of all the directors of graduate studies, the medical school deans, and the dean of the graduate school about what the graduate student stipends should be. After the meeting I talked to a male colleague who then decided to write a letter to Yale's president about the lack of financial support for the graduate program. He showed me the letter, but I didn't sign it. He simply asked me whether I thought it would be okay to send it. Two days after this colleague sent the letter, the phone rang and it was the dean who screamed and yelled at me and fired me as director of graduate studies. He said he would have nothing more to do with me. Can you imagine?! He just assumed that since this letter came from our department that I must be behind it. Isn't that unbelievable? Our department chairman went to work and said, "You can't fire her." Eventually it got sorted out. I wrote down some of the incredible names the dean called me, and I still have them in a box somewhere for when I write my memoirs. He said that I had no professional sense. He would never have done that to a man.

When I asked Steitz to what factors she attributed the enormous success she has achieved as a scientist, she responded:

I attribute my success to being in a good institution and a good department, where I have been able to get good graduate students and good colleagues, and to the fact that I think today it is slightly easier for women to do well. I have been reasonably successful at using people in my lab, not in a pejorative sense. I know a lot of male colleagues who run into a lot of interpersonal problems with some of their graduate students and postdocs. In that respect it may help to be female, but on the other hand not all females succeed, and there are certainly a lot of males who succeed very well.

I now have women colleagues whom I consider my friends at other institutions . . . whereas in the seventies it was very lonely. That has really changed in the last 10 years. I have also gotten older, so I sit on more committees . . . where you get to know who these people are. There really is sort of a female structure within the biological sciences that wasn't there at all before.

Joan Steitz decided to study molecular biology because she had become fascinated by the subject in the course of doing a research rotation as an undergraduate. In the 1960s she never expected to be anything other than a research assistant. When she realized in the 1970s that she was being seriously recruited as a faculty member she was "flabbergasted" and very scared but decided to rise to the challenge. She even saw certain advantages to being a woman because women were suddenly in demand, and if, as a woman, you achieved good results, you were noticed and did not blend in with the crowd. Today she is a leader in her field.

## NANCY J. KOPELL

Nancy Kopell is an applied mathematician. She graduated from Cornell University in 1963 and earned her doctorate at the University of California, Berkeley, in 1967. From 1967 to 1969 she was an instructor in mathematics at MIT, and from 1969 to 1986 she was on the faculty of Northeastern University. Since 1986 she has been a professor of mathematics at Boston University. She has lectured widely, has held numerous visiting appointments in the United States and abroad, and has served on many editorial boards and advisory committees. From 1990 to 1995 Kopell held a MacArthur fellowship. She was elected to the National Academy of Sciences in 1996 and is one of only two women among the 60 male members in the Academy's applied mathematical sciences.

Kopell is a mathematical biologist who uses mathematical analysis to reveal new principles of biological organization. She has helped to develop new methods in the qualitative theory of differential equations and has applied these methods to study the dynamics of networks of neurons. Her recent work has focused on problems at the boundary between mathematics and neurophysiology, especially networks of neurons that participate in rhythmic electrical activity. Such networks are important in motor behavior, sensory processing, and cognition.

I spoke with Kopell on the telephone in September 1996. She was most gracious about talking with me. When I inquired about influences on her career, she told me that her parents had discouraged her early intense academic involvement on the grounds that it would be too competitive for her. Yielding to her parents' wishes, she passed up an opportunity to attend the highly competitive Bronx High School of Science in New York and instead attended a large city high school. She graduated before she turned 17 and entered Cornell the next fall. She recalls feeling somewhat aimless in college but, after toying with majors in chemistry, economics, and visual arts, decided to major in mathematics. Both her mother and sister had been mathematics majors, and her own high school teachers had encouraged her to go into mathematics.

At Cornell she enrolled in a small mathematics honors program, the only woman in a group of five. Her mentor was male, and she recalls that even then she was aware of the absence of other women. Kopell attributes her career success to serendipity and to her innate intensity. She looks back on her decision to go to graduate school as, in part, a way to find an alternative to the more traditional life her family expected for her. She had originally applied only to graduate schools in the East and was admitted to all but one program, but, at the urging of a fellow student, she decided to go to the West Coast instead. She was admitted to Berkeley with a fellowship and earned her doctorate there four years later.

At Berkeley, Kopell passed her exams with honors and soon became known as the "bright female." Nevertheless, she described herself as "floundering" during the early stages of her dissertation work. Eventually she switched supervisors in order to work for Stephen Smale, a distinguished mathematician. This decision marked a turning point in Kopell's career. Smale suggested a new problem to Kopell and strongly encouraged her. She then almost singlehandedly solved the problem he had suggested. This, in turn, led to her dissertation in the field of dynamical systems and launched her career. Kopell describes Smale's mentoring as key to her success at Berkeley and as a paradigmatic example of the critical role that the well-timed intervention of a mentor can play in the success of students, especially women.

Following graduate study, Kopell returned east to accept an instructorship at MIT. Again she credits mentors with being key factors in her career. Her first collaborator at MIT, Lou Howard, helped Kopell reinvent herself as an applied mathematician. She continued:

> Later, it was my husband-to-be who provided the encouragement I needed to change fields from my thesis work to an area that was not populated enough even to be called a field. I cannot imagine that I could have survived the early years of my career psychologically or intellectually without the help of these two people. Mentoring played a critical role in my career.

At age 35, after she had been awarded tenure at Northeastern, Kopell married a fellow tenured faculty member. She acquired two stepchildren as a result of the marriage, but, since she was a custodial parent only for brief periods, she did not face the difficulties of juggling child care and a professional career.

When I asked Kopell whether being female had affected her career, she replied, "Yes, in subtle ways." During her preschool years she had a serious eye problem that had forced her to struggle, and so from early childhood on Kopell always considered herself on the margin. Later, being a woman in science emphasized her marginality. She described her contributions to mathematics, except for her dissertation, as out of the mainstream as well. "Eventually," Kopell said, "the mainstream caught up with me." She believes that these early personal experiences enabled her to weather being on the margin. Recent studies have demonstrated that even outstanding women scientists often consider themselves marginal.

Kopell would like to see greater institutional flexibility to reduce the tensions between career and family. More couples should be hired by the same institution, and policies to extend the tenure decision should be implemented. Like many of the women members of the National Academy of Sciences, she views day care as a critical issue for professional women who contemplate having children and strongly supports policies that will help women with this issue, even though she personally did not have to grapple with the child care problem.

Kopell echoed the views of many that science today entails tooth-and-claw competition and views this as bad for science. She believes competition affects women even more than men. In her own work Kopell tries to counter this trend by encouraging group activities and research that bridges more than one discipline, such as mathematics and neuroscience or mathematics and engineering. Students who participate in these endeavors tend to be very cooperative, even if they are predominantly male. Kopell also makes sure that all individuals who contribute to a project have their names on the resulting paper.

Kopell thinks that science is a human, not a gender-specific activity, but that men and women have different perspectives as a result of different cultural backgrounds. Women tend to be less hierarchical than men, and men therefore often attach more importance to the rank of "problem posers" than women. In Kopell's opinion this may affect the choice of problems in science as well as the style in which science is carried out. She believes that part of the reason there are still relatively few women in the physical sciences, mathematics, and engineering may be that it is easier to pose one's own research problems in the biological disciplines than in physics and mathematics. Hierarchical rank may thus be less important in achieving recognition in the biological sciences.

Standard training in mathematics is very narrowly focused, so many researchers work alone. In Kopell's view, a group of talented colleagues and an immersion in mathematics culture that leads to collaborative thinking are essential. Because it takes so much perseverance to survive the early phase of any science career, she would like to see more personal and intensive mentoring to facilitate careers in all fields of science, especially for women.

Nancy Kopell describes herself as someone who, as a result of a childhood health problem, learned to cope with being "different" at an early age. She attributes her success as a woman mathematician, working on problems out of the mainstream of her field, in part to this ability and in part to the help of mentors at key stages of her career. She doubts that she would have survived psychologically or intellectually without the encouragement those mentors provided. Like so many others, Kopell believes that tooth-and-claw competition is destructive to science and even more so for women scientists than for men.

## SUSAN S. TAYLOR

Susan Taylor is a protein chemist and structural biologist. She graduated from the University of Wisconsin with a major in chemistry in 1964 and obtained her Ph.D. degree from Johns Hopkins University in 1968. She has been on the faculty at the University of California at San Diego since 1972 and was promoted to full professor there in 1985. Taylor is an active participant in national scientific affairs and has lectured widely in the course of her career. From 1995 to 1996 she served as president of the American Society of Biochemistry and Molecular

Biology. She became a member of the National Academy of Sciences and the Institute of Medicine in 1996. In 1997 Taylor was selected in a national competition to be an investigator with the Howard Hughes Medical Institute. Hughes investigators conduct biomedical research in cell biology, genetics, immunology, neuroscience, and structural biology at institutions throughout the country.

Taylor has applied technological advances in computation to important biological questions. Her lab has been studying an important family of regulatory enzymes called protein kinases. In living systems this family of enzymes regulates processes, including cell growth and division, tissue differentiation in embryos, memory and thought, and most of the complex instructions for cellular changes from birth to death. In 1991 a team of researchers led by Taylor solved the three-dimensional structure of a member of the kinase family. Since then the structure has been used as a template to solve and model the structures of other kinase molecules. Faulty regulation of kinases has been linked to several diseases, including immunodeficiency diseases, diabetes, cancer, Alzheimer's disease, and Lou Gehrig's disease. The findings of her research offer avenues toward the rational rather than the trial-and-error design of drugs that are capable of regulating these enzymes.

I talked with Taylor in January 1997 and asked her to reflect on the factors early in her life that led to her success as a scientist. She described a home in which she was encouraged to do what she wanted to do. Her father was an engineer and her mother a librarian. She has one younger sister with very different interests from hers, but both daughters were equally encouraged and valued by their parents. Taylor was a good science student at the public high school she attended and never thought she was doing anything exceptional by going into science. Like many other scientists I spoke with, Taylor thinks that the early stages of her career were determined by happenstance. She is unclear why she decided to attend the University of Wisconsin after rejecting an offer to go to Wellesley College. She does recall that from the time she was little she wanted to go into medicine and that she still had this goal when she graduated from college with a chemistry major. Taylor chose chemistry as her major because she had a wonderful chemistry professor, Charles Sorum, for her freshman honors chemistry course. He taught the regular chemistry lectures, the lab, and her section and in her words "was totally committed to his career in teaching." Although there were more men than women in her classes, Taylor never felt that she did not belong or that it was unusual for her to be there.

In the summer of her senior year at the University of Wisconsin, Taylor began to date the man who would become her husband. He was about to complete his Ph.D. and had already accepted a position at the National Institutes of Health (NIH) in Bethesda, Maryland, when they became engaged in the winter of her senior year. Taylor had applied to several medical schools, but Johns Hopkins had not been among them. By the time she decided to get married, it was too late to apply to the medical school at Johns Hopkins but not too late to apply to its graduate school. She promptly changed her plans and decided to study for her doctorate in physiological chemistry at Hopkins, with the idea that she would go to medical school later. When she earned a Ph.D. from Johns Hopkins in 1968, she still intended to go to medical school. "I loved the science, had a very good mentor, Edward Heath, and became a good experimentalist, but I did not want to spend my life working in the field in which I did my doctorate." Taylor emphasized that while she knew what she wanted, she remained flexible and ready to adapt to changing circumstances. She attributes her career success, in part, to such flexibility.

By the time she completed her doctorate, her husband had become interested in an advanced training program in molecular pharmacology in Cambridge, England. Unfazed, she again postponed her medical school plans to join him in England.

> I didn't really consciously choose my career in terms of what I was going to do. I followed. I looked up who was in Cambridge and wrote to two people at the prestigious MRC lab there. I didn't know very much about the lab at the time and I didn't know much about proteins, DNA, or RNA, which is what most people there worked on. I didn't come from a lab that sent postdoctoral fellows there, but I wrote to two people there, and one of them, Brian Hartley, said, "Well, you can't

start in September, but you could start in January." To this day I don't know why he took me because I didn't have any training in proteins.

Taylor attributes much of her success to luck rather than her own initiative and ability. I wondered whether this is truly how she perceives herself or whether she deliberately tried not to appear threatening or pushy. In any event, Susan Taylor's decision to follow her husband to England marked a critical turning point in her career. She was so stimulated by the talented scientists with whom she worked at the MRC that she never again thought of leaving research or attending medical school. She became and has remained a protein chemist, and she loves the work she is doing. After two years in Cambridge, Taylor and her husband returned to the United States. She described the job hunt that ensued:

> Because my husband was a little more senior than I was, he applied for positions and interviewed in pharmacology all around the country and then ended up coming to the University of California at San Diego (UCSD). I didn't know anybody there, and I don't remember being much involved in the decision. I had never even been to California, but I fortuitously started doing an extra year of postdoctoral work with Nate Kaplan, a very eminent biochemist at the University of California, San Diego. That was really the work which led to my tenure. . . . My life has been a series of these little chances, very serendipitous.

Taylor went on to explain how she happened to end up working with Nate Kaplan. Just after Taylor's husband decided to go to San Diego, a crystallographer, Michael Rossman, visited the MRC lab in Cambridge. He gave a talk about an enzyme structure he had just solved and mentioned that Nate Kaplan at UCSD was trying to sequence it. When Taylor mentioned to him that she was going to San Diego but wasn't sure what she was going to do, he suggested that she contact Kaplan, which Taylor promptly did.

Susan Taylor is the mother of three children, who were 24, 22, and 14 at the time of our interview. The oldest, a girl, born two days before Taylor started her faculty appointment at UCSD, was in medical school. The second child, a son, was a senior at the University of Colorado majoring in fine arts, and her youngest son was in high school. Taylor had just completed a year as president of the American Society for Biochemistry and Molecular Biology, and her husband was serving as chair of the Pharmacology Department at UCSD. It was the first year in which they had not had an au pair at home. She described her husband as "very supportive" and their lives as "very busy." I asked her how she had coped with three children while both she and her husband pursued such demanding academic careers. Her account follows:

> When we came here, you could buy property close to the university, so we lived not too far away. UCSD is a very convenient campus for that. We had au pairs from the time our oldest, Tasha, was three months old until just about a year ago, so there was always someone in our home. We had a Danish girl who actually stayed with us for quite a few years while she went to school. We had a girl from Israel who stayed one year in San Diego, went with us for a sabbatical year in Cambridge, and then came back to go to school in the United States. She comes back to visit us often and was just back with her baby last Christmas for a week. By now we have quite an extended international family. . . . We learned a lot from them. . . . Each was more like an older sibling for the children. . . . Sometimes it would bother me if the child would go to the au pair rather than to me, but I think you have be confident of your relationships with your children. You have to be willing to share them and not be bothered by it.

I asked Taylor how her life had been affected by the fact that she is a woman. She responded:

> I have always thought being a woman is helpful. I think women can focus on different levels at the same time more easily than men in general. Having children also forced me to keep a balanced perspective. I would come home when the children were little and would read to them at night and I would never

feel guilty about it. Instead of reading journals, I would read stories and sing to them. I can switch back and forth easily. I like to cook, too, so I usually come home and cook dinner for the family every night. That provides a good contrast. . . . You have to balance many things to succeed in an academic career. . . . However, you don't have to do all the things that I do, either. I have always had a sense of obligation to the larger scientific community as well because that community has given a lot to me.

I am not consciously aware that I was hurt by being a woman. My mentors were all men, but they were very supportive. I didn't come to UCSD looking for a specific faculty position. After a year or so, however, I did get a faculty position. That was just fortuitous. If I hadn't gotten a faculty position at UCSD, if that postdoctoral fellowship hadn't evolved into a faculty position, then it would have been a hard decision to make. . . . I don't remember that I worried very much about it. I think young people today seem to worry so much about each step, what they are going to be doing five years from now. You encourage the young people these days, but there are too many choices for them.

Taylor has worked full time throughout her career. What did her female colleagues do?

One of our new young faculty members is in her third year now. During her first year she taught two classes and had a baby and took three graduate students. She just had a second baby. Another woman just got tenure. She's not married but has many other outside interests. Another woman, a theoretical physical chemist, had two children, and I don't believe she took time off when they were born. She also served as chairman of the department. Another full professor, a physical chemist, doesn't have a family. Other young women faculty members in pharmacology, for example, are either starting families or have young children. None of them have taken extended time off. . . . I think it is important what you establish as your routine when you first have a child. If you begin working right away as part of the routine for yourself and your child, I think you just accept it. For my children that is the way it has always been. Whereas if you were home for a year, then you really bond with that child in a different way. Returning to work at a later time is then a very difficult transition for both you and your child.

Would Taylor describe herself as a high-energy person? Without hesitation she responded:

Yes. Definitely a high-energy person! It takes a lot energy, especially if something goes wrong. My children were well adjusted and didn't have any major illnesses. You don't have much buffer room. If something goes seriously wrong, you couldn't continue at the same pace. Then you would have to readjust.

I asked Taylor to tell me about the careers of the students trained by her. She thought for a moment and then replied:

Most of them have finished and gone into some level of science. One of my very good students who just finished has started law school. He will definitely have a good career, although it was not what he or I would have predicted when he started graduate school. Young people are concerned now that there are too many scientists, too many biochemists, and there are not enough jobs for them. Although support for NIH research has been increasing steadily, it is very difficult scrambling for grants.

The example cited by Taylor illustrates the fact that men as well as women, when faced with the demands of careers as academic scientists, consider other options and may leave science altogether. Taylor spotted opportunities and ran with them. She repeatedly rerouted her career plans in response to changed circumstances. Although she describes herself as a mere follower, she obviously opened doors for herself. Compared to other Academy members in her age group, Taylor was among those who felt most comfortable in her institutional setting. Her comfort level may be due in part to her own personality and in part to a supportive atmosphere at her institution. She is tenacious yet flexible, adaptable, optimistic, and full of drive and energy, as well as lucky, but even her career could easily have been deflected at many points.

## JANE LUBCHENCO

Jane Lubchenco, a marine biologist, graduated from Colorado College in 1969 and began graduate study at the University of Washington. There she met and married Bruce Menge, a fellow marine biologist who was completing his doctoral work in marine ecology. When her husband left Seattle to take a position as a postdoctoral fellow at the University of California in Santa Barbara, Lubchenco continued her doctoral work there. In 1971, when her husband accepted an assistant professorship at the University of Massachusetts in Boston, she accompanied him and completed her graduate studies at Harvard. She earned her Ph.D. in marine biology there in 1975. Jane Lubchenco joined the Harvard faculty as an assistant professor immediately after completing her doctoral degree. She left Harvard voluntarily two years later to accept a position at Oregon State University. Looking back, she thinks she benefited from her exposure to different departments and institutions in the course of her graduate study. Jane and her husband have two sons, both born after they moved to Oregon.

Lubchenco's research focuses on conservation biology and environmental protection. As a marine biologist she has contributed to our understanding of intertidal communities, foraging tactics, coevolutionary interactions between plants and herbivores and between predators and prey, and numerous other aspects of population and community ecology. She has been actively involved in policy analysis and formulation in conservation sciences and has served on many national boards and committees addressing these problems. She has served as president of the Ecological Society of America and the American Association for the Advancement of Science.

Her achievements have brought her a long list of honors, including several honorary degrees. Early in her career she was a corecipient with her husband of the George Mercer Award of the Ecological Society of America. In 1993 she became a MacArthur fellow and a Pew scholar. In 1996 she was elected to the National Academy of Sciences.

I spoke with Lubchenco by telephone in January 1997. She and her husband both grew up in large families. She is the oldest of six girls, and he is the oldest of five siblings. When I asked her what had enabled her to become a successful scientist, she mentioned her parents, both of whom are physicians. Her father, a surgeon, worked full time, while her mother, a pediatrician, worked part time. They helped Jane and her sisters to take risks and explore and encouraged them to participate in sports, something that was still rare for girls at the time. Lubchenco sees many similarities between academia and sports and says that having played both individual and team sports was invaluable preparation for functioning in the academic world. She attended an all-girls Catholic high school and valued the excellent intellectual environment there. An active Girl Scout in a troop led by her mother, Lubchenco developed leadership, camping, and other skills at a young age. She described her mother as a strong and wonderful person who provided love, encouragement, and a role model.

Lubchenco recalls liking everything in high school. As an undergraduate at Colorado College, she was part of an experimental program for 20 students who were given freedom to do what they wanted. During her sophomore year, she became interested in biology, an interest that was strongly encouraged by a woman professor whom she describes as stern, demanding, and gruff but very supportive. This woman arranged for Lubchenco to spend time at Woods Hole so that she could get research exposure. Lubchenco also attended two coeducational National Science Foundation camps.

At the time Lubchenco and her husband married during graduate school, each made a commitment to support the other's professional career. Having grown up in large families, both knew they wanted children. They therefore decided to look for positions that would permit a sharing of professional work so they would have time with the family they hoped to have. To achieve this goal they decided to leave their respective jobs in Boston and find two joint positions in which each could work half time. They had watched many other couples in which one spouse worked full time while the other did only research but rejected this model. Although the central administration at one leading eastern private university was open to their idea, the department involved opposed it. Fortunately, after some persuading, Oregon State University came through with an offer of two half-time tenure-track positions, which they accepted in 1977.

For 10 years each worked half time. They were given great flexibility, and both reduced their teaching and committee work by half. Each also did research. When their boys were very young, they set up a nursery in their laboratory. Colleagues were very supportive, but this arrangement was no longer feasible once the children were toddlers. They then split child care between them, with each spending half a day at home while the other one worked on campus. They had cleaning help and sometimes used babysitters so they could work during their time at home and shared the child care. Both attended fewer out-of-town meetings when the children were small. Until 1983 they took both children on field trips to Panama each winter and summer quarter. Once their children started school, they tried to restrict fieldwork to Oregon. They spent a sabbatical leave in New Zealand in 1995 to 1996 with the boys, who were by then high school age. They now alternate travel so that one parent is always at home. Lubchenco emphasizes that her husband's total commitment to shared parenting is a key to its success. By the time they married, he had been living independently and had become skilled at cooking and doing housework.

Lubchenco pointed out that because universities tend to be conservative, they need to be pushed. She and her husband had to make their case and sell it to succeed. She credits a former Oregon State University dean, Robert Krauss, and the current dean, F. H. Home, for being enlightened and flexible. The fact that both she and her husband had good credentials and a record of publications also helped. Oregon State University has since offered joint appointments to other faculty, and Lubchenco and her husband have been invited to accept attractive joint appointments elsewhere—signs that demonstrate that such arrangements can work. In retrospect, Lubchenco thinks that two three-quarter-time appointments are a better option professionally and economically than half time, in part because of the increased income that results. She stressed the importance of protecting one's time and resisting demands that exceed the time commitments agreed upon.[1]

Throughout her career Lubchenco has dealt with negative vibes by ignoring them. She stressed the importance of fostering the presence of women and minorities in science because the greater the diversity, the greater the pool of creativity and new ideas. She is committed to bringing science into the political and public arenas, something in which she believes the scientific community still shows relatively little interest. She was therefore especially pleased to be awarded the MacArthur award and a Pew fellowship in 1993, validating her contributions in this area.

Lubchenco and her husband symbolize a new trend among the younger generation of scientists. They were aware that their needs clashed with the traditional expectations of established institutions. Rather than accepting the status quo, they have successfully begun to change it.

## PAMELA A. MATSON

Pamela Matson, a biogeochemist, is interested in the cycling of nutrient elements between rock, soils, plants, water, and the atmosphere. She studies the biogeochemical consequences of land-use change, agriculture, and nitrogen deposition in the tropics, including their effects

on processes within ecosystems and on emissions of trace gases that are critical to atmospheric chemistry and the greenhouse effect. Together with soil scientists, hydrologists, and environmental engineers, she tries to understand the factors regulating the transfer of nutrients from land to water. She also works with social scientists in the development of land management alternatives that reduce the negative environmental effects of agriculture.

Matson graduated magna cum laude from the University of Wisconsin-Eau Claire in 1975 with a double major in biology and English. She earned a master's degree in 1980 at Indiana University and a Ph.D. in forest ecology at Oregon State University in 1983. She spent the next 10 years as a research scientist at the National Aeronautics and Space Administration (NASA) Ames Research Center in Palo Alto, California. In 1993 she left NASA to accept a professorship at the University of California, Berkeley. She recently moved from Berkeley to her present position as a professor of geological and environmental sciences at Stanford.

Matson serves on numerous committees dealing with global change, ecosystems, and other environmental issues. She has published widely, occasionally jointly with her husband, Peter Vitousek, a faculty member of the Department of Biological Sciences at Stanford and also a member of the National Academy of Sciences. She was elected to the National Academy of Sciences in 1995 and received a MacArthur fellowship for her work the same year.

I interviewed Pamela Matson in March 1995, shortly before the birth of her second child. Friendly and outgoing, she was a pleasure to talk with. It came as no surprise when she told me that she loves science and that it is her life. Her parents did not specifically encourage her scientific interests but always gave her and her four siblings the feeling that they could do anything they wanted to do.

> They gave me self-confidence through my whole childhood and young adulthood. My parents were supportive without pushing anything. My father has a college education; my mother doesn't. I don't think they originally thought of me as going on, getting a Ph.D. Not that kind of family. I never got the sense that anybody was questioning whether I could do it.
>
> I decided that I liked biology when I was very young. My grandmother was my mentor. She used to take me out walking in the forests of Wisconsin, and we would pick spring flowers. I loved spring flowers, and I always wanted to know about them and why they grew in certain places. By the time I got into high school I knew I wanted to be a biologist.

As an undergraduate, Pamela Matson had no women professors, although she was taught by a woman lecturer. This woman had only a master's degree, but Matson thought she was clearly the best teacher in the department. In retrospect, she thinks that the unjust and unfair treatment of this woman, the fact that she was so good but not acknowledged, provided a negative example that was more useful than anything. Matson did have a male professor as an undergraduate who was a great botanist and loved biology.

> He showed that he loved the subject in everything that he did. He encouraged me in it and knew that I really liked it. I still think about him as being definitely the most important person for me as an undergraduate.

Once Matson had her bachelor's degree in biology, she became disheartened because she had a degree in biology but no job prospects as a naturalist. Her male undergraduate adviser had told her to get teaching credentials because teaching would be the only job she would be able to get with a degree in biology. She managed a music store for a year after that, until she realized that she really wanted to be a biologist. She described herself as "very driven" and very much influenced by Paul Erlich's work, by Carson's *Silent Spring*,[2] by all the environmental issues raised in the late 1960s and early 1970s. As a result she decided to get a master's degree at Indiana University in environmental science and to "do something useful with that."

> There I started research for the first time in my life and loved it. It hooked me. The research that I have done has always been related to the effects of change and disturbance on the way ecosystems work, whether driven by human activity or natural occurrences.

After Matson earned her doctorate at Oregon State University in 1983, her husband was offered a position at Stanford University. At the same time, a position opened up for her at the nearby NASA Ames Research Center. She recalled:

> There just happened to be a position that had my name on it. They were looking for someone with my combination of skills

and I was there. For me it was strictly fortuitous that I ended up there. . . . We were very lucky.

Matson stayed at NASA for the next 10 years and echoed the opinion of several other Academy members that women tend to do better in government laboratories than in universities. I asked her why. Government laboratories, she said, foster the development of women. She was given a lot of freedom to move ahead scientifically in the laboratory in which she worked and, at the same time, was free of the tight academic promotion time frame.

Pamela Matson's first child was born after she had been at NASA for several years. By then she had proved she was capable of doing good work, and NASA was eager to keep her. As a result the agency was very flexible about her scheduling needs, so that she was able to stay home for six months after her son was born, with the full support of her boss. She described how she coped after she returned from a six-month leave:

> For two years after that, my husband stayed at home one day a week, and I stayed at home another, and we had in-home child care, not live-in but in-home. The reason we did that is because our son has cystic fibrosis, a serious lung disease. He's healthy right now, but it is an added strain and worry. The one good thing that came out of it is that it drove us to have in-home child care, and it's like having a third parent. It made not only his health better but everything else about our lives easier.
>
> People say to me, "How do you do it? How do you have a child and do all this?" I almost hate saying this, but you have to have enough money to do it. We have two good incomes, relatively speaking, and when I am talking to graduate students who ask "How do you do it?" I almost feel guilty saying, "You hire a third parent." It really made it possible for us. We will do that again with this child. Now we have new family members, two young women, who have become so dear to us and so a part of our family that we will never lose contact with them. It is important to find that right person and to make

sure that they are happy. I think the key to keeping our longest-running child care person was treating her like a third parent. She was involved in decision making, and we asked her for advice and we treated her like a professional.

My area of fieldwork is incredibly intensive, and we tend to work really long hours, nonstop; there's no such thing as a weekend. When we're not in the field, we work just about every night. Our son goes to bed at 9:00, and we work for three to four hours after that. That's what we have to do to keep things going. We changed our work style on weekends because we have a little six year old who wants to go bike riding or hiking. I think both of us have slowed down.

In 1993 Berkeley recruited Matson to a position as full professor. She is confident that had she been a nontenured faculty member who came up through the ranks she would have survived the tenure promotion process but is happy to have avoided the stress that this would have entailed. At the time of our interview in 1995, Matson was living in Palo Alto and commuting to Berkeley. She admitted that this was not easy but said it was possible because her department chair, Mary Firestone, was supportive and flexible and permitted her to figure out how she could make the arrangement work. She normally spent three days a week at Berkeley and worked at home the other two days, keeping in touch by e-mail, fax, and telephone.

Matson realizes that her own situation is very special. Because she sees her husband and a few other men sharing home responsibilities completely, she starts to assume that everyone is like that. She sometimes thinks that it should be as easy for other women, but she realizes that other women do not necessarily have that kind of support. She knows several women whose marriages broke up in graduate school because their husbands just could not understand their dedication, the time they spent on research. She went on to explain that her husband's mother was a judge and his father was a lawyer. She never saw her mother-in-law cook and is very aware that her husband was exposed to a very different family situation from most men. "If you love science and want to keep it up," she says, "then it is critical that you not marry a man who automatically puts himself first."

Matson has been trying to teach herself to say "no" for the past several years and has even succeeded, but it is difficult. Each year she receives more and more requests to speak or to serve on committees, activities she is eager to participate in. She admits that science is a passion for her. "Do the men feel as passionate?" I wanted to know. "Yes," she replied, "but most of them are not juggling as many things as I am."

Two years after our interview she wrote to tell me that she had a second child, a wonderful two-year-old daughter. She explained that, much as she had loved Berkeley, the commute had become more than she could handle, and she had therefore accepted her present position at Stanford. The MacArthur fellowship she received soon after our interview in 1995 allowed her to move ahead on some interdisciplinary projects as well as to obtain quality child care and bring her children and her child care giver along on some research trips.

Pamela Matson's career reflects the changes that are taking place in the lives of younger women scientists. Matson earned her doctorate in the early 1980s and the trajectory of her professional career parallels that of her male peers. She considers herself lucky, but she also sees the need for further change. It is easy to understand why other women might have abandoned science after an interval of running a music store or after the birth of a child with a serious health problem. Matson's extraordinary optimism, passion, and energy enabled her to sweep aside obstacles that would have derailed many other aspiring scientists.

⟫•⟪

Certain themes recur in the profiles of each of the women in this chapter. All married before they had established their careers, and most tagged along with their husbands early on. Klinman went to Israel, and Steitz and Taylor went to England, while Lubchenco moved from Oregon to California to Boston as a graduate student. Their aspirations changed once they had experienced the thrill of doing independent research and had developed self-confidence. Klinman, Steitz, and

Taylor recall distinctly that when they were students they never expected to become full-fledged faculty members. Yet at some point each of these women abandoned traditional expectations and became ambitious scientists in their own right. In retrospect each of the women profiled in this chapter attributes her success in large part to luck, rather than to her own talents or efforts.

The profiles of the women in this chapter form a sharp contrast with those of prior generations of Academy members. They illustrate the changes that have taken place in the lives of women scientists since the 1970s. External barriers have all but disappeared, but at the same time new issues have arisen. Today, the competition in science is such that part-time work is rarely a realistic option for someone who aspires to become a committed research scientist. The women in this generation who combined career and motherhood no longer remained in peripheral positions in the early stage of their careers. Susan Taylor and Pamela Matson both coped by sharing their domestic responsibilities with surrogate parents. Jane Lubchenco and her husband persuaded a university to hire both of them on a part-time basis and demonstrated that nontraditional options are feasible. Although the outstanding women profiled in this chapter are not typical of the average woman who earns a science doctorate, their experiences illustrate the unresolved issues that continue to confront women scientists who wish to raise children—issues that our institutions have just begun to address.

# 8

# SHARED
# EXPERIENCES AND
# CONCERNS

Women elected to the National Academy of Sciences tend to be rugged individualists pursuing their personal hopes and dreams. They are pioneers as scientists and as women. As revealed in their profiles, the careers of women scientists are closely tied to the era in which they grow up and work, and the careers of the older generations of women differ in important ways from those of younger members. I wondered whether any common threads would emerge from their stories. Would I learn anything from talking with them that would help me understand how they had become scientists and what had contributed to their success? Would they have advice that might be useful to young women aspiring to become scientists in the twenty-first century? Despite individual differences and differences linked to a particular era, certain themes did emerge from the stories of these women that were unrelated to the ages, scientific disciplines, or particular lifestyles of individual women.

Academy members constitute an elite group. They are likely to have encountered fewer obstacles along the way than most women scientists and to minimize those they did encounter. However, the factors that helped these women to succeed and the difficulties even they encountered and recall are relevant to the careers of all contemporary and future women scientists.

*171*

Whether male or female, members of the National Academy of Sciences love the excitement of pursuing knowledge, formulating and testing theories, and making discoveries. All possess the qualities required for election to the Academy—outstanding talent and training as well as recognized scientific achievement. They are creative and daring. But the women in the Academy were quick to remind me that scientists are, above all, unique individuals and that even within a single branch of science they approach their work in a myriad of different ways. The theme that intellectual and creative abilities are unique to each scientist, and that the differences between individuals are much more significant than the differences that may exist between groups of men and groups of women, emerged again and again in the course of our conversations.

## Family Influences

Some of the Academy members are American born; others are foreign born. Some are single; most are married. Among the latter a majority have children. Some come from large families, others from small ones. Most have siblings, but some do not. Members include oldest, middle, and youngest children in a family. Some come from highly educated professional families. Many come from families in which they are the first member of a generation to have attended college. A strikingly large number are daughters of immigrants whose parents had been deprived of an education and as a result were determined that their children, whether male or female, would obtain the education they themselves had missed. Parents who experienced the Great Depression were particularly insistent that their daughters, not only their sons, attend college and become economically self-sufficient.

The importance of parental influence recurred in the comments of virtually every Academy member. Most had heard clear messages as children that they could succeed in any endeavor they wanted to undertake. For some the father's influence was dominant, for others the mother's. In many cases both parents had supported or encouraged them. The recollections of Pamela Matson, one of the youngest women in the Academy, were typical. She described her parents as being supportive, without ever pushing anything. They never thought of her as going on to get a Ph.D., but she never got the sense that anybody questioned whether she could do it.

The recollections of many other women in the Academy were similar. Some attributed their own success in part to the strong work ethic of their parents, although none recalled having being pressured by a parent to become a scientist. Carol Gross, a geneticist on the faculty of the University of California, San Francisco, went to high school in the 1950s. Her family thought she could do anything and encouraged her strongly. She knew from a young age that she wanted to go into biochemical genetics and was inspired by working in the garden with her grandmother and by trips to the Brooklyn Botanical Garden.

While the majority of women received encouragement at home, a significant minority, even among the younger members, persevered in the face of parental opposition or at least without encouragement because one or both parents did not believe that a science career was suitable for a woman. Several mentioned having to overcome family pressures to marry and settle down, while others were discouraged from further study for financial reasons. The expense and the long period of study required to obtain an advanced degree plus the resulting delay in becoming gainfully employed were a concern for many families. This was particularly true of parents who hoped that their daughters would get married and settle down to become homemakers.

For some women graduate school provided an escape from family pressures or from an unpleasant home environment. One member who had been told by her father, himself a scientist, that she could not succeed in science, told me that her father's discouragement had made her determined to prove him wrong. Her goals were supported by an aunt who was "a very strong supporter of professional women," and she now attributes her success in part to her father's attitude. Because these women had few role models to show them the way, the encouragement of parents, teachers, and friends proved especially important to many.

## Educational Backgrounds

The women who were elected to the Academy received their education at a great variety of institutions in the United States and abroad. Of the 86 women in the Academy, 13 received their undergraduate degrees from foreign institutions. Of the remaining 73, about half graduated from large public or private American universities and one-quarter from small private coeducational colleges. Ten women graduated from formerly tuition-free New York City colleges, including six from Hunter College, one from Queens, and three from Brooklyn College. Fourteen graduated from private women's colleges including 10 from independent women's colleges and four from university-affiliated women's colleges. Members earned doctorates from an equally broad range of public and private institutions, both in the United States and abroad. Seven of the women earned M.D. degrees rather than Ph.D.s, and two, Nobel laureate Gertrude Elion and MacArthur award winner Jane Richardson, never had formal training beyond the master's degree.

That the graduates from the independent women's colleges were all born before 1940 and therefore do not include any of the younger Academy members raises questions regarding the current role of these colleges in preparing women for scientific careers. No conclusions can be drawn based on this limited sample, but the problem bears watching.

## Getting Hooked and Keeping Going

For many of the women in the Academy their first interest in science was sparked by hearing about Marie Curie or by reading books by Rachel Carson. Others were inspired by visits to zoos, botanical gardens, or museums of natural history. For some, family friends or peers sparked the initial interest in science. Dorothy Horstmann, a noted virologist, became interested in medicine as a girl when a physician friend of her family took her on rounds. One woman had a classmate who was helping out in a high school biology lab and enrolled in the biology course at the friend's suggestion. She promptly fell in love with the subject and is now a renowned geneticist. Many women members recalled a specific moment when they got "hooked on" science. For some this point occurred very early, sometimes before high school. Geophysicist Susan Solomon, for example, recalled that she decided to become a marine biologist at the age of 9 after watching Jacques Cousteau on public television. She switched to chemistry in high school because she preferred a more quantitative discipline. For the majority of women the decision to go into science came at a later stage.

In many instances, high school or college teachers first detected and fostered a student's talent for math or science. A member who was born in the 1920s became interested in science when her high school teacher permitted her and some fellow students to "fool around in the laboratory after hours." She described him as generally enthusiastic, although, in retrospect, not well grounded in chemistry. A high school biology teacher steered another student, now a plant biologist, to a college she could afford. There were others, even among the youngest cohort of members, who, like Pamela Matson, enjoyed science and wanted to pursue it but were advised to get a teaching degree or to forget science altogether because "there was no future for a woman in scientific research." The women elected to the Academy include only those persistent enough to resist such negative advice. Many others who were more compliant undoubtedly changed their goals in response.

By no means all of the women had clear career goals by the time they entered college. I was amazed by the broad range of possible majors many of the Academy members considered before making a commitment to science. Nancy Kopell, a mathematician, toyed with majors in chemistry, economics, and visual arts at Cornell before deciding on mathematics. A number of women became science students after abandoning their original goal—teaching. A woman who ultimately became a distinguished geneticist had first considered majoring in linguistics or art history. Myriam Sarachik found it hard to choose between romance languages, literature, mathematics, music, and physics when she was a student at Barnard. She eventually chose physics because it really challenged her. She knew she would never excel as a musician and thought that for her, having been born in Belgium, a language major would be too easy.

Gertrude Elion earned a master's degree in chemistry, but the contributions for which she was awarded the Nobel Prize in Physiology or Medicine were made in the areas of biochemistry, pharmacology, immunology, and virology. Mildred Cohn majored in chemistry and minored in physics at Hunter. She tried to study chemical engineering at Columbia University, but when she was told by the department that women would not be admitted, she returned to her first love, physical chemistry, to earn her doctorate. Some women switched fields even after they had earned a doctorate. Some moved into new areas they found more interesting, others to fields they found more hospitable. Such changes are by no means unique to women, but women often switch for different reasons than men.

That many of the female Academy members developed concrete career goals at a relatively late stage parallels findings among former National Science Foundation postdoctoral fellowship holders that a higher proportion of women than men tended to enter careers step by step rather than having clear career goals at the outset.[1] For many women, career plans remain closely intertwined with personal plans. Men in our society face greater pressure than women to define their career goals early. Marrying and becoming a parent, once the primary goal for many women, has never been an acceptable career goal for men.

Hands-on experience in a research laboratory at an early stage persuaded many women to become scientists. Mary Gaillard spent a summer at Brookhaven National Laboratory as an undergraduate at the suggestion of a woman faculty member at Hollins College. Joan Steitz and Susan Taylor had both planned to study medicine before they became hooked on research. Taylor decided to abandon her medical school plans while working at a well-known laboratory in Cambridge, England, and Steitz when she obtained a position working for Joseph Gall in a biological laboratory in the summer before she had planned to enter medical school. Gall gave Steitz her own project to work on, and she soon found herself happily working nights and weekends. By August she had switched her plans and decided to go to graduate school.

The influence of a mentor who was helpful and who made a critical difference at one or more stages of their careers surfaced in the stories of many of the women. Such mentors included junior high school teachers who recognized outstanding mathematical or scientific ability; teachers who encouraged a student to attend college or undertake graduate study; and leaders in a field who went out of their way to help a protégée secure fellowships, employment, or appointment to a prestigious panel or committee. Mary Gaillard credits a female faculty member at Hollins College who persuaded her to spend time at Brookhaven and at a Paris research laboratory with putting her in the right places at the right times. Nancy Kopell says she cannot imagine how she could have survived the early years of her career, psychologically or intellectually, without the help of several key people, including her first collaborator at MIT, who helped her reinvent herself as an applied mathematician, and later her husband-to-be, who provided the encouragement she needed to change fields to an entirely new area.

A number of women who had children during the early phase of their careers believe that they would have abandoned their scientific careers had it not been for a sympathetic faculty member who had quietly made special arrangements to lighten teaching duties, to permit part-time work, or to temporarily defer entry to the regular tenure track. A mother of four wrote to me as follows:

> My chairman at the time when I had four children under the age of seven years offered me the opportunity of reducing my commitment to the department for a few years while leaving me all the dignity of a well-accepted and integrated member of the department and the certainty that I would get into the regular tenure-accruing track when I was ready. He did this in such a way that my colleagues were, for the most part, unaware that I was in a special position and thus accepted me as an equal colleague. This support was the most important factor in allowing me to continue in an academic career. I am

often saddened to see young female colleagues who, lacking such support, are faced with a choice between family and career. If the first wins, then there goes one possible good scientist; if the second, we may have an unhappy scientist. With all the progress made by the women's liberation movement, the need for this type of special consideration and support has, I believe, been overlooked.

Having a cohesive, inspiring group of fellow students with similar interests, such as the Swarthmore peer group described by Maxine Singer, encouraged other women to pursue their interests in science. Women who achieved success late in life frequently attributed the delay in part to their exclusion from the "old boys" network at the early stage of their careers and to the resulting lack of mentoring and visibility.

## Passion, Persistence, and Independence

A passionate commitment to scientific research characterized each of the Academy members. When I asked Myriam Sarachik what had helped her to succeed as a scientist, her instant response was a "love of science plus tenacity." Both, she said, were "absolutely indispensable." Pamela Matson described science as "the core of her life." All spoke of their work as something they loved.

Yet Academy members are not entirely immune to prevailing cultural attitudes and pressures. One Academy member who finished her professional training in the early 1980s told me that she remembers walking home from elementary school in tears on numerous occasions because she had been "the feisty kid who always had her hand up first and gave answers even if not called on." She was chastised by her teacher for being so eager and inquisitive. Her personality, she said, kept her going at whatever cost and pain, but in her opinion a lot of children are still getting squelched and girls more than boys, an opinion supported by recent studies indicating that girls still receive different messages than boys from many of their elementary and high school teachers.[2] I recently had a conversation with the wife of a male member of the National Academy of Sciences who complained to me that her daughter, a 1998 college graduate, had just decided to study medicine. The mother had hoped that her daughter would find a husband and raise a family. Subtle pressures steering young women away from science and other professions persist.

Nevertheless many members of the National Academy of Sciences managed to have distinguished careers even at a time when there was still widespread overt discrimination against women scientists. Gertrude Goldhaber is a typical example of these early pioneers. She was born in Germany in 1911, educated in Europe, and immigrated to the United States in 1939 with her husband, Maurice Goldhaber, a fellow physicist. She and her husband spent virtually their entire careers at Brookhaven National Laboratory. Gertrude Goldhaber died recently, more than 26 years after she was elected a member of the Academy in 1972.

I was fascinated when I read the wedding announcement of her granddaughter, which appeared recently in the *New York Times*. From it I learned that Gertrude's granddaughter, Sara, planned to begin medical studies at Harvard and that Gertrude's son (Sara's father) is a professor of theoretical physics. The announcement went on to note that both Gertrude and her husband Maurice did prominent work at the Brookhaven National Laboratory, she in nuclear physics and he in high-energy particle physics. Gertrude Goldhaber, mother of two other sons besides Sara's father, obviously managed to raise a family while she and her husband had outstanding careers as physicists years before equal opportunity law had entered the picture and careers for women became the norm. She was by no means unique in this achievement.

In order to pursue their dreams as scientists, female Academy members had to be nonconformists, and they are very aware that they had to defy societal expectations to succeed. Most succeeded in part because they developed the ability to live their lives in unconventional ways, to stray from the accepted norm, and to set their own rules. They did not accept "no" for an answer when told, as many were, that their career goals were "unsuitable for a woman," nor did they let popularizers of maternal attachment theory tell them how to raise their children. They neither sought nor required constant approval from family, friends, colleagues, or superiors. Many admitted that overcoming disappointments or outright rejection had often been difficult but that they persisted nonetheless.

Several members said they persevered because their parents had encouraged them to become risk takers and to be willing to compete. Carla Shatz, a neurobiologist and the first woman to be named a full professor in a nonclinical department at Stanford Medical School, recalled that her parents had encouraged her to become a nonconformist early on and believes that this helped her to be comfortable as a woman scientist. The pressures another pioneering woman faced at the Stanford Medical School have been described vividly by a professor of neurosurgery there.[3]

Members who were born abroad and subsequently immigrated to the United States remarked that being raised in another country had allowed them to pursue their careers in the United States free of traditional expectations. Either they were unaware of or did not feel bound by these cultural norms because as immigrants they already considered themselves outsiders. Philippa Marrack, an immunologist working at the Howard Hughes Medical Institute in Denver, came to the United States in 1971, after having earned her doctorate in England. She was elected to the National Academy of Sciences in 1989. In 1995 she wrote to me:

> You ask if my career has been affected by the fact that I am a woman. Of course! On the whole, for me, as a non-U.S. citizen it has been a help to be a woman. Because I was not born and bred in the USA, I do not have to follow, and sometimes do not even know, the rules of conduct for American women. This has allowed me to break all sorts of rules and get away with it.

Myriam Sarachik had this to say about the fact that she had been transplanted from Europe:

> My travels . . . left me a misfit. . . . I decided I may as well accept myself for who I am, and if I don't fit in with most, then so be it. When the time came to make choices, I had

already come to terms with not fitting in, so going into science was just a small additional step.

Elizabeth Neufeld, chair of the Department of Biological Chemistry at the University of California at Los Angeles, came to the United States from France as a child. She attributes her willingness to embark on a science career to having been born abroad and raised by refugee parents who never quite felt at home in the United States. She either did not understand or tuned out the negative cultural pressures of the 1950s that discouraged her American women contemporaries from becoming scientists. Nancy Kopell got used to being "on the margin" because she had a serious eye problem as a child and, as a result, later felt comfortable in a male-dominated field in which she did research that was on the margin and out of the mainstream as well.

Whatever lifestyles women Academy members chose, they did not let cultural messages about appropriate female roles and behaviors stop them from pursuing their dreams. These women are comfortable as nonconformists in a "man's world." They defied societal norms, whether they remained single, combined motherhood and career, or married and remained childless. They have a "Teflon" reaction to setbacks and criticism that enables them to tune out negative messages. Again and again women told me that they attribute their success to their innate stubbornness and persistence, and their ability to ignore "negatives." To what extent this ability to be autonomous and inner directed is the result of inborn traits and to what extent it is the result of upbringing and external circumstances are difficult to determine. In most cases it is undoubtedly a combination of both factors.

## Cultural Hurdles

Even as we begin the twenty-first century, women continue to be socialized to be ladylike, not to be aggressive, pushy, or too inquisitive. They are taught to be nurturing, to be compliant, and to put the needs of others before their own. Until very recently, few girls participated in team sports. As the late Marian Koshland observed:

> When something comes along and is really important to your
> career and important to science, important enough so that
> lots of other people are working on it, you have got to do it in
> a short time. You have got to get in there and run experi-
> ments quickly and get published. That is the killer instinct. I
> do not think women have that part of it. Part of it comes from
> sports. It's like scoring a goal.

Men, on the other hand, have always been encouraged to be manly
and to stand up for themselves. Participation in competitive sports
teaches boys early on how to be aggressive and how to win. It is
therefore not surprising that many women dislike the competitive atmosphere they encounter in male-dominated institutions.

Mary Ellen Avery believes that women are risk averse and tend to
work slowly, carefully, and systematically and that, as a result, many
are relegated to technician roles regardless of their experience and
training. Men then strive to get ahead on the women's shoulders.
While she was department chair, she found that although women
needed money as much as men, they did not use money in the same
competitive way as men. Women welcomed a raise, but they rarely
came to her as chair to say, "I need a raise." Men, on the other hand,
requested raises for all sorts of reasons. They also routinely used outside offers as an opportunity to obtain raises, while women rarely did.
The resulting disadvantages of such behavior for women are obvious,
although they are in large part due to women's own reluctance to be
assertive.

Beyond outstanding ability, training, and creativity, the women
elected to the National Academy of Sciences needed unusual persistence, resilience, stamina, and a strong sense of self in order to rise to
the top of their professions. None accepted the popular definitions of
what it means to be a woman, a wife, or a mother. Successful women
are often criticized for being overly aggressive, but until women
achieve true equality in the workplace, they need toughness to persevere, especially in fields such as some of the sciences in which they still
constitute a distinct minority.

The vast majority of the women Academy members vigorously
rejected the notion that there is any validity to the concept of a "male"

versus a "female" science and believe that differences between individual scientists far outweigh any differences that may exist in the innate scientific aptitudes between men and women as a group. As Judith Klinman predicted, "Once there are no barriers to women whatsoever, women will play in the big time the same way men always have." While Academy members unanimously regard substantive science as unaffected by gender, a fair number remarked on the differences they had observed between the research styles of men and women. They described laboratories run by women as less hierarchical and more collaborative than those run by men and noted that students tend to view women faculty as more approachable and easier to talk to than male faculty.

Differences in the way male and female scientists are perceived or treated were mentioned frequently in the course of my interviews with Academy members. Numerous women remarked that men have difficulty evaluating the credentials of women candidates correctly and that female candidates are criticized more readily than men for being either too aggressive or too reticent. They attribute the inability to assess women fairly to the subconscious application of different success criteria for men and women rather than to overt prejudice.

When women collaborate with male colleagues there is often the perception that the man made the creative contributions to the project rather than the woman. Rosalyn Yalow had to prove that she could continue research on her own after the sudden death of her long-time collaborator, Solomon Berson, with whom she had developed the radioimmunoassay technique that revolutionized the treatment of diabetes. She was vindicated when she was awarded the Nobel Prize in 1977.

There is ample evidence that unconscious hypotheses about sex differences affect our expectations of men and women and our evaluations of their work. In a 1995 study of applicants for postdoctoral fellowships awarded by the Swedish Medical Research Council, women were rated below men on scientific competence by the senior scientists who judged the applications. When the applications were analyzed, it was found that to be rated equal to the males the women needed 100 or more points for combined productivity and journal prestige compared to 20 or fewer points by the men, giving the males a five to one edge over the females.[4]

There are other ramifications that result from differences in how men and women are perceived. Women tend to be more cautious, even perfectionist, and want to tend to every detail to avoid being faulted. Such caution may in part result because women's competence is questioned more often than men's and may explain the finding that women publish somewhat fewer papers on average than men but that their papers tend to be longer and more comprehensive than those written by men.[5]

The women Academy members were remarkably modest about their success and minimized both the difficulties they overcame and their personal contributions to their achievements. Almost every member I spoke with attributed her success to a greater or lesser extent to luck, to having been "in the right place at the right time." Most described themselves as lucky rather than brilliant, helped by others rather than propelled by their own desire to search and to know. Many credited a mentor who had played a key role in their ultimate success by offering support at an early stage of their careers. However, when I asked them what traits enabled women scientists as a group to succeed, all stressed ability, hard work, persistence, and discipline.

The traits that were typical of the women members of the National Academy of Sciences closely parallel gender differences found among other groups of women scientists. The female scientists surveyed by Sonnert and Holton had a significantly lower self-assessment of their ability than their male counterparts. Almost three-fourths of the women in the survey reported that they had experienced gender discrimination at some point in their careers, compared to one-eighth of the men. Not surprisingly, 25.3 percent of the women but only 4.6 percent of the men said that in retrospect they should have been more assertive and confident. The study revealed that women often make choices that anticipate and circumvent perceived disadvantages.[6] Since women reported a far higher incidence of negative experiences than men, and since the appropriate strategy for dealing with negative experiences is resilience and hard work, it is not surprising that women put a greater emphasis on the need for resilience and hard work.

# The Uneven Distribution of Women Among Disciplines

I asked Academy members to speculate about the reasons for the uneven distribution of men and women in different scientific disciplines. Many believe that the newer interdisciplinary areas of science tend to attract younger more adventurous researchers who may be more welcoming to women. They regard these areas as less hierarchical, more flexible, and more hospitable to women than older disciplines such as chemistry and physics. All agreed that once there is a critical mass of women in a field or department women are readily integrated and no longer feel that they are outsiders. When there is a critical mass of women in a discipline, that discipline attracts ever more women, thereby further accentuating the uneven distribution of women.

Gertrude Elion and Rosalyn Yalow both told me that in their opinion the opportunities available to women scientists have a direct effect on the fields women go into. It is thus possible that the current disproportionate number of women in the biological sciences is in part a reflection of the relatively greater opportunities available to women in these fields at a time when women could not find employment in the other branches of science. Before 1970 many women who earned doctorates began their careers as research assistants in laboratories run by men. Since physical scientists, mathematicians, and engineers rarely employed research assistants, many of the women scientists who worked as research assistants before the 1970s worked in the biological and medical sciences, fields in which positions were open to them. This may in turn have contributed to the higher proportion of women found in the biological sciences.

A number of Academy members attributed the uneven distribution across disciplines to women's failure to obtain the mathematics background required for the physical sciences and engineering, but others disagreed. The fact that there are many instances of women who earned doctorates in the hard mathematically based sciences and later moved into more biological research areas indicates that many women possess the required mathematical background. Some of these women switched fields because they saw greater challenges and opportunities in the newer biological sciences, others because they were drawn toward more "socially relevant" areas of research. Some simply left a field in which there were few opportunities for women for one that was more welcoming to them. It is too early to predict whether the uneven gender distribution among disciplines will persist once women are equally at home in all disciplines.

In those scientific disciplines or institutions in which women remain a minority, women face disproportionate demands on their time. There is an understandable desire to have women represented at all levels of an institution, but as long as women remain underrepresented they remain burdened by an unequal share of committee assignments, student advising, and other administrative responsibilities.

It is apparent from the comments of several women in the Academy that they prefer not to be the sole woman in a department and therefore take departmental diversity into account when making career decisions. A young woman who was being heavily recruited by a department at a major university on the West Coast, heard rumors that a female professor in the same department had just decided to leave. The job candidate was so concerned that she called the senior woman to say that a major reason she was thinking of coming was that she would have a female colleague. When she was reassured that the rumor was false, she accepted the offer. Mary-Lou Pardue told me that in 1972 a major factor in her decision to accept a position in the biology department at MIT rather than elsewhere was that at MIT she would not be the only woman in the department.

That career patterns and experiences of women scientists depend on the particular discipline in which they work was borne out by the Sonnert and Holton study. The authors concluded that a glass ceiling effect operates in the physical sciences, mathematics, and engineering but not in the biological sciences. They speculate that the relatively high number of women in the biological sciences seems to protect women from being treated as outsiders, confirming that, while the female members of the Academy are truly exceptional, their experiences nevertheless parallel those of other women scientists in many respects.

## The Brain Drain

It is apparent from the comments and concerns of women in the National Academy of Sciences that the prevailing scientific climate is driving many young, creative, and highly talented people out of academic science. Joan Steitz is one of many members who is concerned about the impact of her current lifestyle as a female scientist on her students. This is what she told me:

> The fact that there are now successful role models means that more women should be going into science. Why they are not, I don't know. It's not an easy life for women or for men. We would all like to have a wife at home. It is still true that women, even when they have the most sharing husband on the face of the earth, end up doing slightly more at home and it's damn hard. There is now flexibility so that there is half-time maternity leave. That is hard because people are really working full time but only getting paid for half time. . . .
>
> There is another thing I worry about a lot. I've let myself admittedly get overcommitted. I do too much. I work harder than I should work . . . and I really worry about how that affects the perspective of students. I feel terribly guilty about some of our women students who decided to go into industry, when everybody thought they would be wonderful in the academic scene. I wonder whether it was my fault, letting them watch me turn myself inside out.

Outstanding women who do very well and complete postdoctoral fellowships seem to disappear from the pool of applicants for faculty positions. Mary-Lou Pardue sees a black hole for women at the end of the postdoctoral period. Like Steitz, she believes that lots of people, male and female, are having second thoughts about pursuing scientific careers in the current pressured competitive environment. Janet Rowley is another Academy member who is troubled by the disproportionate loss of women at every level after the postdoctoral stage. Some questions she would like answered are "Do women quit because a mentor discourages them? Do they quit because they do not like the lifestyle they see as the accepted norm? Are they repelled by the high level of aggressive behavior that is displayed by some colleagues for whom success is the only goal, no matter what the price?" She emphasized the need for solid information before remedies can be devised.

The experiences of women scientists as a group still differ from those of similarly talented men in important respects. Although the women elected to the National Academy of Sciences mastered the art of deflecting criticism and outright harassment without becoming derailed, like most women scientists they recalled experiencing self-doubt and a sense of isolation at some stage of their careers. The necessity for finding the time, the energy, and the help to care for children while pursuing a demanding career as a research scientist proved to be the major challenge many Academy members had encountered and overcome and remains the single most difficult challenge facing young women scientists today. Chapters 9 and 10 contain suggestions advanced by the women in the National Academy of Sciences when I asked them to dream about ways to increase opportunities for young women aspiring to become scientists.

# BALANCING
# CAREER AND FAMILY

The dominant theme that pervaded interviews with women of all ages and all disciplines is the dilemma women encounter in balancing career and family responsibilities. The tension between personal life and career exists for many women but is especially acute for women in competitive professions such as scientific research and was a significant issue for all of the women I contacted—whether married or single, with or without children. Most considered it to be the major difficulty facing young women scientists today.

Almost four-fifths of the women in the Academy married, and more than three-fifths had children. These numbers should dispel the myth that women scientists cannot succeed if they marry and have children. The family constellations among Academy members are similar to those among women scientists surveyed by Sonnert and Holton and among senior women business executives.[1] The issue of whether and when to have children is closely intertwined with the career plans for most women scientists since the childbearing years coincide with the period in which tenure decisions are made. The majority of the older members of the Academy married and had children while they were still in graduate school or even earlier. Many of those who made a choice to remain single, or to marry but not raise a family, now resent the fact that they felt forced into making such a choice and are among the strongest advocates for implementing family-friendly policies. The younger Academy members, those born after World War II, have smaller families and had children relatively late in life, many in their late thirties or early forties. Many delayed childbearing until their careers were well established or even until they obtained tenure. Some then discovered too late that the biological clock had run out.

The intense competition among contemporary research scientists described in Chapter 2 compounds the stresses faced by young women who choose academic or other high-level careers. A six- or eight-week maternity leave alone does not solve the problem. Even when institutions permit longer leaves or part-time schedules, many women are unwilling to accept them because they are afraid that they will lose out in the competition for results and funding if their productivity slackens, even temporarily. Such fears are not entirely unfounded. The irony is that, as overt barriers to women's advancement have disappeared, new obstacles have taken their place. Over and over again I was told that today many young women and an increasing number of young men are unwilling to take on the frenetic lifestyle they see among scientists at elite institutions or that they simply lack the stamina to do so.

Geophysicist Mary Lou Zoback is among the few younger women in the Academy who worked less than full time when her children were young. She is married to a fellow scientist. Her children were 13 and 10 when she wrote to me in 1995:

> I feel strongly that a valued woman (or man) should be able to make choices about their life and career, not having to abandon childrearing to pursue a successful career (or vice versa). My personal compromise, which has been supported now for 13 years by the United States Geological Survey and my husband, was to work only part time after having kids. I chose to work half time when they were young (less than 2.5 years; they are about three years apart) and since then I have worked about six hours a day. I come home with them every day after school and we share that time together. My husband

is very supportive, helps out a lot around the house, and most importantly adapts to my part-time schedule when I have to travel. We have no family nearby so we've done it all on our own.

This was, of course, our choice. I think each woman needs to work out the compromise that best suits her and her spouse. I hope my election to the National Academy demonstrates that a variety of career and life choices can be "successful," and this is what I view as the true impact of the women's movement.

Zoback's sentiments echo those of many women I contacted. Rosalyn Yalow views the availability of quality day care as a key issue for women scientists and other working women. In her opinion, combining career, family, and children is more difficult today than when her children were young because it is harder to find competent help now than formerly, a result of widening employment opportunities for women who were once restricted to doing housework. When her own children were young, Yalow relied on live-in help. She was emphatic that we must find a way to enable bright young women to have careers and children.

How do married women scientists with children cope? Virtually all Academy members agreed that the single most important factor for married women is their choice of a spouse. Many mentioned that they might have dropped out if they had not had a supportive encouraging husband who helped them to persevere. They emphasized that the pursuit of a scientific career is not compatible with marriage to a nonsupportive husband. A biologist who is now in her fifties and the mother of three put it this way: "He [the husband] must believe in her and accept that science is the core of her life." Another member put the problem bluntly: "If a husband does not support his wife's career as a scientist, the wife has only two choices—give up her career or give up the husband." There is no data about how many trained women scientists have chosen the first option since they are by definition excluded from the sample I selected.

The majority of Academy members who raised children used daytime household help, day care, or a combination of both. Live-in help was rare. In isolated instances grandparents or other family members helped out. Very few of the younger members of the Academy worked part time or took time off while their children were young, although many of the older women did so. A mother of two, now in her mid-forties, told me that she and her husband "just cobbled together what they could, the way most people do." When I asked if she had taken time off when her children were born, she said:

> No, but I was prepared to if I needed to. I wanted to have a very common-sense approach. Sometimes your health needs it. Sometimes your child might not be well. I don't have any dogma about what I can or cannot do.

Said another:

> Stress the message that you can't do everything. A high-level science career requires help with home and kids. Women must be willing to accept this.

The women in the Academy were candid and sensible about the need for help when their children were young. Cathleen Morawetz believes that American men are more helpful at home than European men, but she thinks they are also more resistant to hiring adequate household help. Her husband came from Europe, where having help was common, and that made it easy for her to hire help for her children. As one young mother put it, "You hire a third parent." With the commitment and long hours that a research career requires today, most of these women entrusted the care of their children partly to others. As one Academy member put it: "You have to be willing to share them [the children] and not be bothered by it."

The availability of adequate financial resources often proved critical. For many Academy members the award of a National Science Foundation fellowship enabled them to continue their studies. A few women received financial help from their own or their husband's families, but the majority did not. When Pamela Matson was awarded a MacArthur fellowship, she used part of the proceeds to hire help so that her children could accompany her on some of her travels.

Maxine Singer and her husband had no financial help from their families. They paid for household help out of their combined incomes by restricting all other discretionary expenses. Singer commented on the differences between young people in her generation and the expectations of young people today:

> My female postdocs have much higher expectations with respect to their own standard of living than I had. When I grew up, if you wanted to be in a scholarly profession you didn't expect that you were going to make a good income. We never went out to eat. We almost never went to the movies. We did very little that cost any money. We certainly didn't go on costly vacations. I think today the young people have grown up more affluent. They have very often had a long period of being single or married without children, so they get used to a high standard of living. The percentage of their incomes that they are willing to spend for help is much less than ours. It is also, of course, true that help is more costly.

It is truly remarkable how many personal crises some women can survive without being derailed from their goal as scientists. Many overcame illness, divorces, and personal tragedies. One member had a shotgun wedding while still in high school. Both her husband and her parents objected adamantly to her plans to go to college, but she persevered despite them and without their help. Before she was able to obtain a divorce, she had another child whom she gave up for adoption. Following her divorce, she supported herself and her first child by doing translating, giving music lessons, and playing professionally in a symphony orchestra.

With the help of a tuition scholarship and a small grant in aid, she managed to complete college and to graduate as the salutatorian of her class. The award of a National Science Foundation fellowship eventually enabled her to earn a doctorate from a major university, but before she had completed her degree, she remarried and had yet another child. She divorced again and now found herself supporting two children on a postdoctoral fellow's income. Despite such a troubled start, she forged a successful career. As a single mother she helped her two children complete college. Through sheer coincidence she was recently reunited with the child she had given up for adoption, by now a successful professional in his thirties. Today this woman is remarried and working at a leading university where both she and her husband hold faculty positions. She was elected to the Academy before she turned 50.

The career outcomes—measured by academic rank, employment status, and related factors—of the 461 men and women scientists surveyed by Sonnert and Holton were unaffected by marital or parental status, although 21 percent of the women compared to 3 percent of the men mentioned family demands as a career obstacle.[2] The women members of the Academy successfully combined marriage, children, and career, an ability they share with many women in other demanding occupations.

## Dual-Career Issues

Many of the women members of the Academy are married to other scientists, including a number who are also Academy members. Sonnert and Holton have aptly described the dilemma that women scientists married to fellow scientists face when they try to synchronize three separate clocks—their biological clock, their career clock, and the career clock of their spouse. Among the group of science doctorates Sonnert and Holton surveyed in the late 1980s, 62 percent of the women had husbands who also had science doctorates, but only 19 percent of the men had wives who had science doctorates.[3] Since male scientists are less likely than their female colleagues to have scientist spouses, they are also less likely to encounter the time pressures that result when there are two scientists in a family.

Dual-career couples who have children must juggle three careers —two professional careers plus the career of caring for home and children and assuming other sundry duties—responsibilities formerly assumed by stay-at-home spouses. Mothers tend to have primary responsibility for arranging child care and making substitute arrangements when necessary.[4] When both spouses have equally demanding

careers, wives more frequently than husbands assume a disproportionate amount of the domestic duties.

There is a growing trend among younger couples to equalize child
care and other domestic responsibilities. However, as long as universities and other employers maintain policies based on the assumption
that every man has a full-time traditional wife at home, it will remain
difficult for men, no matter how well intentioned, to free up enough
time to achieve an equal sharing of family responsibilities. Women
scientists with children therefore continue to face overwhelming demands on their time and energy, especially if they live in localities
lacking adequate child care and other support services.

On the other hand, they have certain advantages. Such couples
have shared interests and goals and can therefore understand and respect each other's professional obligations. Some, although by no
means all, collaborate in their work. The spouse of one member admitted that he welcomed the fact that his wife had demanding professional commitments because it enabled him to work long hours without feeling guilty. The social and professional lives of these couples
often overlap. Marriage to a fellow scientist can also be a source of
emotional support. Many women recalled that there had been moments when they might have given up science if their husbands had
not urged, even pushed them to persevere. It is undoubtedly easier
for a fellow scientist to support his wife's scientific career at a time of
crisis than for someone less familiar with the daily demands of a research career. Such support can be critical in overcoming the difficulties and disappointments that are an integral part of all research.

Women who marry nonscientists benefit in different ways. Professional pressures may be less intense when two disparate careers are
meshed and a couple's life is not focused entirely on science. One
intense career per couple may be easier to manage than two. Husbands who freelance as writers, artists, or consultants are usually more
mobile than academics, and this can simplify relocation issues.

Finding positions for both husband and wife in the same geo-
graphic location can be a major hurdle. Today, husbands as well as
wives often face the issue of trying to relocate with a spouse. The

comment that both government and industry are more flexible than academia in accommodating family needs recurred throughout the interviews. The husbands of several Academy members refused prestigious academic appointments at institutions that were unwilling to offer more than token positions to their wives and instead accepted appointments at government laboratories where both spouses were able to pursue their research and rise to top positions without facing the tight timetable for promotion to tenure. Several Academy couples, the Karles and the Goldhabers among them, remained at a government laboratory throughout their careers. Pamela Matson and Patricia Goldman-Rakic are examples of women who established their careers in government laboratories and later moved into tenured positions at academic institutions.

Until both partners have permanent positions, the "two-body" problem can recur. Relocation is difficult when both spouses have to find positions, move, and reestablish a new set of support systems for the family, including day care and household help in addition to facing the usual problems involved in a move. Some solve the problem by moving to large urban areas where there are opportunities for both spouses. Occasionally spouses accept positions in separate locations hoping that such an arrangement will be temporary, but not all marriages survive such a separation. Since the most talented scientists have the widest choice of opportunities and are in the greatest demand, the elite group of women members of the National Academy of Sciences probably had a somewhat easier time solving the two-body problem than other women scientists.

Married women in demanding nonscience careers encounter many of the same pressures as women scientists, but doctors, lawyers, and business people have a wider choice of employers, are more geographically mobile, and are less dependent on outside funding sources. They frequently have substantially higher incomes than academics, so it is easier for them to pay for child care and household help. Reentry after a break in a scientific career is especially difficult because scientific knowledge and techniques undergo constant, rapid change.

Many Academy members talked proudly about the accomplishments of their children and their families. A high proportion of their children, sons as well as daughters, have successfully embarked on their own similar high-level careers in science, medicine, business, and other leadership positions. When I asked women to explain why so many children of Academy members had embarked on demanding careers of their own, several interviewees told me that they had involved their children in their work and travels at an early age and that the children had experienced the joy and satisfaction their parents derived from their work. The profiles of Mildred Cohn, Isabella Karle, Marian Koshland, Cathleen Morawetz, and many others reveal the important role that children and families play in the lives of these busy accomplished women. For women who overcome the early career struggles, the ultimate rewards, both personally and professionally, are very fulfilling.

## Issues for Single Women

Unmarried women scientists face different problems. Men tend to view all young women as potential wives and mothers. To the extent that some men still harbor conscious or unconscious prejudices against women scientists because they view all young women as potential mothers, such prejudices affect all young women, whether married or single. A number of single women commented that informal professional interaction with peers is difficult when men view them as unattached females on the prowl rather than as colleagues. The recent emphasis on sexual harassment undoubtedly aggravates this problem when it results in the exclusion of women from important informal information networks. Social interaction with colleagues is often more difficult for single women than for their married women colleagues. A divorced scientist wrote:

> Sexual harassment is a problem because it interferes with collegial interactions. You don't realize how much energy is used in avoiding situations where a pass might be made, or in recovering from the humiliation of passes that are made, until you get older and the harassment stops. I can be normally friendly to people now without being misinterpreted.

Women who are not in a marriage or other steady relationship lack the emotional support that a partner can provide at a time of crisis. Although it may be simpler for single women to find positions than it is for two people as a couple, when single women move they must adapt to a new environment without a spouse to help them. It is often easier for a single male to reestablish a social life, especially in a university community, than for a single woman. An unmarried female scientist remarked that she had sacrificed comforts and friendships in her early thirties when she relocated twice in order to take advantage of professional opportunities.

Single women in the Academy were more willing to talk with me about discrimination they had encountered during the course of their careers than were many of their married peers and were at least as concerned with the problems of balancing careers with family commitments as their married colleagues. It is possible that those women who had raised children found it difficult to distinguish obstacles resulting from their family obligations from those based on their gender or that they were reluctant to admit that it had not always been easy to balance competing demands.

Whether married or single, female Academy members were unanimous that more must be done to address the conflicting demands of home and family. Their suggestions for implementing changes that might make it easier to strike a balance between these demands are discussed in the next chapter.

# RIGHTING THE BALANCE

If substantive science is gender free, as many Academy members believe, why does the gender of scientists matter? Why does it matter that women scientists remain conspicuously absent from the top echelons of the profession? Leaving aside the obvious issues of equity and the right of each individual to develop her or his full potential, gender matters because we need a pool of highly trained scientists in order to maintain our role as a leading industrial nation. All aspects of our economy—health care services, communications, transportation, protection of the environment, among others—depend on the availability of talented scientists and engineers. In every field, whether sports, the arts, business, or science, the likelihood of finding truly outstanding individuals increases as the pool of potential talent increases. Since women constitute half of the talent pool, it is imperative for us to explore and try to understand the causes for their continued underrepresentation in many areas of the sciences and to take prompt steps to correct it.

Women's advocacy groups have been aware of the unequal status of women faculty for a long time, but until recently their findings were often dismissed as anecdotal unsubstantiated reports. It took almost five years of pressure and hard work by women faculty to persuade the Massachusetts Institute of Technology to launch a study in response to their allegations that gender-based inequalities persisted among MIT's science faculty. A key finding of that study was that each generation of young women, including those that are now senior faculty, began by believing that gender discrimination had been "solved," yet found when they attained senior status that the playing field was not level after all.[1] It is not until women reach the upper ranks in industry or academia, where there continue to be very few women, that they become aware they are disadvantaged in many subtle ways in comparison to men of the same age, rank, and achievement.

## Affirmative Action and Beyond

There has been a dramatic increase in the number of women at the lower ranks of academia and elsewhere. However, women remain scarce at the tenure ranks of university faculties and at the upper echelons of industry. There are notable exceptions, but they are rare. Rensselaer Polytechnic Institute recently named Shirley Ann Jackson, a black woman, as its president; Hewlett-Packard's new CEO is a 45-year old woman, Carly Fiorina; Carolyn Porco heads the camera team of NASA's (National Aeronautics and Space Administration) Cassini space probe; and Rita Colwell is the director of the National Science Foundation (NSF). The observations made 30 years ago by a feminist political scientist remain relevant today, especially in academia:

> The lifestyles of the population of intelligent, highly educated women are more heterogeneous than those of men. Yet the University is geared to serving the needs of men or of those who most closely resemble them. Only women who can organize their own lives, however uncomfortably, into the environment created for men, can succeed there.[2]

Thirty years have passed since legislation was enacted outlawing discrimination based on gender and requiring colleges and universities receiving federal funds to formulate affirmative action plans designed to increase the recruitment, hiring, and promotion of women. The effect of this legislation has been dramatic. The unequal treatment of women that had long been overlooked was seriously addressed for the first time. Between 1970 and 1995 the number of science doctorates awarded to women grew sixfold. For the first time, recent women doctorates were actively recruited to career-track positions in academia, industry, and government. Most Academy members attribute these changes to affirmative action requirements and the advent of the women's movement. Barring a precipitous lowering of academic standards in doctoral programs or a sudden mutation of women's genes, it is difficult to explain the changes that came about for women in the past three decades on any other basis. Nevertheless, affirmative action has become a highly charged issue.

Academy members expressed conflicting opinions regarding the desirability of continuing affirmative action requirements to improve the status of women in science. Several women who believe that they obtained academic appointments as a result of affirmative action told me that they had hated feeling like a token and would not wish that on anybody. On the other hand, Pamela Matson spoke for many younger Academy members when she said:

> At every level, at the university level, at the National Academy, you are assumed to be there because you are a woman. It is not something that has bothered me very much. I think one of the reasons that I have been able to ignore it is because of all of the women who have paved the way before me, who have had to fight tooth and nail to be heard. . . . Women have come a long way, but we have to be careful that we don't think we have come further than we have. I have been given some wonderful breaks. I have had male mentors suggest my name for things, for this meeting or that committee. Maybe I wouldn't have been asked at the age I was if I hadn't been a woman. But I certainly wouldn't have been invited back over and over again if I weren't good at what I do. I think women need to remember that . . . luck gives everybody a start, but then it's up to you to keep it going. It is too easy for women to doubt whether they should or would have been there if it had not been for affirmative action. They need to recognize that they are taking the opportunities and running with them.

Another Academy member wrote as follows:

> I strongly suspect that my career has been helped for the past 25 years. In the biomedical sciences, there has been a generally sincere and effective effort on the part of a majority of academic departments, NIH [National Institutes of Health], NSF, professional societies, and other national and regional organizations to bring women into the mainstream. As a visible senior woman . . . my visibility has very likely been higher than it might otherwise have been. There's no question the affirmative action tic, "Do they want me because I'm best or because I'm a woman?", inevitably goes through my mind at each invitation to be a candidate for society office, or serve on a panel. . . . On the other hand, the issue vanishes when I do a creditable job and I have never had the sense that my colleagues in such activities began or ended our association with anything less than the most collegial and cordial respect.

She believes that consciousness raising, largely in response to affirmative action, has influenced not only the establishment but also young women students to enter careers in science and concludes that affirmative action should be continued.

Although members were divided on the question of whether affirmative action for women should be continued, all were adamant that affirmative action should never involve a lowering of standards. Most emphasized the continuing need for affirmative action in those areas of science in which women remain underrepresented and for minorities in all fields. Some, though not all, noted that women as a group still receive lower salaries, fewer perks, and slower promotions than male colleagues with the same level of experience. One member at a large state university, now retired, described her situation thus:

> The jobs I have gotten and two massive equity raises (20 and 30 percent) in the course of my career resulted from the civil rights laws. Opportunities opened up as civil rights laws were enforced. Also my own behavior changed as I learned to value myself more. I found that there were other academic women around and developed collegial relationships with them and was no longer so isolated.

When I had a faculty position, I felt very hesitant to ask for anything because I was made to feel that I was only tolerated on the faculty. Low wages helped to reinforce this impression. For example, the first year that I had a faculty position I applied to the NSF for travel funds to an international conference to which I had been invited. I was turned down, which disappointed me very much, and I canceled my participation in the conference, although I was on the program. I drifted away from the field altogether in subsequent years. Later I found out that the university routinely paid for travel for faculty to such conferences and would have given me the money if I had asked. I believe that the isolation that many women faculty members feel prevents them from learning about opportunities analogous to this, so they do not benefit from them. But male faculty are quite unconscious of the fact that the women do not know about all the opportunities that are available.

The number of women scientists at the top ranks of academia and elsewhere depends not only on the number of women doctorates in the pipeline but also on the number of women who seek such positions and, once hired, on the ability of institutions to retain them. The existing dearth of women at the upper echelons of science has a chilling effect on the aspirations of potential women scientists and thereby decreases their numbers. Academy members, like most women, do not want to fill the role of being the token woman. Efforts to increase the number of women scientists must therefore be directed to both entry-level and upper-rank positions, since progress at the entry level is closely intertwined with progress at the top.

The proposals advanced by Academy members for adapting university policies to meet the needs of increasingly diverse faculties are almost identical to proposals for family-friendly policies previously advanced by numerous university committees, government agencies, and women's advocacy groups. There is surprisingly little difference between the proposals for improving the status of women issued in 1971 by a faculty committee at Harvard and those contained in recent reports seeking to increase the participation of women in science and engineering, such as the MIT report referred to earlier, a 1998 report of the Association of Women in Science, and a report issued in 1992 by a committee of the National Research Council.[3] The recommendations of the Harvard report addressed the same agenda as the reports issued in the 1990s and included:

- Appointment of a limited number of part-time assistant, associate, and full professors.
- Optional extension of nontenured appointments for one year for each pregnancy, not to exceed two years total.
- Unpaid full- or part-time maternity leave without reduction of benefits.
- Appointment of a university administrator of child care, a setup fund for the start-up costs of day care centers, and provision by the university of space, utilities, and liability insurance for child care centers approved by the administrator.

Why do we still grapple with problems that have been evident for more than 30 years? Women's desire for greater flexibility clashes with the prevailing scientific climate. Many departments continue to regard family responsibilities as incompatible with the total commitment to research they expect and prize, and proposals for helping to integrate women have thus not been high on the list of faculty and institutional priorities. In this respect, academia lags behind industry and government research laboratories.

This message is not lost on young women who fear that the seriousness of their commitment as scientists would be questioned if they were to take more than a brief leave of absence after the birth of a child or to request a temporary reduction in their teaching or administrative responsibilities. Even at universities that have adopted flexible leave or promotion policies few faculty members dare take advantage of them because parents are afraid they might jeopardize their future careers if they were to deviate from the "normal" (i.e., male) career path. Since decisions regarding hiring, promotions, and the allocation of perks are determined primarily at the departmental level, their fears may not be entirely unjustified. Science careers today are more competitive for everyone, but because of long-standing cultural and gender role expectations the competition causes greater obstacles for women. The pressures are greatest in those fields where there are still relatively few women.

Many of the women who were born in the first third of the twentieth century, among them Mary K. Gaillard, Margaret Kidwell, Marian Koshland, Ruth Patrick, and Janet Rowley, did not enter mainstream science until after their children were in secondary school. Mildred Cohn, mother of three, was a postdoctoral fellow and research assistant for more than 21 years. These women did not have to juggle teaching, administration, research, and countless hours writing grant applications while their children were very young.

Today, spending such extended periods in off-ladder positions is no longer a viable option for women who want to pursue careers at the forefront of science. Mildred Dresselhaus, a professor of electrical engineering at MIT, echoed the view of many Academy members who believe that there continue to be relatively few women in some areas of science because women ask themselves whether they want the pressures of the current scientific climate and view other careers as more compatible with their desired lifestyles.

It is apparent from the observations made by Academy members that the lives of women scientists continue to differ from those of their male colleagues in some significant ways. I asked members what changes they would make to facilitate careers for women scientists if they had sufficient money and power. Their suggestions fell into three general categories:

- Policies designed to encourage more young women to become scientists and to overcome internal barriers rooted in traditional attitudes.
- The adoption of family-friendly policies by institutions in order to attract and retain scientists who are currently leaving academia for positions they view as less pressured and more compatible with other responsibilities.
- Policies designed to promote more women to senior positions and to equalize other opportunities by including women in significant numbers at all levels of decision making.

## Overcoming Internal Barriers

Academy members believe that aspiring women scientists should be helped to overcome the internal barriers that continue to hamper many along the way. Self-doubt, timidity, and dislike of conflict do not contribute to success in the competitive arena of scientific research. In the words of one member, "Women contribute to the image of who women are as much as men." Said another:

> Some of this is quite insidious. After a lifetime of not feeling entitled to having our scientific careers, we can use that against ourselves. . . . We have to get the word out that women can trust their own voice and then follow it.

As I spoke with members and listened to their stories I realized that these women differ from other talented but less successful women scientists precisely because each of them learned relatively early in life how to overcome or totally disregard such internal barriers. Having done so they were able to pursue the work they loved with passion and without expending energy dealing with self-doubt or guilt.

It is evident from the experiences of Academy members described earlier that in many schools boys and girls are still treated differently based on gender-related expectations. Children internalize these messages, and girls lose interest in math and science as a result. Members stressed the importance of improving science education from elementary through high school for all students in order to encourage talented girls as well as boys to consider science, mathematics, and engineering as possible future careers. The training of science teachers should address the special needs of women students and help them recognize and dispel stereotypical attitudes that can undermine girls' confidence and interest in mathematics and science. Requiring mathematics and science courses rather than offering them as electives might help female students avoid the social pressures that steer them toward more "feminine" subject areas. One member noted that in Italy, and in other countries where four years of high school science are mandatory for all students, more women tend to go into the sciences.

Maxine Singer, who has launched a science program for inner-city children in Washington, D.C., advocates using a problem-solving rather than a didactic approach in the classroom.

> I think it is important to get women to do technical things in their early years. Young girls don't take things apart. Nobody gives them screwdrivers to play with. Building circuits and things that used to be consigned to manual or vocational training in schools are what we try to do in our program.

Exposing students to hands-on science at an early age is important for all students but especially girls, who are less likely than boys to get such experience on their own. Women should therefore be encouraged to participate in summer science programs and summer internships in order to get an in-depth exposure to the thrill of discovery that science can offer when it is properly taught.

Academy member May R. Berenbaum, head of the Department of Entomology at the University of Illinois at Urbana-Champaign, studies the chemical warfare between plants and insects. She recalled a visit to an elementary school class at which she described how insects move, a description that was initially greeted by cries of "Yucky!" as the bugs squirmed in a container on a table. Soon, however, the children were arguing over who would hold the sphinx moth caterpillar next and were shouting "Pass down the maggots!" They not only asked perceptive questions but by the end of her visit two of the children had decided to become entomologists—at least for the moment. Berenbaum's approach typifies the kind of science instruction to which children readily respond. She is aware that attempts to popularize science are often viewed as frivolous by researchers, but she remains determined to reach out to the public through films, lectures, and visits to schools.

The role of supportive mentors is of paramount importance to women scientists in light of the internal barriers that continue to hamper many. To function effectively, scientists must become part of the national and international community of researchers in their field. Traditionally, scientists are introduced to these fellow researchers by their dissertation supervisors and the professors under whom they do their postdoctoral work, a group that continues to be predominantly male.  Although many Academy members were helped by mentors in the course of their careers, others recalled incidents in which they had been actively discouraged by a teacher or faculty member from pursuing their scientific interests in high school, college, graduate school, or even later.  These "mentors" viewed the roles of mother and scientist as incompatible and discouraged women from continuing their studies.  Those women who attained Academy membership obviously ignored such advice, but other female students undoubtedly abandoned dreams of becoming research scientists in the face of similar discouragement.  It is therefore essential that faculty members, whether male or female, are made aware of the vital role they play in shaping the future careers of their students, so that they can address the special concerns of women students.  The more diverse faculties become, the easier this task should be.

When students see couples in which the husband holds a professorship while the wife is a lecturer supervising laboratory sections, the implicit message is not lost on them.  The models that students observe can have a greater impact on them than what they are told.  One Academy member who became aware of the subservient position of a female scientist at the college she attended resolved to avoid such a fate herself, but it is easy to imagine that other women might take away a different message.  Every effort must be made to offer both members of a couple responsibilities commensurate with their talents and training.  This not only combats discrimination but also helps erase negative messages that hamper women.

## Achieving a Critical Mass

Minority status easily translates into marginal status and thus has a cumulative negative effect on women's careers by limiting visibility, self-confidence, and productivity.  Grateful to have found a niche in which they can pursue their scientific work, many women remain reluctant to rock the boat. Because they often underestimate their own abilities and achievements, many are less willing to speak up for themselves than men.  As a result, differences in salary, research space, awards, and perks persist between men and women of comparable achievements. Academy members agreed that once women approach a critical mass among students, faculty, committee members, and at the administrative level they tend to be treated more equally. In many of the biological sciences women graduate students and young women faculty now feel that they "belong," while in those disciplines in which women constitute a distinct minority, the culture around them remains relatively unaffected by their presence, and their status remains marginal.

Scientists like to believe that, as reasonable individuals, they base promotions, selection of department chairs, salaries, and other professional rewards purely on merit, but several Academy members emphasized that there is no such thing as hiring based solely on merit. They stressed the importance of including women on all selection committees in significant numbers because the old boys' network is just that, and many men are simply unaware of talented women scientists. Even when women are considered, men who have not had the opportunity to work closely with female colleagues are often unable to evaluate them fairly. Many unintentionally overlook and thus disqualify able women candidates in hiring, promotions, and awards; in selecting speakers for distinguished lectureships; and even in proposing women for membership in the National Academy of Sciences. Several members suggested that institutions that have few women faculty add outside members to all selection committees on an ad hoc basis until their faculties become sufficiently diversified.

## Family-Friendly Policies

The widespread impression among women Academy members that a significant number of highly promising women decide to leave academia soon after they complete their postdoctoral training was discussed earlier (see Chapter 8). As Janet Rowley and others pointed out, it is impossible to remedy this apparent "dropout" problem without first obtaining data documenting what happens to the women who seem to disappear. Do they move out of academia to other positions? Do they drop out temporarily and then reenter? Do they change careers? We simply do not know.

All contemporary research scientists face the pressures of a tight job market; competition for promotions, funding, and recognition; and the ever-increasing pace of change in science, but because women still assume the primary responsibility for rearing children, these pressures affect their lives and careers more than men's, and policies that appear neutral on their face can have a disparate impact on women. There was a consensus among the women Academy members that inflexible career ladders in academia are a serious obstacle for many women, and that the needs of parents with young children must be addressed in order to attract and retain more women.

Academy members emphasized that there is no single policy that fits the need of all women or all scientific disciplines and that flexible options should be offered. Parents who want to share child care in the early years should have the option to reduce their schedules temporarily in order to do so. One or both of such parents may need relief from teaching or administrative duties so that they can maintain their professional activities while caring for their children during infancy. Many women, even those who had worked part time themselves, were ambivalent about the feasibility of taking extended time off in rapidly moving, competitive fields and urged that some form of reduced workload be offered as a more viable alternative.

The difficulties of devising an ideal solution to the overload problem faced by women are reflected in the comments of Mary Osborn, professor and head of the Department of Microbiology at the University of Connecticut Health Center. She views women's reluctance to commit to a full-time competitive career during the childbearing years as a major impediment for them but does not wish to see professional commitment or standards compromised. She commented:

> Although it is just possible (though very difficult) to return . . . after taking time off, I don't believe a fully independent productive career in this experimental science—in which both knowledge and methodologies are advancing very rapidly— can be sustained on much less than a full-time basis. . . . Not that it can't be done—I know at least two eminent women scientists (Academy members) who have done it—but they

have gone the route of taking purely research-track nonfaculty positions, made their research reputations, and then moved into the faculty track at a senior level when their time and effort became less constrained. I do think it is unrealistic as a general rule to expect to step into a regular faculty position after such a hiatus as though no time had been lost. On the other hand, promotion and tenure committees, as well as administration, must be willing to stretch the usual time limits for young women faculty with small children.

Today, few couples are fortunate enough to be able to rely on extended family members for child care. Academy members emphasized the importance of providing quality affordable day care, preferably onsite, for faculty and other employees. Administrators should take the initiative in exploring new options and policies jointly with faculty members in order to accommodate individual situations. The women Academy members agreed that whatever family-friendly policies are instituted, they should be offered equally to both men and women. One member suggested that flexible work options should also be made available to the growing number of employees who assume responsibilities for the care of aging parents or ill spouses.

Jane Lubchenco and her husband, Bruce Menge, left full-time positions on the East Coast and persuaded Oregon State University to offer them two part-time tenure-track positions. Few young faculty are willing to take the risks or have the stamina that such a job search involves. Lubchenco spoke for many Academy members when she emphasized that, since there are many possible ways to provide relief from the pressures caused by the overlap of the tenure timetable with a woman's childbearing years, families should be offered a choice among viable options. She added that flexible options should be offered routinely and that their availability should never depend on the luck of finding sympathetic department chairs or deans. Parents should not have to devise solutions on their own on an ad hoc basis. The availability of flexible options is often buried in annual pro forma statements in personnel manuals or in statements describing affirmative action policies, but merely having such policies on the books is not enough. Unless administrators and department chairs actively encourage faculty, both male and female, to take advantage of flexible options, such options have little or no impact.

Mary Ellen Avery would like to see mothers who decide to take extended maternity leaves encouraged to attend seminars and to maintain contact with students and colleagues while on leave and believes that they should be eligible for a subsidy to cover any resulting child care costs. For young parents whose combined income is limited, and for mothers who want to return to work soon after the birth of a child and need full-time help to care for an infant, the availability of some form of financial subsidy for child care expenses can make a critical difference.

The cost of providing day care, temporarily relieving faculty from teaching, or providing other support for parents could be offset by the savings that result from greater success in recruiting and from reduced faculty turnover. The criticism often voiced that child care subsidies are unfair to employees who have no children is without merit. Universities routinely provide benefits to faculty and staff even though only a fraction of all employees ever derive a benefit from them. Single employees derive no benefit from insurance coverage available for spouses. On-campus parking is subsidized although it is rarely used by staff who ride bicycles or live near the campus. Sports programs and scholarships for faculty children likewise benefit only a fraction of all faculty members.

## Initiating Change

In order to address the difficulties in attracting and retaining women faculty, a woman faculty member at the Johns Hopkins University School of Medicine initiated a study in 1990 that led to a long-range program for improving the status of women at that institution.[4] A careful factual analysis of existing problems preceded the changes that were implemented at Johns Hopkins. This study documented "multiple, complex, and often subtle" gender discrimination and structural career obstacles for women faculty in the Department of Medicine. Eighty percent of the women, compared to 34 percent of men, listed a sense of isolation as a reason for seriously considering leaving academic medicine. The study also disclosed a major gender-based difference in the mentoring experience. One-third of the women reported that their mentors used the woman faculty member's work for the mentor's own career benefit, rather than to benefit the woman's career, but only 10 percent of men reported similar experiences. When new mentoring programs were established, it was found that men as well as women benefited from them. Analogous differences in the experiences of male and female scientists were documented in the Sonnert and Holton study cited earlier.[5]

Among the interventions designed to remedy these and other findings at Johns Hopkins were strong and visible leadership by the department chair regarding the necessity of eliminating gender-based obstacles, steps designed to legitimize concerns and to help the faculty understand the nature of gender-based discrimination and bias, steps to motivate faculty to develop skills in order to accomplish necessary change, and steps to achieve equity in salaries and promotions. The program addressing these issues resulted in a fivefold increase in the number of women at the associate professor level with no alteration in promotion criteria as well as in a substantial decrease in the proportion of women anticipating that they would leave academic medicine. Useful interventions were quickly generalized to include men as well as women. The faculty was helped to recognize that, since women constitute half the talent pool, failing to draw proportionally from that pool limited the institution's competitiveness and excellence.

Outreach efforts designed to attract more women to the sciences are important, but, as the ongoing absence of women at the upper ranks of the sciences demonstrates, they are not sufficient to level the playing field. There is an urgent need for data documenting what happens to able highly trained women scientists who seem to disappear. Most Academy members believe that greater flexibility by institutions is needed if we hope to attract and retain more women to university faculties. The experiences at MIT and the Johns Hopkins University School of Medicine demonstrate that institutional change is possible, given strong leadership and a serious commitment to progress. Similar strategies have been undertaken by many industrial firms. The proposals of the women members of the National Academy of Sciences echo those made previously by numerous groups seeking to improve the status of women scientists. It is time to heed the proposals.

# CONCLUSION

The achievements of the women elected to the National Academy of Sciences parallel those of their male colleagues. All have made major contributions to the advancement of science and attained positions of leadership among their fellow scientists. They are truly stars. The Academy members were drawn to science because they loved the challenge and excitement of exploring the unknown, of solving puzzles, of increasing our understanding and knowledge of the natural world, and by a desire to be useful. All are passionately committed to their work. However, in order to achieve success as scientists, these women had to overcome barriers that their male colleagues did not face. Many were denied access to educational and employment opportunities. They were told again and again that, as women, they did not belong in science. Yet they persisted, persevered, and succeeded. The majority married and raised families while pursuing their careers. It easy to see why the women elected to the Academy are often portrayed as heroines.

Despite their outstanding achievements, female Academy members have a great deal in common with professional women everywhere, whether in medicine, law, the arts, sports, or business. They dream of a day when their lives as scientists and as women will mesh seamlessly so that they will no longer have to straddle two separate worlds. What distinguishes this group of women from other women scientists is their phenomenal passion, drive, and persistence, which, with a little luck, enabled them to stay the course despite the obstacles they encountered. They dared and they took risks. Each found a way to deflect negative messages without losing her bearings. Their success demonstrates that it is possible, though not easy, to thrive in the triple roles of scientist, wife, and mother. As the sociologist Suzanne Keller once observed, "It is very difficult to be mother, maid, and Madame Curie."

The experiences of the women Academy members reflect the era in which they grew up. The lives of the older generations of women are dramatically different from the lives of members who launched their careers after the enactment of civil rights legislation and the advent of the women's movement in the early 1970s. Earlier generations of women scientists were systematically denied equal access to educational and employment opportunities and forged careers in the face of overwhelming obstacles. When barriers based on gender became illegal, there was a surge of women students at graduate and professional schools and institutions suddenly recruited the women they had previously shunned. Today, women and men earn advanced degrees in many fields in almost equal numbers. Even in fields in which men still outnumber women by a significant margin, such as engineering and the physical sciences, the proportion of women doctorate recipients has increased significantly.

The changing climate in which contemporary women scientists work is reflected in how they view their roles as women. Women's caucuses or committees have been formed in many professional societies. Women scientists are willing, often eager, to talk about their experiences as women, whether favorable or unfavorable. Academy members were candid about further progress they would like to see, and many work with colleagues in order to implement needed changes. Their eagerness to participate in my study and to have its results published is an indication of their growing sense of power and belonging.

Academy members born in the 1940s and 1950s feel at home in their disciplines and believe that civil rights legislation and the women's movement are primarily responsible for the change in their status. Their career paths parallel those of their male contemporaries. A minority, primarily in the biological sciences, now believe that women have an easier time than men in obtaining positions, awards, and other honors. As one such member put it:

> In recent years it became fashionable to be female. As far as I can surmise, my status as a woman has been at least as helpful as hurtful. I have been fortunate to be in situations where ability was recognized and respected, irrespective of gender. My field (molecular biology) is relatively new and is probably less susceptible to "old boy" attitudes than others.

Many people expected that the implementation of gender-neutral policies together with concerted efforts to attract women to science would result in a level playing field for women. However, women still progress through the ranks at a slower pace and disappear from mainstream science more often than men do. Most female Academy members are aware that subtle discrimination persists in hiring, salaries, promotions, invitations to prestigious lectureships, nominations for awards, and other opportunities for career advancement, especially in those disciplines in which there are still relatively few women, even though overt barriers have essentially disappeared. They remain overburdened with committee appointments and administrative responsibilities because a woman is needed on every committee and in most departments there are not enough to go around. When these issues are brought out into the open and taken seriously by senior faculty and administrators they can be addressed and remedied, as demonstrated by the changes recently implemented at MIT and Johns Hopkins.

Subtler obstacles to women's progress rooted in long-standing gender stereotypes ingrained in our culture persist. Such obstacles are widespread and harder to eradicate because they cannot be changed by fiat. Young women internalize stereotypes that dampen their aspirations and cause them to wonder whether they belong in science at all. The proposals in Chapter 8, including better education and mentoring, are designed to help women recognize and overcome these internal barriers.

Today, there are opportunities for science doctorates in many areas beyond academia—in government, industrial and pharmacological laboratories, environmental agencies, and elsewhere. Scientists are needed as patent attorneys, science writers, policy advisers, and in many other areas and can mesh job opportunities with their personal plans and aspirations. A growing number of men and women scientists are becoming entrepreneurs, forming their own companies or working as consultants. However, for women equal opportunities will not become a reality until the lingering myth that women must forego marriage and children in order to succeed at the cutting edge of science is relegated to history and the glass ceiling vanishes.

A careful reading of the profiles in this book makes it apparent that even for the highly talented members of the National Academy of Sciences the playing field is not yet level. Women scientists remain scarce on tenured faculties of universities and at the upper echelons of industry and government, even though the number and proportion of women earning advanced science degrees have increased severalfold during the past three decades. The scarcity of women at the top can no longer be blamed on a scarcity of women in the pipeline. More than 5,000 women now earn science doctorates each year. The proportion of women scientists moving into entry-level positions approaches their proportion among recipients of science doctorates, but women progress through the ranks at a slower rate and disappear from mainstream science more often than their male peers. If we are committed to maximizing the pool of available scientific talent and to providing equity for women, the reasons for this discrepancy must be explored. The stories of the women related in this book contain partial answers to the recurring question "Why so few?"

Universities and research facilities were established for men by men. Their policies are based on the once-valid premise that each scientist has a wife at home to whom all responsibility for family and domestic responsibilities would be delegated. Expectations for faculty members, researchers, and other professionals tacitly continue to rest on this premise, a premise that is no longer appropriate for any woman or for most younger men. Although institutions today encourage and support women's participation, few have adapted their policies and schedules to the changing structure of contemporary families. They ignore expectations and policies that, although neutral on their face, disadvantage women by not taking the realities of their lives into account. In this respect, relatively little progress has been made in the past 25 years, especially in academia. The difficulty of combining family and career responsibilities remains a major obstacle for women scientists who must continue to find ways to fit their lives into an environment designed for men.

The women scientists who attained membership in the National Academy of Sciences did so by adapting their lives to prevailing expectations through ingenuity, doggedness, and extraordinary energy. Many acknowledged that a supportive spouse had been indispensable to their success. Female Academy members are acutely aware that students, male as well as female, see them as role models and that many decide not to follow in their footsteps because they believe that the demands of academic research careers today are incompatible with a balanced lifestyle. Providing more flexible work patterns, onsite day care, and other policies to ease the pressures for scientists with young children would help men as well as women. The vast majority of female Academy members view such support as essential if we hope to persuade more talented women to pursue high-level scientific careers and to retain promising young scientists, male and female, in academia and elsewhere.

Academy members are aware that few women (or men) currently avail themselves of part-time or leave options even when they are offered because, given the prevailing competitive pressures, students and young faculty are afraid to damage their career prospects by deviating in any way from established work patterns. Many women who had worked part time themselves in the 1940s or 1950s when they had young children now characterize part-time work as a highly desirable but unrealistic option, given the fast pace of current scientific research. They would therefore like to see institutions provide and subsidize quality affordable child care and to offer options that would enable young faculty to lighten teaching and administrative burdens temporarily while maintaining their research programs on a full-time basis. Because most institutions have been reluctant to address the issues brought about by changing lifestyles among their employees, women scientists must either juggle roles as scientists, wives, and mothers without help from the institutions in which they work or forgo having children. No male scientist has to confront such a Hobson's choice.

The women in the Academy forged individual solutions and managed the work overload in a variety of different ways. Some solved the dilemma by hiring a "third parent," someone with whom they could share domestic responsibilities. One couple found two half-time academic positions while their children were small and then later resumed a normal workload. In rare instances couples relied on grandparents for help. Most simply muddled through by using day care, household help, working late at night, and strictly limiting their nonprofessional activities to those directly related to their careers or their families. Older members look back nostalgically to the days when it was possible to do independent research without having any responsibility for teaching or administration while one's children were young and to postpone entering the mainstream until midcareer, an option rarely available in today's competitive environment.

Although the overload problem pervades all areas of science, there is a consensus that having a critical mass of women in a department or discipline makes it easier for women to cope and to be treated as integral members of the scientific community. It lessens the pressure of being a token female presence. As Judith Klinman put it, "When you are alone you start to think you may be crazy." The ability to network bolsters self-confidence and offers the possibility of concerted pressure for change.

Efforts have recently been made to encourage doctorate recipients to seek employment beyond academia and the scientific establishment, in areas such as science writing, consulting, or at the interface of public policy and science. These are important, but they should not be used to channel students into alternative careers on the basis of gender or race. It would be regrettable if now that women can finally choose freely whether to become physicians or nurses, science faculty or technicians, we were once more to encourage employment segregation among young scientists by race or gender.

Academy members in all age groups would like to see a more

humane environment for everyone. More collaboration, less emphasis on competition, and more flexibility regarding workloads and the promotion timetable were among their proposals, but many conceded that their wishes were unlikely to be implemented given the current intense competition for jobs, recognition, and funding. The women elected to the National Academy of Sciences are grateful to have the opportunity to pursue the science they love among colleagues who share their interests. The suggestions they advanced for change are designed to minimize conflicts between career and family in order to make science more hospitable for women, rather than to bring about fundamental changes in the institutions in which they work.

Time, improved science education, better mentoring, more support for young families, and the elimination of gender inequality in salaries, promotions, and the allocation of perks will undoubtedly increase the number of women at the forefront of science, whether in academia, industry, government, or elsewhere, but I predict that further progress will be slow unless we also take a fresh look at how science today is organized and funded. The proportion of white males in the pool of future scientists is shrinking. Increasingly young men as well as women are taking lifestyle considerations into account when making career plans, and there is considerable anecdotal evidence that highly trained women scientists are leaving academia to seek employment elsewhere. So far efforts to attract minority students to science have had little success. Outreach efforts are not righting existing imbalances. New strategies are needed.

Our universities have a long and distinguished history. Many evolved from monastic institutions into hierarchical academies. Their expectations and policies were designed for male faculties and male students in a different era, based on a model that by its very nature severely disadvantages women. The twentieth century has witnessed dramatic changes. We are moving toward an ever more diversified work force, in part as a result of the civil rights struggle and the women's movement. For the first time in history women can plan whether and when to bear children. Advances in medicine have lengthened the average lifespan significantly. The fraction of women's lives devoted to childbearing has been correspondingly reduced. If we hope to attract bright and creative individuals to faculties in the future we must take a critical look at the policies under which today's universities operate.

Serious questions should be asked about whether the intensely competitive culture that dominates scientific research today promotes or hinders scientific creativity. We should examine whether the way science is funded steers investigators away from tackling fundamental problems toward those that promise quick payoffs. Could the granting system be simplified in order to provide support for longer periods from a single source in order to eliminate the considerable time now devoted to writing multiple grant applications? Do professors take on ever-larger research groups in order to assure that they will have enough publications to obtain more funding, greater prestige, and coveted awards and invitations? How much supervision and instruction can individual students get when they work in research groups numbering 30 or more? Who benefits when the award of a doctorate takes five years or more? Students? Faculty supervisors? Anyone?

Scientific research has made much of the progress of the twentieth century possible. To maintain the pace of progress in the future we must find ways to attract and retain talented scientists irrespective of gender, race, or ethnic background. We are unlikely to achieve this goal unless we take a fresh look at the scientific enterprise and reexamine the assumptions on which it operates.

3. *New York Times,* February 10, 1999, p. B1.

4. *Ibid.,* March 1, 1999, p. A1, B5.

5. Vicki Schultz, "Reconceptualizing Sexual Harassment," *The Yale Law Journal,* 107:1762, 1998.

6. Nancy Hopkins et al., Members of the Committee on Women Faculty in the School of Science, *A Study on the Status of Women Faculty in Science at MIT,* Massachusetts Institute of Technology, Cambridge, Mass., 1999; also online at <http//web.mit.edu/fnl/women.html>.

## Chapter 4

1. E. M. Burbidge, K. Esau, G. S. Goldhaber, G. Henle, R. Levi-Montalcini, B. Scharrer, S. G. Waelsch, and C. S. Wu.

2. Debra C. Cleveland, "Remembering Katherine Esau, Pioneer in Plant Biology," *UC Davis Biological Sciences,* 5(3):4-5, 1997.

3. Steven Wissig, *In Memoriam for Berta Scharrer,* American Association of Anatomists, <www.anatomy.org/anatomy/dberta.htm>.

4. Rita Levi-Montalcini, *In Praise of Imperfection: My Life and Work,* Basic Books, New York, 1988.

5. Sharon Bertsch McGrayne, *Nobel Prize Women in Science: Their Lives, Struggles, and Momentous Discoveries,* Birch Lane Press, New York, 1993, p. 208.

6. Ibid., p. 223.

7. M. Cohn, "Atomic and Nuclear Probes of Enzyme Systems," *Annual Review of Biophysics and Biomolecular Structure,* 21:3, 1992.

8. Ibid., p. 22.

9. Gertrude B. Elion, *Les Prix Nobel,* Nobel Foundation, Stockholm, Sweden, 1988, pp. 233-266; also online at <http://www.nobel.se/laureates/medicine-1988-2-autobio.html>.

10. McGrayne, op. cit., p. 288.

## Chapter 5

1. "In Memoriam: Marian Koshland, 1927-1997," *Journal of Immunology,* 161(2):545-546, 1998.

2. Deborah C. Fort, ed., *A Hand Up: Women Mentoring Women in Science*, Association for Women in Science, Washington, D.C., 1993, p. 76.

3. Ibid., p. 77.

## Chapter 6

1. Benjamin Spock, *Baby and Child Care*, Simon and Schuster, New York, 1946.

## Chapter 7

1. Jane Lubchenco and Bruce A. Menge, "Split positions can provide a sane career track—a personal account," *BioScience*, 43(4):243, April 1993.

2. Rachel Carson, *Silent Spring*, Houghton Mifflin, Boston, 1962.

## Chapter 8

1. Gerhard Sonnert and Gerald Holton, *Gender Differences in Science Careers,* Rutgers University Press, New Brunswick, N.J., 1995, p. 139. The Sonnert-Holton study is based on data collected in the late 1980s from 699 male and female scientists who had been awarded National Science Foundation postdoctoral fellowships between the mid-1950s and the mid-1980s.

2. Susan McGee Bailey, *How Schools Shortchange Girls: The AAUW Report—A Study of Major Findings on Girls and Education*, Center for Research on Women, Wellesley College, Wellesley, Mass., 1995.

3. Frances K. Conley, *Walking Out on the Boys,* Farrar, Straus and Giroux, New York, 1998.

4. Valian, op. cit., pp. 234-235.

5. Sonnert and Holton, op. cit., pp. 149-151.

6. Ibid., p. 139.

## Chapter 9

1. Sonnert and Holton, op. cit., p. 156; *Women in Corporate Leadership: Progress and Prospects*, Catalyst, New York, 1996.
2. Sonnert and Holton, op. cit., pp. 156-157.
3. Ibid., p. 158.
4. Valian, op. cit., p. 39; Londa Schiebinger, "Women in Science: The Clash of Cultures," *Research/Penn State*, September 1995, p. 4.

## Chapter 10

1. Hopkins et al., op. cit.
2. W. Todd Furniss and Patricia Albjerg Graham, eds., *Women in Higher Education*, American Council on Education, Washington, D.C., 1974, p. 129.
3. *Report of the Committee on the Status of Women*, op. cit., pp. 68-70; Hopkins, op. cit.; Catherine Jay Didion, Mary Anne Fox, and Mary Ellen Jones, "Executive Summary—Cultivating Academic Careers: AWIS Project on Academic Climate," *AWIS Magazine,* 27:22-27, Winter 1998; Marsha Lakes Mayas and Linda Skidmore Dix, eds., *Science and Engineering Programs—On Target for Women?*, National Academy Press, Washington, D.C., 1992, pp. 115-117.
4. Linda P. Fried et al., "Career Development for Women in Academic Medicine: Multiple Interventions in a Department of Medicine," *Journal of the American Medical Association*, 276(11):898, 1996.
5. Sonnert and Holton, op. cit., pp. 107, 136.

# APPENDIXES

# ACADEMY MEMBERS SURVEYED, LISTED ALPHABETICALLY

*Dates in parentheses denote year elected to the academy.*

Avery, Mary Ellen (1994), Harvard Medical School, Boston, Mass.

Berenbaum, May R. (1994), University of Illinois, Urbana

Burbidge, E. Margaret (1978), University of California, San Diego

Chilton, Mary-Dell (1985), Novartis Seeds, Inc., Research Triangle Park, N.C.

Cohen, Carolyn (1996), Brandeis University, Waltham, Mass.

Cohn, Mildred (1971), University of Pennsylvania School of Medicine, Philadelphia

Conwell, Esther M. (1990), University of Rochester, Rochester, N.Y.

Davis, Margaret B. (1982), University of Minnesota, St. Paul

Dresselhaus, Mildred S. (1985), Massachusetts Institute of Technology, Cambridge

Edmonds, Mary (1991), University of Pittsburgh, Pittsburgh, Pa.

Elion,† Gertude B. (1990), Glaxo Wellcome, Inc., Research Triangle Park, N.C.

Esau,† Katherine (1957), University of California, Davis

Faber, Sandra M. (1985), University of California, Santa Cruz

---

†Deceased

Farquhar, Marilyn Gist (1984), University of California, San Diego

Federoff, Nina (1990), Pennsylvania State University, University Park

Fox, Marye Anne (1994), North Carolina State University, Raleigh

Franzini-Armstrong, Clara (1995), University of Pennsylvania School of Medicine, Philadelphia

Fuchs, Elaine (1996), University of Chicago, Chicago, Ill.

Gaillard, Mary K. (1991), University of California, Berkeley

Gantt, Elisabeth (1996), University of Maryland, College Park

Geller, Margaret J. (1992), Harvard-Smithsonian Center for Astrophysics, Cambridge, Mass.

Giblett, Eloise R. (1980), Puget Sound Blood Center, Seattle, Wash.

Goldhaber,† Gertrude S. (1972), Brookhaven National Laboratory, Upton, N.Y.

Goldman-Rakic, P. S. (1990), Yale University School of Medicine, New Haven, Conn.

Graybiel, Ann M. (1988), Massachusetts Institute of Technology, Cambridge

Gross, Carol A. (1992), University of California, San Francisco

Guthrie, Christine (1993), University of California, San Francisco

Hay, Elizabeth D. (1984), Harvard Medical School, Boston, Mass.

Henle, Gertrude (1979), Children's Hospital of Pennsylvania, Philadelphia

Horstmann, Dorothy M. (1975), Yale University School of Medicine, New Haven, Conn.

Jan, Lily Y. (1995), University of California, San Francisco

Jones,† Mary Ellen (1984), University of North Carolina, Chapel Hill

Karle, Isabella L. (1978), Naval Research Laboratory, Washington, D.C.

Kidwell, Margaret G. (1996), University of Arizona, Tucson

Kieffer, Susan W. (1986), Kieffer & Woo, Palgrave, Ontario, Canada

Kimble, Judith (1995), University of Wisconsin, Madison

Kleckner, Nancy (1993), Harvard University, Cambridge, Mass.

Klinman, Judith P. (1994), University of California, Berkeley

Kopell, Nancy J. (1996), Boston University, Boston, Mass.

Koshland,† Marian E. (1981), University of California, Berkeley

Kustu, Sydney (1993), University of California, Berkeley

Leeman, Susan E. (1991), Boston University School of Medicine, Boston, Mass.

Leopold, Estella B. (1974), University of Washington, Seattle

Levelt Sengers, Johanna M. H. (1996), National Institute of Standards and Technology, Gaithersburg, Md.

Levi-Montalcini, Rita (1968), Institute of Neurobiology C.N.R., Rome, Italy

Long, Sharon R. (1993), Stanford University, Stanford, Calif.

Lubchenco, Jane (1996), Oregon State University, Salem

Margulis, Lynn (1983), University of Massachusetts, Amherst

Marrack, Philippa (1989), National Jewish Medical and Research Center, Denver, Colo.

Matson, Pamela A. (1994), Stanford University, Stanford, Calif.

Mintz, Beatrice (1973), Fox Chase Cancer Center, Philadelphia, Pa.

Morawetz, Cathleen S. (1990), Courant Institute, New York University, New York, N.Y.

Navrotsky, Alexandra (1993), University of California, Davis

Neufeld, Elizabeth F. (1977), University of California, Los Angeles

New, Maria I. (1996), Cornell University Medical College, New York, N.Y.

Osborn, M. J. (1978), University of Connecticut Health Center, Farmington

Pardue, Mary-Lou (1983), Massachusetts Institute of Technology, Cambridge

Patrick, Ruth (1970), Academy of Natural Sciences, Philadelphia, Pa.

Ranney, Helen M. (1973), Alliance Pharmaceutical Corporation, San Diego, Calif.

Ratner, Marina (1993), University of California, Berkeley

Ratner,† Sarah (1974), Public Health Research Institute, New York, N.Y.

Richardson, Jane S. (1991), Duke University Medical Center, Durham, N.C.

Rowley, Janet D. (1984), University of Chicago Medical Center, Chicago, Ill.

Rubin, Vera C. (1981), Carnegie Institution of Washington, Washington, D.C.

Russell, Elizabeth S. (1972), The Jackson Laboratory, Bar Harbor, Maine

Russell, Liane B. (1986), Oak Ridge National Laboratory, Oak Ridge, Tenn.

Sager,† Ruth (1977), Dana Farber Cancer Institute, Boston, Mass.

Sarachik, Myriam P. (1994), City College of the City of New York, New York, N.Y.

Scharrer,† Berta V. (1967), Albert Einstein College of Medicine, Bronx, N.Y.

Shapiro, Lucy (1994), Stanford University School of Medicine, Stanford, Calif.

Shatz, Carla J. (1995), University of California, Berkeley

Singer, Maxine F. (1979), Carnegie Institution of Washington, Washington, D.C.

Solomon, Susan (1992), National Oceanic and Atomospheric Administration, Boulder, Colo.

Stadtman, Thressa C. (1981), National Institutes of Health, Bethesda, Md.

Steitz, Joan A. (1983), Yale University, New Haven, Conn.

Stubbe, Joanne (1992), Massachusetts Institute of Technology, Cambridge

Taylor, Susan S. (1996), University of California, San Diego

Uhlenbeck, Karen K. (1986), University of Texas, Austin

Vaughan, Martha (1985), National Institutes of Health, Bethesda, Md.

Vitetta, Ellen S. (1994), University of Texas Southwestern Medical Center, Dallas

Waelsch, Salome G. (1979), Albert Einstein College of Medicine, Bronx, N.Y.

West-Eberhard, Mary Jane (1988), University of Costa Rica, Ciudad

Witkin, Evelyn M. (1977; retired), Rutgers University, Rutgers, N.J.

Wu,† C. S. (1958), Columbia University, New York, N.Y.

Yalow, Rosalyn S. (1975), Veteran Affairs Medical Center, Bronx, N.Y.

Zoback, Mary Lou (1995), U.S. Geological Survey, Menlo Park, Calif.

# ACADEMY MEMBERS SURVEYED, LISTED BY SCIENTIFIC DISCIPLINE

*Parenthesized numbers following section titles refer to the number of women members/total number of members in each discipline as of July 1, 1996.*

**Applied Mathematical Sciences (2/48)**
Kopell, Nancy J. (1996), Boston University, Boston
Morawetz, Cathleen S. (1990), Courant Institute, New York
    University, New York, N.Y.

**Applied Physical Science (1/73)**
Sarachik, Myriam P. (1994), City College of the City of New York,
    New York, N.Y.

**Astronomy (3/65)**
Burbidge, E. Margaret (1978), University of California, San Diego
Faber, Sandra M. (1985), University of California, Santa Cruz
Rubin, Vera C. (1981), Carnegie Institution of Washington,
    Washington, D.C.

---

†Deceased.

### Biochemistry (14/170)

Cohen, Carolyn (1996), Brandeis University, Waltham, Mass.

Cohn, Mildred (1971), University of Pennsylvania School of
    Medicine, Philadelphia

Edmonds, Mary (1991), University of Pittsburgh, Pittsburgh, Pa.

Jones,† Mary Ellen (1984) University of North Carolina, Chapel Hill

Klinman, Judith P. (1994), University of California, Berkeley

Neufeld, Elizabeth F. (1977), University of California, Los Angeles

Osborn, M. J. (1978), University of Connecticut Health Center,
    Farmington

Ratner,† Sarah (1974), Public Health Research Institute,
    New York, N.Y.

Richardson, Jane S. (1991), Duke University Medical Center,
    Durham, N.C.

Singer, Maxine F., (1979), Carnegie Institution of Washington,
    Washington, D.C.

Stadtman, Thressa C. (1981), National Institutes of Health,
    Bethesda, Md.

Steitz, Joan A. (1983), Yale University, New Haven, Conn.

Stubbe, Joanne (1992), Massachusetts Institute of Technology,
    Cambridge

Taylor, Susan S. (1996), University of California, San Diego

### Cellular and Developmental Biology (6/72)

Farquhar, Marilyn Gist (1984), University of California, San Diego

Fuchs, Elaine (1996), University of Chicago, Chicago, Ill.

Hay, Elizabeth D. (1984), Harvard Medical School, Boston, Mass.

Kimble, Judith (1995), University of Wisconsin, Madison

Shapiro, Lucy (1994), Stanford University School of Medicine,
    Stanford, Calif.

Waelsch, Salome G. (1979), Albert Einstein College of Medicine,
    Bronx, N.Y.

### Chemistry (2/182)

Fox, Marye Anne (1994), North Carolina State University, Raleigh

Karle, Isabella L. (1978), Naval Research Laboratory, Washington, D.C.

**Engineering Sciences (3/88)**
Conwell, Esther M. (1990), University of Rochester, Rochester, N.Y.
Dresselhaus, Mildred S. (1985), Massachusetts Institute of Technology, Cambridge
Levelt Sengers, Johanna M. H. (1996), National Institute of Standards and Technology, Gaithersburg, Md.

**Genetics (10/64)**
Gross, Carol A. (1992), University of California, San Francisco
Guthrie, Christine (1993), University of California, San Francisco
Kleckner, Nancy (1993), Harvard University, Cambridge, Mass.
Kustu, Sydney (1993), University of California, Berkeley
Mintz, Beatrice (1973), Fox Chase Cancer Center, Philadelphia, Pa.
Pardue, Mary-Lou (1983), Massachusetts Institute of Technology, Cambridge
Russell, Elizabeth S. (1972), The Jackson Laboratory, Bar Harbor, Maine
Russell, Liane B. (1986), Oak Ridge National Laboratory, Oak Ridge, Tenn.
Sager,† Ruth (1977), Dana-Farber Cancer Institute, Boston, Mass.
Witkin, Evelyn M. (1977; retired), Rutgers University, Rutgers, N.J.

**Geology (3/56)**
Kieffer, Susan W. (1986), Kieffer & Woo, Palgrave, Ontario, Canada
Navrotsky, Alexandra (1993), University of California, Davis
Zoback, Mary Lou (1995), U.S. Geological Survey, Menlo Park, Calif.

**Geophysics (1/76)**
Solomon, Susan (1992), National Oceanic and Atomospheric Administration, Boulder, Colo.

**Mathematics (2/90)**
Ratner, Marina (1993), University of California, Berkeley
Uhlenbeck, Karen K. (1986), University of Texas, Austin

**Medical Genetics, Hematology, and Oncology (4/71)**
Giblett, Eloise R. (1980), Puget Sound Blood Center, Seattle, Wash.
Henle, Gertrude (1979), Children's Hospital of Pennsylvania,
    Philadelphia
Ranney, Helen M. (1973), Alliance Pharmaceutical Corporation, San
    Diego
Rowley, Janet D. (1984), University of Chicago Medical Center,
    Chicago, Ill.

**Medical Physiology and Metabolism (5/48)**
Avery, Mary Ellen (1994), Harvard Medical School, Boston, Mass.
Elion,† Gertrude B. (1990), Glaxo Wellcome, Inc., Research
    Triangle Park, N.C.
New, Maria I. (1996), Cornell University Medical College, New
    York, N.Y.
Vaughan, Martha (1985), National Institutes of Health,
    Bethesda, Md.
Yalow, Rosalyn S. (1975), Veterans Affairs Medical Center,
    Bronx, N.Y.

**Microbiology and Immunology (4/70)**
Horstmann, Dorothy M. (1975), Yale University School of Medicine,
    New Haven, Conn.
Koshland,† Marian E. (1981),  University of California, Berkeley
Marrack, Philippa (1989), National Jewish Medical and Research
    Center, Denver, Colo.
Vitetta, Ellen S. (1994), University of Texas Southwestern Medical
    Center, Dallas

**Neurobiology (5/55)**
Goldman-Rakic, P. S. (1990), Yale University School of Medicine,
    New Haven, Conn.

Graybiel, Ann M. (1988), Massachusetts Institute of Technology, Cambridge

Levi-Montalcini, Rita (1968), Institute of Neurobiology C.N.R., Rome, Italy

Scharrer,† Berta V. (1967), Albert Einstein College of Medicine, Bronx, N.Y.

Shatz, Carla J. (1995), University of California, Berkeley

**Physics (4/162)**

Gaillard, Mary K. (1991), University of California, Berkeley

Geller, Margaret J. (1992), Harvard-Smithsonian Center for Astrophysics, Cambridge, Mass.

Goldhaber,† Gertrude S. (1972), Brookhaven National Laboratory, Upton, N.Y.

Wu,† C. S. (1958), Columbia University, New York, N.Y.

**Physiology and Pharmacology (3/39)**

Franzini-Armstrong, Clara (1995), University of Pennsylvania School of Medicine, Philadelphia

Jan, Lily Y. (1995), University of California, San Francisco

Leeman, Susan E. (1991), Boston University School of Medicine, Boston, Mass.

**Plant Biology (4/45)**

Esau,† Katherine (1957), University of California, Davis

Federoff, Nina (1990), Pennsylvania State University, University Park

Gantt, Elisabeth (1996), University of Maryland, College Park

Long, Sharon R. (1993), Stanford University, Stanford, Calif.

**Plant, Soil, and Microbial Sciences (1/45)**

Chilton, Mary-Dell (1985), Novartis Seeds, Inc., Research Triangle Park, N.C.

**Population Biology, Evolution, and Ecology (9/57)**

Berenbaum, May R. (1994), University of Illinois, Urbana

Davis, Margaret B. (1982), University of Minnesota, St. Paul

Kidwell, Margaret G. (1996), University of Arizona, Tucson
Leopold, Estella B. (1974), University of Washington, Seattle
Lubchenco, Jane (1996), Oregon State University, Salem
Margulis, Lynn (1983), University of Massachusetts, Amherst
Matson, Pamela A. (1994), Stanford University, Stanford, Calif.
Patrick, Ruth (1970), Academy of Natural Sciences, Philadelphia, Pa.
West-Eberhard, Mary Jane (1988), University of Costa Rica, Ciudad

TOTAL = 86 female members out of 1,576 as of July 1, 1996.

# SUGGESTIONS FOR FURTHER READING

Abir-Am, Pnina G., et al., eds., *Creative Couples in the Sciences*, Rutgers University Press, New Brunswick, N.J., 1996.

Astin, Helen S., *The Woman Doctorate in America: Origins, Career, and Family,* Russell Sage Foundation, New York, 1969.

Byrne, Eileen M., *Women and Science: The Snark Syndrome*, The Falmer Press, London, 1993.

Chira, Susan, *A Mother's Place,* Harper Collins, New York, 1998.

Conley, Frances K., *Walking Out on the Boys,* Farrar, Straus and Giroux, New York, 1998.

Crosby, Faye J., *Juggling,* The Free Press, New York, 1991.

Eisenhart, Margaret A., and Elizabeth Finkel, *Women's Science: Learning and Succeeding from the Margins,* University of Chicago Press, Chicago, 1998.

Epstein, Cynthia Fuchs, et al., *The Part-Time Paradox: Time Norms, Professional Life, Family, and Gender,* Routledge Publishing, New York, 1998.

Fort, Deborah C., ed., *A Hand Up: Women Mentoring Women in Science,* Association for Women in Science, Washington, D.C., 1993.

Furniss, W. Todd, and Patricia Albjerg Graham, eds., *Women in Higher Education,* American Council on Education, Washington, D.C., 1974.

Gornick, Vivian, *Women in Science: Portraits from a World in Transition*, Simon and Schuster, New York, 1983.

Henrion, Claudia, *Women in Mathematics: The Addition of Difference,* Indiana University Press, Bloomington, 1997.

Herschbach, Dudley R., "Imaginary Gardens with Real Toads," *Annals of the New York Academy of Sciences,* 775:11-30, 1996.

Hrdy, Sarah Blaffer, *Mother Nature: A History of Mothers, Infants, and Natural Selection*, Pantheon Books, New York, 1999.

Hubbard, Ruth, *The Politics of Women's Biology*, Rutgers University Press, New Brunswick, N.J., 1990.

Keller, Evelyn Fox, *Reflections on Gender and Science,* Yale University Press, New Haven, Conn., 1985.

Kuhn, Thomas S., *The Structure of Scientific Revolutions*, Second Edition, University of Chicago Press, Chicago, 1970.

Kundsin, Ruth B., ed., "Successful Women in the Sciences: An Analysis of Determinants," *Annals of the New York Academy of Sciences*, 208:1-255, 1973.

Levi-Montalcini, Rita, *In Praise of Imperfection: My Life and Work,* translated by Luigi Attardi, Basic Books, New York, 1988.

Lowman, Margaret D., *Life in the Treetops: Adventures of a Woman in Field Biology*, Yale University Press, New Haven, Conn., 1999.

Mayas, Marsha Lakes, and Linda Skidmore Dix, eds., *Science and Engineering Programs: On Target for Women?*, National Academy Press, Washington, D.C., 1992.

McGrayne, Sharon Bertsch, *Nobel Prize Women in Science: Their Lives, Struggles, and Momentous Discoveries,* Birch Lane Press, New York, 1993.

Rossiter, Margaret, *Women Scientists in America: Before Affirmative Action, 1940-1972,* Johns Hopkins University Press, Baltimore, Md., 1995.

Rossiter, Margaret, *Women Scientists in America: Struggles and Strategies to 1940*, Johns Hopkins University Press, Baltimore, Md., 1982.

Sayre, Ann, *Rosalind Franklin and DNA*, Norton, New York, 1978.

Schiebinger, Londa, *Has Feminism Changed Science?*, Harvard University Press, Cambridge, Mass., 1999.

Schultz, Vicki, "Reconceptualizing Sexual Harassment," *The Yale Law Journal*, 107:1683-1805, 1998.

Sime, Ruth Lewin, *Lise Meitner: A Life in Physics*, University of California Press, Berkeley, 1996.

Sonnert, Gerhard, and Gerald Holton, *Gender Differences in Science Careers,* Rutgers University Press, New Brunswick, N. J., 1995.

Sonnert, Gerhardt, *Who Succeeds in Science? The Gender Dimension*, Rutgers University Press, New Brunswick, N.J., 1995.

Strauss, Erich, *Rosalyn Yalow Nobel Laureate: Her Life Work in Medicine: A Biographical Memoir,* Plenum Press, New York, 1998.

Tobias, Sheila, *Faces of Feminism: An Activist's Reflections on the Women's Movement,* Westview Press, Boulder, Colo., 1997.

Valian, Virginia, *Why So Slow? The Advancement of Women*, MIT Press, Cambridge, Mass., 1998.

Wasserman, Elga, Arie Y. Lewin, and Linda H. Bleiweis, eds., *Women in Academia: Evolving Policies Toward Equal Opportunities,* Praeger Publishers, New York, 1975.

Zuckerman, Harriet et al., eds., *The Outer Circle: Women in the Scientific Community*, W. W. Norton, New York, 1991.

# INDEX

## A

Abzug, Bella, 147
Academia
  administrative positions, 4, 6, 28,
    71, 108, 116-117
  career trajectories of women, 18,
    20, 21-23, 28, 32, 34, 35, 36, 39,
    41, 45, 52, 53, 57-58, 65, 71, 74-
    76, 82, 92, 101, 103, 105, 110,
    177-178, 200
  demands on women's time, 98-99,
    130, 186, 217
  extension of nontenured
    appointments, 204
  influence of, 18-19
  family-career conflicts, 5, 20, 28,
    65-66, 70, 75-76, 103, 110, 177-
    178, 189-190
  joint appointments, 161-163,
    169
  medical schools, 28, 32, 41, 45
  selection committee composition,
    209
  sexism/discrimination in, 1, 28, 43-
    44, 45, 51-52, 69-70, 78, 82, 84-
    85, 99-100, 126, 148-149

team sports as preparation for, 161
undergraduate women at Ivy
  League colleges, 19-21, 43
underrepresentation of faculty
  women, 1, 7, 98-99, 218-219
Academy of Natural Sciences, 36, 39,
  240
Acyclovir, 47
*Advances in Immunobiology*, 35
Affirmative action, 10, 19, 29, 39-40,
  52, 66, 70, 76-77, 102, 108, 131-
  132, 135, 200-206, 211-212,
  216-217
Albert Einstein College of Medicine,
  35, 236, 239
Albright, Madeleine, 13
Algae research, 38-49
Alliance Pharmaceutical Corporation,
  238
Alzheimer's disease, 154
American Association for the
  Advancement of Science, 120,
  160
American Association of Anatomists,
  85
American Association of
  Immunologists, 54

# C